JERUSALEM AND THE NATIONS

Hebrew Bible Monographs, 16

JERUSALEM AND THE NATIONS

STUDIES IN THE BOOK OF ISAIAH

Ronald E. Clements

SHEFFIELD PHOENIX PRESS

2011

Copyright © 2011 Sheffield Phoenix Press

Published by Sheffield Phoenix Press
Department of Biblical Studies, University of Sheffield
45 Victoria Street
Sheffield S3 7QB

www.sheffieldphoenix.com

A CIP catalogue record for this book
is available from the British Library

Typeset by Forthcoming Publications
Printed by Lightning Source

ISBN 978-1-905048-81-6
ISSN 1747-9614

CONTENTS

Part III
THE BOOK OF ISAIAH IN A PERSIAN CONTEXT

PREFACE

Another collection of essays on the book of Isaiah requires some word of explanation, especially as this represents some late reflections on a subject to which I have returned on several occasions during the past two decades. The difficult and problematic literary nature of the prophetic books of the Old Testament is not a recent perception, but the extent to which the study of them has, over more than two millennia, influenced debate between Judaism and Christianity is immense. The book of Isaiah has figured prominently in such efforts. In a half-century of Jewish-Christian dialogue when sincere and determined efforts have been made to heal past wounds and correct past misconceptions the contemporary era of fresh thinking on the subject may hope to make some contribution to these wider concerns. In this connection the Christian ideal of presenting a 'biblical theology', or even an 'Old Testament theology', has relied heavily on the relationship between the prophetic literature of the Old Testament and related citations and allusions to them in New Testament writings.

Furthermore the extent to which the more extreme expressions of contemporary Christian political movements have claimed to find support for their viewpoints in the Old Testament prophetic writings has aroused widespread disquiet and alarm. Of all the writings of the prophets the book of Isaiah stands firmly in the forefront of such interest. When seen in retrospect those many, highly readable, nineteenth-century volumes purporting to uncover the 'Life and Teaching' of the prophet Isaiah of Jerusalem now look remarkably inadequate. Biblical exegesis has never lacked its quota of wishful thinkers and even well-intentioned scholars are sometimes tempted to follow them.

A very special word of thanks is due to Professors David Clines and Philip Davies of Sheffield for their patience and encouragement. The former scholar suggested in the first instance that I might consider writing this book, and both scholars have maintained encouragement when other scholarly interests have drawn me into other fields of enquiry.

The essays included here develop topics and themes which I have dealt with earlier and several of them have earlier been published elsewhere in *Festschrift* volumes of limited circulation. In others I have sought to re-examine issues in the light of earlier responses and questions about my publications. Much of the incentive to look again at some well-researched issues has been the conviction that the division of Isaiah into two, or three, separate books has been a deceptively attractive path, which ignores other major features. The concern to look again at issues regarding the events of 701 BCE reflect my own deep disquiet that biblical interpretation has fallen deeply into a narrowly historicist approach with a serious undervaluing of its literary and theological richness.

Like all students of Isaiah I am conscious of the scale of my debt to others who have worked on this book. To have met some of them and to have shared their enthusiasm for it has been a great privilege. I well recall a happy day spent with Professor and Mrs Hans Wildberger in Switzerland in 1971 and the many hours of fruitful discussion since then with Professor Brevard Childs. Similarly Graham Davies, Hugh Williamson and Marvin Sweeney have greatly enriched my understanding of it, as have others too numerous to mention. To all of them I express my thanks. We have travelled hopefully and I for one have not been disappointed.

R.E. Clements,
Cambridge, July, 2010

ACKNOWLEDGMENTS

Several of the chapters appearing in the present volume have been published elsewhere, sometimes in a slightly different form. These reprinted studies are used here with the permission of the original publishers.

Chapter 2, 'Max Weber, Charisma and Biblical Prophecy', was earlier published in Y. Gitai (ed.), *Prophecy and Prophets: The Diversity of Contemporary Issues in Scholarship* (SBL Semeia Series; Atlanta: Society of Biblical Literature, 1997), pp. 89-108.

Chapter 3, 'Isaiah: A Book without an Ending?', was originally published in *JSOT* 97 (2002), pp. 109-26.

An earlier version of Chapter 4 was published in E. Ben Zvi and M.H. Floyd (eds.), *Writings and Speech in Israelite and Ancient Near Eastern Prophecy* (SBL Symposium Series, 10; Atlanta, Society of Biblical Literature, 2000), pp. 89-101. It is here presented in an extensively revised and rewritten form.

Chapter 5, was previously tited 'The Politics of Blasphemy: Zion's God and the Threat of Imperialism' and originally published in I. Kottsieper *et al.* (eds.), *"Weristwie du, Herr, unter den Göttern?"*. *Studien zur Theologie und Religionsgeschichte Israels. FS für O. Kaiser zum 70. Geburtstag* (Göttingen: Vandenhoeck & Ruprecht, 1994), pp. 231-46.

Chapter 11, 'Isaiah 14.22-27: A Central Passage Reconsidered', was first published in *The Book of Isaiah. Les Oracles etleursRelectures. Unitéet Complexitè de l'ouvrage* (BETL, 81; Leuven: Leuven Univeristy Press, 1989), pp. 253-62.

Chapter 12, 'Isaiah 53 and the Restoration of Israel. was earlier published in W.H. Bellinger Jr and W.R. Farmer (eds.), *Jesus and the Suffering Servant: Isaiah 53 and Christian Origins* (Harrissburg, PA: Trinity Press International, 1998), pp. 39-54.

Chapter 13, 'A Light to the Nations: A Central Theme of the Book of Isaiah', was earlier published in P.R. House and J. Watts (eds.), *Forming Prophetic Literature: Essays on Isaiah and the Twelve in Honor of John D. W. Watts* (JSOTSup, 235; Sheffield: Sheffield Academic Press, 1996), pp. 57-69.

Chapter 14, 'Zion as Symbol and Political Reality', was earlier published in J. van Ruiten and M. Vervenne (eds.), *Studies in the Book of Isaiah: FS W.A.M. Beuken* (Leuven: Leuven University Press, 1997), pp. 3-18.

ABBREVIATIONS

AB	Anchor Bible
ABD	David Noel Freedman (ed.), *The Anchor Bible Dictionary* (6 vols.; New York: Doubleday, 1992)
AOAT	Alter Orient und Altes Testament
ATD	Alte Testament Deutsch
BETL	Bibliotheca ephemeridum theologicarum lovaniensium
BJRL	*Bulletin of the John Rylands University Library of Manchester*
BZAW	Beihefte zur *ZAW*
CBQ	*Catholic Biblical Quarterly*
ConBOT	Coniectanea biblica, Old Testament
EBib	Etudes bibliques
EglTh	*Eglise et Thkologie*
ETL	*Ephemerides theologicae lovanienses*
FAT	Forschungen zum Alten Testament
FOTL	The Forms of the Old Testament Literature
FRLANT	Forschungen zur Religion und Literatur des Alten und Neuen Testaments
HAT	Handbuch zum Alten Testament
HKAT	Handkommentar zum Alten Testament
ICC	International Critical Commentary
JBL	*Journal of Biblical Literature*
JSJSup	Journal for the Study of Judaism in the Persian, Hellenistic and Roman Period Supplement Series
JSOT	*Journal for the Study of the Old Testament*
JSNTSup	Journal for the Study of the New Testament Supplement Series
JSOTSup	Journal for the Study of the Old Testament Supplement Series
JSSM	Journal of Semitic Studies Monographs
JTS	*Journal of Theological Studies*
LHBOTS	Library of the Hebrew Bible/Old Testament Studies
LUÅ	Lunds Universitets årsskrift
NCBC	New Century Bible Commentary
NICOT	The New International Commentary on the Old Testament
NRSV	New Revised Standard Version
OTG	Old Testament Guides
OTL	Old Testament Library
OTS	Old Testament Studies
PTMS	Pittsburgh Theological Monograph Series
SBLSS	Society of Biblical Literature Symposium Series
SBS	Stuttgarter Bibelstudien
SBT	Studies in Biblical Theology

SOTSMS   Society of Old Testament Study Monograph Series
TynBul   *Tyndale Bulletin*
VT   *Vetus Testamentum*
VTSup   *Vetus Testamentum*, Supplements
WBC   Word Biblical Commentary
WMANT   Wissenschaftliche Monographien zum Alten und Neuen Testament
ZAW   *Zeitschrift für die alttestamentlichen Wissenschaft*

PART I

PROPHECY IN NEW PERSPECTIVE

Chapter 1

PROPHECY INTERPRETED:
RECENT STUDY OF THE PROPHETIC LITERATURE

On any reckoning the prophetic writings of the Hebrew Bible are the most complex books among the many that the Bible contains. These long prophetic compositions were unique in antiquity, since, although many stories about the activities of prophets and diviners exist, and many letters and documents recording their utterances have been preserved, the remarkable feature of these writings is their length and the intricate interweaving of themes and poetic imagery which they display.

1. *From Prophetic Word to Prophetic Book*

Prophecies were originally relatively short sayings, or occasionally written messages addressed to specific situations and events. They made extensive use of metaphors and sometimes included signs that would serve to confirm future events. They usually had in mind a specific context of events and a particular addressee, or social group. If the king were the subject then this obviously had far wider implications than some event that was exclusively personal. Bringing together a number of such sayings to form books, as has happened in the Hebrew Bible, was an unusual step and it is this process of growth and linking-up which evidently passed through several stages.

While it is often possible to discern the originating situation of a particular prophecy, the work of collecting together several prophecies and forming them into books is a little known and largely unrecorded procedure at that early period of literary development. How, by whom, and to what purpose this literary assemblage was done is far from clear. Nevertheless it is this process of forming collections of short prophecies into long books that has given them a lasting significance and which has occupied an increasing level of scholarly attention during the past century. Initially it was taken for granted that no very great gap separated the activity of the originating prophet and the formation of a collection of his major sayings into a book.

The main purpose of this task was assumed to have been that of preservation—retaining a record of unique sayings by inspired individuals.[1]

Increasingly, however, it has become clear that this was not the case. The form of the books as they now appear was the end result of a long process in which a considerable number of intermediary scribes and editors took part. The books that we now have are essentially revised and re-formulated versions of earlier books and the structure and shape of these earlier books still shows through! The book of Isaiah is a particularly instructive example in this respect because from as far back as the Middle Ages the point was recognized by a leading Jewish scholar (Ibn Ezra 1092/3–1167) that it comprises two books (this was later revised in the nineteenth century to three). This perception, however, only partly covers the relevant literary facts regarding this particular example. The reasons for this are discussed more fully below in Chapter 3, but the general point is relevant to the Old Testament prophetic books as a whole: the form in which they now appear is not their original form, nor even a particularly early one. It is a relatively late, superimposed form on collections of sayings and narratives which at one time existed in shorter, carefully edited writings. There are 'books within the books'!

Tracing back the evidence that is still discernible of these older forms of prophetic books, or 'booklets' shows that forming prophetic books was a drawn-out process in which collections of sayings were edited, supplemented and commented upon over a long period of time. Moreover the words of prophets were 'living words' so that the message they contain was not simply preserved as a record of wisdom from the past, but as a fresh, and ever-relevant, message about past, present and future events.

The work of making short collections of prophetic sayings into books was combined with the further task of making cross-references between many of the most important sayings—a procedure that has come to be described as intertextuality. This practice was particularly—even uniquely—relevant to prophecy because prophecies were believed to contain hidden meanings, or sometime multiple meanings. In the course of time this linking together of prophecies was extended to the point of establishing comprehensive links between large numbers of prophetic sayings from different periods. Of course there were dangers in this procedure which could lead to falsifying

---

1. M.A. Sweeney, *Isaiah 1–39 with an Introduction to Prophetic Literature* (FOTL, 16; Grand Rapids: Eerdmans, 1996); Susan Niditch, *Oral World and Written Word: Ancient Israelite Literature* (Louisville, KY: Westminster/John Knox Press, 1996); Karel van der Toorn, *Scribal Culture and the Making of the Hebrew Bible* (Cambridge, MA: Harvard University Press, 2007); Ehud Ben Zvi and M.H. Floyd, *Writings and Speech in Israelite and Ancient Near Eastern Prophecy* (SBLSS, 10; Atlanta: Society of Biblical Literature, 2000).

the original intention of a prophet, but broad guidelines and controls were eventually put in place.

The idea of a canon formed around a set of core principles became essential to establish the basic outlines of 'true' prophecy.[2] This is what has happened in the Hebrew Bible so that preserving 'old' prophecies was not simply aimed at preserving past literary treasures, but was also needed to serve as a guide and check showing how they should be interpreted. This shows one of the reasons why there are prophetic books which include many comments and additions from a time after the originating 'source' prophet had lived. This procedure has acquired for itself the title of 'developmental exegesis'. Of course some measure of uniqueness and individuality has been retained since prophets were individuals and they did not all live at the same period or face the same challenges. Nevertheless the main purpose of prophecy was to present an overall picture of God's plan and purpose for Israel. This also meant that prophecy had to be interpreted in relation to the wider teachings, rituals and instructions that belonged to the religion of Moses.

The imperfectly known background to the making of the prophetic books provides the reason why scholarship has been much divided about their interpretation and highlights the point that they are a highly distinctive type of literature. They seek to do more than capture the original sayings of a prophet since they aim to be an interpretation of his message to show its relevance to a larger world of events. Individual prophecies were taken to be part of this much larger whole and this is why, by New Testament times, prophecies were usually read in series, or collections, often taken from different books. Comparison with the activities of other historical prophets of the ancient world, or even of contemporary examples, provides useful material for study, but nothing that is comparable to the Old Testament's extensive literary legacy of written prophecy has survived.[3] This has inevitably made these writings a hotly contested forum of debate. The reader is left to work out from evidence within the books themselves how they came to be put together.

Not surprisingly in view of the fact that prophecy claims to uncover the future history of the world, and in particular of the Christian Church, much controversy has surrounded the various interpretations that have been put forward. This sense has been exacerbated still more by the fact that it has, repeatedly throughout the history of the Church, been interpreted to explain

---

2. So especially in the writing of B.S. Childs, *Biblical Theology in Crisis* (Philadelphia: Westminster Press, 1970), pp. 91-148 and, more fully, *Introduction to the Old Testament as Scripture* (London: SCM Press, 1979), pp. 305-498; Stephen B. Chapman, *The Law and the Prophets* (FAT, 27; Tübingen: Mohr Siebeck, 2000).

3. Important comparative examples are given in M.J. de Jong, *Isaiah among the Ancient Near Eastern Prophets* (VTSup, 117; Leiden/Boston: E.J. Brill, 2007).

major world events and the coming of great historical figures, like Napoleon, or Adolf Hitler. When favourite methods of interpretation have been challenged by more cautious conclusions, or when the actual course of events has shown particular interpretations to be dangerous, or blatantly false, then biblical prophecy has suffered in popular esteem. The scholar must take into account how prophecy has been interpreted and misinterpreted throughout history, besides seeking to uncover its religious and historical origins in the Bible itself.

At the outset it is necessary to recognize that, from New Testament times, Jewish and Christian interpretations of prophecy have differed widely. More precisely these different traditions have shared many basic assumptions about prophecy, but have differed over the conclusions to which their respective interpretations lead. For long periods of the history of the Christian Church the paths of prophetic interpretation between these inter-related religions had little to do with each other. Nor should this be a cause for surprise since the preferred title given to Jesus by the early Christians—the Messiah—links him and his life directly to an interpretation of Old Testament prophecy. Most of the interest in Jewish teaching and ideas that re-awakened among Christians in the early nineteenth century was aimed at converting Jews with special attention being devoted to showing that Jesus of Nazareth was the messiah foretold in Hebrew prophecy.[4] It is also worthy of note that the broad title for the Hebrew Bible used by Christians—the '*Old* Testament' divides world history into two eras, labelled ages of 'Promise' and 'Fulfilment', backed up by a particular interpretation of prophecy.

As a feature of the Protestant Reformation of the sixteenth century renewed efforts were made by Christian scholars to rethink and re-examine the nature of prophecy since the Reformation itself was widely believed in Protestant tradition to have been foretold by it. This reinvigorated interest opened up recognition of a tension between some of the key Hebrew texts recorded by Old Testament prophets and the versions of them in the Greek New Testament. A particular example of this lies in the celebrated promise of the birth of a wonder-child to a virgin in Isa. 7.14 which has continued to exercise a great deal of attention from scholars. Christian authors naturally read Old Testament prophecies in ways favourable to their interpretation of the life and work of Jesus The need arose to find out how far, in the time of Jesus this was a widely adopted Jewish way of understanding these texts and

---

4. The background to this development and its close links to Christian missionary activities among Jews is noted in my essay 'A Fruitful Venture: The Origin of Hebrew Studies at King's College, London', in C. Hempel and J.A. Lieu (eds.), *Biblical Traditions in Transmission: Essays in Honour of Michael A. Knibb* (JSJSup, 111; Leiden/Boston: E.J. Brill, 2006), pp. 61-80.

how far this was a consciously Christian application.[5] Inevitably the study of the Old Testament prophets in their own times leads forward to raising questions about the way they were understood in the later biblical period. One reason for paying great attention to the making of the prophetic books, which has been a major goal for scholars in recent years, is that the editorial techniques employed in forming the books provide important clues towards filling this gap.

Prophecy played a major role in the English Civil Wars (1640–1660) of the seventeenth century which opened up a host of fresh questions about its meaning.[6] Some of these were new and some had not previously appeared all that important. It brought to the surface politically radical viewpoints and the Christian dependence on Jewish Hebrew learning drew fresh attention to questions about the textual transmission of the Old Testament books. The key texts in the prophetic books which tell of the coming of a messiah, and which are given a central place in the New Testament, were all placed under fresh scrutiny.[7] Fuller explanations were called for why the Old and New Testament records of particular prophecies frequently appear to say different things, or at least raise questions about their meaning. Perhaps most argued about was the possibility that a prophecy might have more than one meaning—a literal one and a spiritual (or Christian) one. The separate issues that these questions addressed were all placed under close scrutiny by scholars who were, in reality small in numbers and almost without exception caught up in a range of ecclesiastical duties. By the beginning of the nineteenth century the strains and tensions between academic and Church interests began to show and semi-public controversies arose.[8] Not least the question 'What is biblical interpretation and how should it be done?' began to be raised.[9]

---

5. Cf. Craig A. Evans and J.A. Sanders (eds.), *Early Christian Interpretation of the Scriptures of Israel: Investigations and Proposals* (JSNTSup, 148; Sheffield: Sheffield Academic Press, 1997).

6. Cf. especially, Christopher Hill, *The English Bible and the Seventeenth Century Revolution* (London: Allen Lane, 1993).

7. Cf. my essay 'The Messianic Hope in the Old Testament', in *Old Testament Prophecy: From Oracles to Canon* (Louisville, KY: Westminster/John Knox Press, 1996), pp. 49-62 (first published 1989).

8. Cf. especially, J. Sheehan, *The Enlightenment Bible: Translation, Scholarship, Culture* (Princeton, NJ: Princeton University Press, 2005). The most celebrated debate focused on an argument between Robert Lowth (1710–1787) and William Warburton (1698–1779) over the poetic nature of the book of Job. The controversy illustrated the point that the book of Job was an oriental work conforming to specific literary conventions.

9. Cf. Stephen Prickett, *Words and the Word: Language, Poetics and Biblical Interpretation* (Cambridge: Cambridge University Press, 1986).

This focused a spotlight on the point that understanding the pre-Christian background to Christian interpretations of prophecies is not simply a matter of understanding how Hebrew words were translated into Greek, but concerns major issues about the forming of books and the transmission and interpretation of sacred scriptures generally. The concepts of 'inspiration' and 'biblical authority' required to be more fully explained in terms of how the biblical books came to be written. It not only entailed researching the nature and meaning of words, since in prophecy individual words and names become particularly significant, but raised wider issues. It asked questions about the change from an 'oral' culture in which most communication is conducted by word of mouth, to a culture in which important ideas, truths and commitments are recorded in writing.

This is why recent study of Old Testament prophecy has focused on asking how the four large books of prophecy—the 'Latter Prophets'—came to be written.[10] Recognizing that some distance separates the great figures from whom these prophetic books are named and their present finished form is simply a first step. The New Testament's interpretations of prophecies, which are a major feature of its writings, are linked closely to the work of the editors and scribes who shaped the extant prophetic books.

2. *What is a Prophetic Book?*

The first, and most basic, question for the modern reader to ask is what exactly a book of prophecy is, and to consider what an ancient scroll or 'book' of this kind might have looked like.[11] The use of long scrolls of papyrus or leather in ancient times was essentially a 'final'—last ditch—solution to a series of complex procedures in making a record of the teaching of prophets who were, in the first instance, preachers. Books of prophecy reflect a secondary stage of their work so that the present eleven books in the Hebrew biblical canon which are ascribed to prophets are the end-product of an extended literary process. One of these—the Book of Daniel—is a book of a highly developed (late) kind of prophecy usually called 'apocalyptic'. The other ten books are divided between the Former

---

10. Besides the works listed above in note 1 see also J.W. Watts and P.R. House (eds.), *Forming Prophetic Literature: Essays on Isaiah and the Twelve in Honour of J.D.W. Watts* (JSOTSup, 235; Sheffield: Sheffield Academic Press, 1996); D.E. Orton (ed.), *Prophecy in the Hebrew Bible: Selected Studies from Vetus Testamentum* (Brill's Readers in Biblical Studies, 5; Leiden/Boston: E.J. Brill, 2000); R.P. Gordon (ed.), *The Place is too Small for Us: The Israelite Prophets in Recent Scholarship* (Winona Lake, IN: Eisenbrauns, 1995).

11. Cf. E.W. Conrad, 'Heard but not Seen; The Representation of Books in the Old Testament', *JSOT* 54 (1992), pp. 53-59.

Prophets (Joshua–Judges–1 and 2 Samuel–1 and 2 Kings) and the Latter Prophets (Isaiah–Jeremiah–Ezekiel–The Book of the Twelve Prophets).The first six of these books are now frequently referred to by scholars as 'the Deuteronomistic History' on account of a widely recognized feature about their relationship to Deuteronomy. However they do not appear to be books of prophecy at all since they take the form a single continuous historical narrative.[12] The Greek (Septuagint) Bible regards them as 'historical books'.

The six separate 'books' into which they are divided resemble chapters of a more modern age of writing. They were not originally separate books which have been joined together but are a piecemeal assemblage put together from a number of ancient documents, but not divided up in the present manner. At one time they formed a single continuous work. They have drawn on several earlier 'books', or 'sources', some of which are explicitly noted and to which the reader is referred. These sources are not correlated directly with the present 'book' divisions. Modern scholars have found a more rewarding comparison to be between this 'Deuteronomistic History' and 1 and 2 Chronicles. The noting of older sources may be an editor's way of affirming the authenticity and reliability of his own work, but there is no doubt that, in ancient Israel and Judaism, a large body of written literature existed and could be used for the composition of further books.

Obviously there were libraries of official or semi-official documents and there was a professional 'scribal' culture.[13] Almost certainly the work of such scribes was highly respected and valued, even by a less literate public. It is widely assumed that, because of the spiritual value of religious texts in ancient Judaism, the role of the scribe was accordingly highly prized and closely linked to education generally.

What is less clear to the modern reader of the biblical texts is in what physical form these ancient documents would have existed and where they would have been kept. Writing materials were scarce and expensive. Pottery,

---

12. The literature on this collection of narrative writings is extensive; cf. especially, A.D.H. Mayes, *The Story of Israel between Settlement and Exile: A Redactional Study of the Deuteronomistic History* (London: SCM Press, 1983); T. Römer, *The So-called Deuteronomistic History: A Sociological, Historical and Literary Introduction* (London/New York: T. & T. Clark International, 2005); *Israel Constructs its History: Deuteronomistic Historiography in Recent Research* (JSOTSup, 306; Sheffield: Sheffield Academic Press, 2000); *Reconsidering Israel and Judah: Recent Studies in the Deuteronomistic History* (Sources for Biblical and Theological Study, 8; Winona Lake, IN: Eisenbrauns, 2000); cf. also my review of some of the issues in 'The Former Prophets and Deuteronomy: A Re-Examination', in J.H. Ellens *et al.* (eds.), *God's Word in Our World: Biblical Studies in Honor of Simon J. De Vries* (London/New York: T. & T. Clark International, 2004), pp. 83-95.

13. Cf. J.L. Crenshaw, *Education in Ancient Israel: Across the Deadening Silence* (New York: Doubleday, 1998).

papyrus and leather scrolls are all possibilities. So also clay tablets with letters cut, or pressed, into them were a readily available material as also were small wooden tablets. What is evident is that, when texts were regarded as of great importance, the use of versatile and durable materials was highly desirable, but also more expensive. The long leather scrolls made familiar to the modern scholar of the Bible by the scrolls from Qumran (The Dead Sea Scrolls) must have been a precious rarity. Any overall reconstruction of the processes of how ancient scribes obtained their materials, gained access to precious official documents and went about their work continues to occasion extensive debate. Similar uncertainties belong to the question of where such writings would have been kept. The citation of 'official' sources in the books of 1 and 2 Kings points to a court, or temple, library, and this would be in agreement with the belief that scribes formed part of an official administrative profession. However, the view has been widely popularised in respect of the prophets that small circles of disciples formed a specific community of followers and exegetes of individual prophets. Certainly the frequency with which prophecies and psalms from several traditions are preserved strongly points in favour of the former view. The transition from the spoken word to the written text was one that was fraught with difficulties and called for a range of skills. The significant feature is that a long work on the scale of the present book of Isaiah must have been assembled in stages from a considerable number of other ancient writings. Yet to call it an 'anthology' misrepresents its character since it has been given a carefully planned order and structure. In the case of the Former Prophets, the present division into six books shows that this division was introduced for literary convenience at a very late stage and not because there were at one time six independent and self-contained books which were simply joined together.

The evidence about the literary form and structure of the Deuteronomistic History, which appears to the modern reader to be a straightforward narrative text, takes on an even greater significance when applied to the book of Isaiah and to the "Latter Prophets" as a whole. These books have no direct counterparts in antiquity even though there is ample evidence of writings about prophets and records of utterances by them. Where the narratives of the Former Prophets refer to several source texts and others can be reconstructed with reasonable plausibility few such helps exist in the case of the Latter Prophets. The book of Ezekiel was at one time regarded as a well-constructed text from a single author, but few would maintain this today.

The task of identifying source documents in Isaiah, Jeremiah and the Twelve Prophets has continually encountered problems and difficulties which have left many questions unanswered. There are nonetheless important markers and guidelines which should be noted. These show up in the form of beginnings and endings; sometimes a central theme stands out clearly, or a particular event links groups of sayings into a coherent unit. The books of the prophets Jeremiah and Ezekiel show a more easily recognizable literary shape than is the case with Isaiah. Nevertheless in the case of Jeremiah similarities in style, subject matter and theological outlook link it closely with the books of 1 and 2 Kings.

In the case of the 'Book of the Twelve Prophets' the level of importance that belongs to its construction as twelve separate books, or 'booklets', has been very variously estimated. It has been put together to make up one book but it seems certain that earlier groupings of its prophecies at one time existed. Words like 'growth' and 'editorial shape' are regularly used to describe the make-up of prophetic books, but it is often very difficult to pin down precisely what they imply about how the books were given their final form. The overall picture is that books in ancient times were very different from those of a modern era in which structural unity, common authorship and a consistent purpose are expected.

Perhaps the most influential of recent perceptions by scholars has been the extent to which 'intertextuality', i.e. the citation of, or allusion to, other texts is evident. This indicates a learned and highly skilled scribal culture with access to collections of books. It also shows a high regard for preserved documents in a variety of forms. The need to preserve, interpret and promote the message of ancient prophecies was obviously keenly felt. In this way the art and skills of the scribe became religious duties which served an important social purpose since prophecy gave hope and upheld a sense of shared identity. This literary culture continued into early Christian history giving rise to the famous libraries and monastic authors of Early and Mediaeval Britain.

3. *From Spoken Word to Written Books*

Almost no independent information is available to show what the procedures and techniques of recording were for written prophecy to reach its present literary form in the earliest years of forming the Hebrew Bible. The scribes who accomplished this task were predominantly self-effacing figures, serving the text and not drawing attention to their methods of work or their personal background. They have left no signatures at the end of a scroll, and few personal features appear. According to a plausible hypothesis the scribes who edited the prophetic books were closely associated with the authors of wisdom.[14] Certainly the accomplishments of education and writing became closely intertwined. The results of their labours are open for all to see in the preserved books of prophecy, but these came at the end of a long process. In

---

14. Cf. B. Gosse, *Structuration des grands ensembles bibliques et intertextualité à l'époque perse* (BZAW, 246; Berlin/New York: W. de Gruyter, 1997).

a well documented passage (Jer. 36.4-32) the manner in which some of Jeremiah's prophecies were written down and recorded appears to provide enough information to explain why prophecies were often written down. The account describes a straightforward and commonplace process of dictation and copying so that an intelligible picture emerges.[15] Yet this notable account concerning an act by Jeremiah poses serious problems if it is used to construct a general picture of the making of the prophetic books. It gives no more than a defensive explanation regarding a first step in the production of a much larger work. This text, or memorandum, may have marked a key moment in the career of Jeremiah, but the book that bears his name was quite evidently made up from a much larger number of written sources than this one and these sources, or 'voices' differed greatly from each other in their style and character. The report of Jeremiah 36 has a specific religious purpose in mind and is more a 'presentation' or 'commendation' of a written text, than a detailed record of how the present book of Jeremiah came into existence.

A comparable presentation of the origin of a sacred 'book' of a rather different kind is to be found in Deut. 31.9-13 (cf. also Deut. 6.6-9; 11.18-21 etc.).[16] This certainly does not mean that there were no written records of prophecy from the time when the original prophets were active. It is a conviction of the present studies that memoranda of the words of prophets from that early period did exist. Some of the arguments for believing this to be the case are discussed below in Chapter 4 in regard to the 'memoir' of the prophet Isaiah, but the final judgements on this issue are indecisive. The existence at an early period of written records of the sayings of prophets falls far short of explaining the origin of the surviving long prophetic books. The extensive debate about Isaiah's written 'memoir', and, more significantly the belief that a major collection of Isaiah's prophecies was made during the reign of King Josiah, provide salutary examples of the complexity of the issues that are raised. Modern study of the prophets at one period became heavily side-tracked into searching for 'inauthentic' passages (called 'glosses') that are present in the surviving prophetic literature. A wealth of internal evidence in Isaiah, and all the prophetic books shows that they have undergone several stages of editorial expansion and revision.

One thing is certain: the earliest collections and editions of the sayings of great prophets like Isaiah and Jeremiah are no longer preserved in their original form. They have subsequently been preserved and re-interpreted in the light of later events and other prophetic sayings have been linked to

15. Cf. R.P. Carroll, *Jeremiah: A Commentary* (London: SCM Press, 1986), pp. 658-68.

16. So especially J.-P. Sonnet, *The Book with the Book: Writing in Deuteronomy* (Biblical Interpretation Series, 14; Leiden/Boston: E.J. Brill, 1997).

them. The result is a comprehensive, but at times confusingly discursive, series of literary compositions. A modern book would have divisions into chapters and appendices, as well as endnotes, or footnotes, which are entirely absent in these historic compositions.

We know very little even of the material form in which the earliest recorded sayings of prophets were made. Contemporary evidence suggests that some may have been little more than short records made on sherds of pottery (ostraca). The gap between these records left by the original prophets and the compilation of their sayings into books has to be filled by what can be gleaned from the evidence of the structures and finished shape of the writings. This amounts to noting that groups of sayings have been assembled into collections and, at times, short notes have been introduced to provide beginnings and endings which served as literary guideposts. These marked out separate units, but the formation of these units conveyed some level of understanding about the events to which the prophecies were related. In several instances sharply contrasted sayings (threats followed by promises) appear together. Had the prophet changed his mind? Or was this the proverbial 'carrot and stick' approach?

Neither explanation can possibly suffice to explain these contrasts since we are faced with texts which have a literary history which aimed at providing some perspective for the sayings.[17] Threats required to be 'wrapped around' by more fundamental reminders of divine assurances. Evidently it is the need of the reader that has governed this awkward literary feature. Without awareness of this the modern reader is faced with what appear as contradictions that render it difficult to make credible sense of the texts. The appearance of disarray is paramount. In some instances, particularly in regard to prophecies from Isaiah, extensive theories regarding the prophet's change of attitude have been put forward. The fundamental claim of these essays is that this appearance of contradiction is to be explained, not by a sudden change of mind on the part of the prophet but by a process of editorial development and revision in the light of events. Prophecy required to be understood as a living dialogue between God and Israel which endeavoured to place warnings and threats in the context of a wider message of assurance and hope. In aiming to achieve this goal prophecies from different times and contexts have been viewed in relation to each other. So 'intertextuality' was

---

17. The tension within the text between citations of earlier prophecies and later applications and developments of them raises serious questions whether a 'final', or 'canonical' form of a passage can be privileged and treated as the definitive expression of it. In some cases such citations relate to broad concepts such as references to a divine 'plan' or 'signal to the nations'. This point is particularly relevant to the discussion regarding the hypothesis that there once existed an 'Isaiah Memoir'. See Chapter 4, below, pp. 53-65.

not simply a word-game, but a serious attempt to discern the mind of God with the help of prophecies read and interpreted in the light of the events that followed them. It is also essential to keep in mind that the present chapter and verse divisions of all the biblical books in modern English language Bibles, which help to some extent to create order and impose a degree of structural system, are a work of later, post-biblical, scribal scholarship.

The task of retracing the steps leading to the composition of the prophetic books is made difficult by the fact that the gap that separates the time of the earliest prophets' active work and the finished form of the books that carry their names is a wide one. Equally lengthy was the interval between the activity in the eighth century BCE of these prophets and the later ones who were active in the Persian period. Prophecy was presumed to reveal some kind of theological 'purpose', or divine 'plan' (cf. Isa. 5.19; 37.26) since God was recognized to be constant and unchanging. As a consequence the task of editorial cross-referencing was important in linking together messages from different prophets. As human beings prophets could display difference and diversity, but as speakers for the One God their messages were expected to show consistency.

It is essential to add to this point recognition that all the texts which have come down to us show that major compilations of prophecy were brought together and edited at critical turning-points in the history of ancient Israel and Judah. Prophecy acquired a special historical significance when events occurred that were thought to confirm, or 'fulfil' what prophets had foreseen. It was believed to offer an explanation for what had happened; as a result it could then be used as a guide to what would happen in the future.

Just as the New Testament writings are heavily influenced by the fact that, in the Roman–Jewish war of AD 66–70 the temple of Jerusalem was destroyed, so the saving of Jerusalem in 701 BCE followed by the city's subsequent destruction in 587 BCE are events that, when taken together, cast a shadow over the entire collection of Old Testament prophecy. The fact that these events were inseparably linked to the fortunes of the royal house of King David added to their significance. Their legacy in the editing, preservation and interpretation of collections of prophecies to create our present long prophetic books provides the key to understanding them.

Knowing about the 'afterlife' of prophecies provides a better basis for understanding them than the often futile attempts to write 'mini-biographies' of the lives of the original prophetic preachers. Since very little is actually known about these persons the attempts to do this have quickly foundered and encouraged rather too much inventiveness on the part of scholars in a desire to accommodate difficult texts. This is as true for the prophets who lived after the disasters of 598 and 587 BCE as it is for those of an earlier date. The events of those years formed so large a turning-point in the history of Jerusalem, Judah and Israel that the entire Old Testament was affected. Even writings that originated before the year when the Jerusalem temple was destroyed were afterwards read in the light of it. The modern reader is well aware how speeches made and opinions expressed by leading public figures before the outbreak of a war appear very differently afterwards. Similarly in the Old Testament, prophecies made before the disasters of the sixth century BCE could not afterwards ignore what had occurred later.

So far as all the Old Testament's books of prophecy are concerned the events that overtook the city of Jerusalem in the sixth century BCE were of over-riding importance in giving them their final shape. They all prominently reflect the events of these years when the Babylonian armies destroyed Jerusalem and removed the last of its Davidic kings. Isaiah is probably the most obvious instance of this, although both Jeremiah and Ezekiel lived through those tumultuous years. Isaiah stands out somewhat from this perspective because his prophecies were taken to have encouraged an optimistic portrayal of Yahweh's incomparable power. This teaching has become inseparably linked to the sparing of Jerusalem from destruction in 701 BCE at the hands of Sennacherib's (Assyrian) forces. To this extent the story of what happened to Jerusalem in 701 BCE, which hinges on words ascribed to the prophet Isaiah, took on a different complexion later when the city was destroyed. The complicated and unbalanced structure of the Isaiah book hinges on the assurance that these disasters could be understood without abandoning hope.

The response to the catastrophes that occurred for Jerusalem in the years 598 and 587 BCE are at the centre of the entire collection of prophecies that are now called 'The Latter Prophets'.[18] This matches closely the point that it is these same events that provide the end-point of the historical books described as 'The Former Prophets'. Both literary compilations show that they have been assembled from older source documents, which are now lost. They reveal the bewilderment when the reprieve afforded Jerusalem in 701 BCE failed to be repeated when the Babylonians came. More precisely, the partial reprieve of 598 BCE provided a first salutary warning that there was no unconditional guarantee either for kings of the lineage of David or for the city from which they reigned. This point is firmly set out in the prophetic book of Jeremiah.[19] After 587 BCE the belief that Jerusalem, its royal head,

18. Cf. on this point E.W. Conrad, *Reading the Latter Prophets: Towards a New Canonical Criticism* (JSOTSup, 376; London: T. & T. Clark, 2003); H. Graf Reventlow and Y. Hoffmann (eds.), *Religious Responses to Political Crises in Jewish and Christian Tradition* (LHBOTS, 444; New York/London: T. & T. Clark, 2008), especially H. Graf Reventlow, 'A Religious Response to Severe Political Crisis: King Ahaz and Isaiah', pp. 36-51.

19. Cf. the perceptions regarding kingship in J. Job, *Jeremiah's Kings: A Study of the Monarchy in Jeremiah* (SOTSMS; Aldershot/Burlington: Ashgate, 2006).

and the existence of a temple to Yahweh were guarantees of protection from the assaults of foreign armies required the most careful qualification. Yet, as the book of Isaiah shows, such a belief did somehow emerge and provided a striking feature of Jewish hope in the Persian period (cf. especially Isa. 14.26-27; 31.8-9).

All these tragic events were, in different ways, linked to belief in the divine promise that had for centuries upheld the Davidic dynasty of kings. Such, at least, is the interpretation reflected in the prophecies of Isaiah. The result is that Isaiah's book is through and through about Jerusalem, its destiny among the nations, and its tradition of kingship—the dynasty of King David—who first raised the city to international importance.

Close study of Isaiah, however, points to a further mysterious episode in the history of Jerusalem and tells something further about the latest stages in the composition of the book. The evidence for it is dealt with below in Chapter 15, but its background and consequences remain shrouded in mystery. It concerns a violent reaction against the authorities who controlled the city of Jerusalem. This has led the book's final editors to burst out in the strongest antagonism to these unknown persons (cf. Isa. 1–4 and 65–66) whose high authority in the city is especially noted (Isa. 1.21-23). The introduction to the book foresees in the imminent future of the city a fearful return of conflict, with the outcome still far from decided. This hostility renews the warnings about its future and stands in sharp contrast to the hope expressed in glowing terms in Isaiah 60–62, and often elsewhere in the book. The shadow of these contrasting events shows that prophecy was not simply concerned with preserving impressive words and memorable poetry about the past, but with using it to understand the present. It is a literature focused on events—for the most part traumatic upheavals which called for explanation through eyes of faith. Its aim was to understand and give meaning to conflicts that ravaged nations; that left lands ruined and its people turned into exiles and fugitives. The events that lie at the back of the great biblical prophets have, throughout Jewish and Christian history, served as paradigms of the triumphs and disasters of the wider human story. It is a literature of hope staring at the realities of human violence and tragedies.

4. Books, More Books and Commentaries

The process of editing, adding to, and elaborating, prophetic texts and themes eventually generated books of unusual length. In the form of continuous scrolls these would ultimately have extended to an inconvenient length for use as a single text. Scrolls could only reasonably remain conveniently accessible when kept within certain boundaries. So the length of books was limited by practical considerations. This fact, combined with the special importance accorded in religious communities to prophetic texts, quickly led

to the appearance of further separate writings and commentaries—a procedure which has continued into the present day. In this way Old Testament
prophecy became the seed-bed for a remarkable class of literature—commentaries and books of prophetic interpretation—that, throughout two millennia,
have remained popular expressions of biblically based piety for Christians
and Jews.

The Old Testament itself bears witness to the fact that prophecies
recorded in relation to one prophet were regarded as of sufficient importance
for other prophets to cite them, using these links to uncover fresh revelations
from God. Prophets themselves probably started such a procedure by recalling and revising their own words. More frequently it is later editors who
have compared one prophet's words with that of other prophets. So words
recorded of Isaiah are alluded to in the books of Zechariah and Daniel. It is
not surprising therefore to find that, alongside the composition of the biblical
prophetic books, an extensive series of further writings appeared in which a
range of new developments with a prophetic character appeared. Prophecy
formed part of a continued quest on the part of succeeding generations of
Jews (and later Christians) to understand human history in relation to a
divine purpose and providence. Events, even the most catastrophic ones,
were looked upon as in some way meaningful expressions of divine judgment and mercy.

Many of the later writings which fall into this category belong to the
'Inter-testamental' period, although this title is misleading. There was
evidently no 'silent' interval between the latest literary activity relating to
the 'Old' Testament and the first writings of the 'New'. Such distinctions, if
they are to be used at all, belong to the parting of the ways between historic
Judaism and the beginnings of Gentile Christianity. Yet throughout the first
and second Christian centuries a remarkable level of cross-fertilisation
between the two communities continued to take place.

Sometimes the prophetic writings of the late Jewish era carry the names
of earlier biblical figures in pseudepigraphic fashion.[20] Two of the most
influential of them are ascribed to Enoch and Elijah—persons who were
believed to have been caught up into heaven and to have seen remarkable
visions of future events. Christians adopted such visionary writings and the
dates and affiliations of many of their surviving versions are unclear since

---

20. Of particular relevance to the prophecies of Isaiah is the text known as *The
Ascension of Isaiah*. Cf. M.A. Knibb, 'Isaianic Tradition in the Book of Enoch', in
J. Barton and D.J. Reimer (eds.), *After the Exile: Essays in Honour of Rex Mason*
(Macon, GA: Mercer University Press, 1996), pp. 217-29, and Knibb, 'Isaianic Traditions
in the Apocrypha and Pseudepigrapha', in C.C. Broyles and C.A. Evans (eds.), *Writing
and Reading the Scroll of Isaiah: Studies of an Interpretive Tradition* (2 vols.; Leiden/
Boston: E.J. Brill, 1997), II, pp. 633-50.

they continued to be used, extended and highly regarded well into the Christian era. They reveal a popular genre of writing which made use of the fact that books of prophecy enjoyed a wide appeal and spawned a range of fantastic imagery which was held in great esteem. It could also be dangerous and disruptive and increasingly fell into disfavour as Christians submitted to political conformity.

In this popular sub-culture old texts took on new life; new applications were found for traditional and well-known metaphors, such as those of the lamb, the vine and the tree. Well-established keywords and themes were repeatedly explored and a whole geography of a heavenly realm was envisaged with a hierarchy of mediating figures.

In similar fashion the concept of an 'evil empire' was attached to new historical powers and notorious names like those of Babylon and Nebuchadrezzar became symbols of new empires and new tyrants. By a process of 'mythologizing', names and titles that had originated in established written prophecy were given an updated contemporary relevance and took on a symbolic dimension. In a related direction a range of themes and images embracing monsters and deities which had their origins in ancient myths and legends were taken up and employed as coded references to more contemporary oppressive powers. Throughout these developments, one of the most distinctive features continued to be the many citations from the canonical prophetic books of the Old Testament among whom Isaiah stands high on the list. Prophetic books became a well-recognized literature of dissent, with its conventions and techniques underlying its subversive message of protest. In Christian history this has continued to give to the biblical prophetic books a special appeal where their dissenting message has, time and again, been raised against abuses of power in Church and State.

One of the great gains for biblical scholarship from the discovery of ancient scrolls at Qumran has been the recovery of a large volume of documents in which the interpretation of prophecy plays a big part. Prominent among them are commentaries on older prophetic texts which apply their message and themes to later situations.[21] Frequently the hidden (coded) nature of this interpretation is carefully maintained, giving to prophecy a quality of mystery and secrecy which is intriguing. The specific citation of an original text, followed by commentary upon it giving it a contemporary, rather than a strictly historical, application established a literary form that will be familiar to the modern reader. Often the new contemporary context remains obscure—a feature noted above in respect of the warnings of Isaiah's opening chapter—and remains open to more than one interpretation.

---

21. Cf. M.A. Knibb, *The Qumran Community* (Cambridge Commentaries on Writings of the Jewish and Christian World 200 BC to AD 200, 2; Cambridge: Cambridge University Press, 1987), especially pp. 207-66.

Throughout these compositions a dependence on the older canonical prophetic books provided a central foundation giving to the new commentaries a degree of authority. They show one of the ways in which new prophecies continued to appear under the guise of extensions and re-applications of those that were already current. The very distinction between what was 'canonical' and what was secondary and derivative became a criterion that only became effective in a period when such an abundance of texts had become commonplace that authoritative rulings and distinctions were called for. The subversive, secretive nature of prophecy made it a dangerous literature on which Church authority has usually frowned. This was very markedly the case after the seventeenth century civil conflicts in Great Britain, and, for a number of reasons has never altogether disappeared.

Critical scholarly opinion has remained divided over the question of exactly how widespread and popular this type of prophetic interpretation was. It reveals a sectarian, divisive spirit and shows a deep-rooted suspicion of contemporary political authority. At the same time it has authentic biblical origins and has served well, alongside satire and ridicule, as a means of opposing the abuses and compromises that human societies experience. Prophecy has usually encouraged and strengthened the faithful more than it has alarmed and frightened those in power. Its importance rests on the fact that it expresses protest and upholds a rich and passionate belief in justice and freedom for the oppressed.

Throughout the development of the many post-biblical compositions that have sought to interpret prophecy, there exists a genuine continuity with the biblical roots of this major class of literature. Prophetic interpretations and commentaries claim a contemporary authority by drawing on the established words of great biblical prophets. Exposition of established writings replaces the forming of new prophecies as a medium of fresh revelation. In this respect new prophetic activities and revelations in Christian communities have seldom won for themselves an equal respect and attention to that given to interpretations of the biblical prophetic books. Early on in the history of the Church the arbitrariness and instability occasioned by endless fresh prophesying required to be curtailed.

The feature that is essential for the modern reader to bear in mind is that, although there are inevitable differences between later commentaries and expositions and the canonical books of biblical prophets, significant continuities are present. The later commentary literature, and the citation of ancient prophecies in liturgies and prayers, has a place as an authentic expression of the phenomenon of prophecy. What is of particular interest for the book of Isaiah is that it can claim to reign supreme as the most frequently cited and popularly recognized of all the books of this type.

Chapter 2

MAX WEBER, CHARISMA AND BIBLICAL PROPHECY

Seen in historical perspective Max Weber's treatment of the concept of charisma has proved to be one of the most wide-ranging and influential of his many insights into the workings of society.[1] Not only is this the case on the broad front of the study of sociology of religion, but particularly is it so in regard to its influence upon biblical studies. It is also a somewhat unsettling influence, since Weber himself did not present any very rounded, or complete, interpretation of what he meant by the concept of charisma or how it was perceived by those who responded to the experience of it. Indeed, it could be argued that it is not possible to offer such, since it is more a matter of working inductively and recognizing where such a characterization applies in particular historical and political situations.

The recognition that a charismatic element has been present in the achievement of certain individuals enables us, in retrospect, to understand why their leadership was so effective. It serves to explain, if only by a broad description, why these individuals were able to command a strong following and why they were able to implement changes that their communities were otherwise reluctant to make. In many of its features such an element of charisma is nebulous and only capable of being loosely defined. It is this lack of definition that has enabled it to be applied in diverse ways and to a great variety of situations.

Nor should we lose sight of the fact that, in a number of respects, the notion of charisma highlights the uniquely personal, and often unforeseeable, factors that affect historical events.[2] It has affinities with the emphasis upon the 'heroic' approach to the interpretation of history which held great appeal to much nineteenth and twentieth century historical writing.

---

1. H.H. Gerth and C.W. Mills, *From Max Weber: Essays in Sociology* (London: Routledge & Kegan Paul, 1948), pp. 245-52; S.N. Eisenstadt (ed.), *Max Weber on Charisma and Institution Building* (Chicago: University of Chicago Press, 1968); M. Albrow, *Max Weber's Construction of Social Theory* (London: Macmillan, 1990).
2. Albrow, *Max Weber's Construction of Social Theory*, p. 172.

1. *Charisma and Kingship*

Weber himself did not develop any special separate treatment of the subject where it could be dealt with comprehensively as a separate topic for examination. It occurs as part of a wider range of analyses of social change and the interplay of authority between individuals and institutions.

The modern reader is well served by the selection and translation of Weber's writings that have a bearing on the topic made by S.N. Eisenstadt[3]

However, it is important to recognize that the most significant *locus* where Weber sought to define charisma and to illustrate its mode of working was presented in less than a half-dozen pages.[4] Nevertheless the main principles of its operation are significant for quite a wide area of Weber's writings.

Our present concern is not primarily to re-examine Weber's own words on the subject, but rather to consider the way in which his observations have been understood in relation to Israelite prophecy. In a rather different connection it is useful to note at the outset that a wide area where the charismatic authority and leadership ascribed to individuals has drawn the attention of biblical scholars concerns the institution of monarchy into the tribal society of Israel.[5] The narrative stories telling how this latter development occurred with the figures of Saul and David make extensive play on authority provided by the charismatic ideal. Yet it is noteworthy that the primary concern of such stories is to show how this ideal was properly transferred to David's descendants in a dynastic succession.[6] By taking for granted the notion that charismatic authority passed to the divinely designated son and heir, a large unit of narrative concerning affairs at David's court is aimed at defending Solomon's claim to be such an heir.

In this fashion the claim to individual charismatic authority linked to the person of David has been carried over in defense of the traditional authority of a royal dynasty. At the same time, it becomes evident that the extent to which Solomon could be properly regarded as entitled to recognition as the legitimate, and divinely appointed, heir of David was widely regarded as questionable. So what has come to be described as 'The Succession

---

3.   Eisenstadt, *Max Weber on Charisma*, *passim*; M. Weber, *The Sociology of Religion* (trans. E. Fischoff; Boston: Beacon Press, 1963), pp. xxxiiiff.

4.   Gerth and Mills, *From Max Weber*, pp. 245-52.

5.   A. Malamat, 'Charismatic Führung im Buch der Richter', in W. Schluchter (ed.), *Max Webers Studie über das antike Judentum: Interpretation und Kritik* (Frankfurt am Main: Suhrkamp, 1981), pp. 110-33.

6.   J. Rosenberg, *King and Kin: Political Allegory in the Hebrew Bible* (Bloomington/Indianapolis: Indiana University Press, 1986); B. Halpern, 'The Political Impact of David's Marriages', *JBL* 99 (1980), pp. 507-28.

Document' takes for granted the principle that the Davidic family is the proper channel through which the royal authority of David is to be upheld. In effect the charismatic principle that applies uniquely to David is carried over to the dynasty descended from him and is used both to support the authority of the monarchy as an institution, and the dynasty to which that institution is to be uniquely tied.

The significance of noting these features regarding the applicability of the concept of charisma to the extensive accounts of how Israel acquired a monarchy is twofold: In the first place the accounts support fully the point made by Weber that charismatic authority tends to pass over into a more institutionalized form of authority, in this case that of a royal dynasty. When this occurs the strength and authority of the original truly charismatic leadership is significantly changed. This may lead to such a weakening of authority that a continued appeal back to the original charismatic figure may become necessary in order to support the much weaker claims attaching to the dynasty that derived from it. The several short-lived royal dynasties of Israel's Northern Kingdom may serve further as illustrations of this.[7] However we should also note the contrasting view of A. Alt.[8]

2. *The Idea of Charisma*

In a second consideration concerning the nature of charisma, it is useful to note some remarks by S.N. Eisenstadt in the introduction he offers to his translation of the extracts from Weber's writings on the subject:

> In much of existing sociological literature it has been assumed that a deep chasm exists between the charismatic aspects and the more ordinary, routine aspects of social organization and the organized, continuous life of social institutions—and that Weber himself stressed this dichotomy. It seems to me, however, that this is a mistaken view and that the best clue to understanding Weber's work and especially his significance for modern sociology lies in the attempt to combine the two and to analyze how they are interrelated in the fabric of social life and the processes of social change.[9]

It is this point concerning the inter-relationship between charismatic and routine aspects of social life and organization that forms the main feature of this essay and which appears to be fully substantiated by the remarks already made concerning Israel's kingship. The stories concerning the dynasty

7.   K.W. Whitelam, 'Israelite Kingship: The Royal Ideology and its Opponents', in R.E. Clements (ed.), *The World of Ancient Israel* (Cambridge: Cambridge University Press, 1989), pp. 119-40.

8.   A. Alt, 'The Monarchy in the Kingdoms of Israel and Judah', in *Essays on Old Testament History and Religion* (Oxford: Basil Blackwell, 1966), pp. 239-59.

9.   Eisenstadt, *Max Weber on Charisma*, p. ix.

founder's unique charisma are directed towards defending the organized continuing life of Israel and Judah under a monarchy.

This observation indicates how the idea of charismatic leadership is important not simply as a distinctive phenomenon in its own right, but as part of the recognition of a continuing interplay between the unique, one-off, leadership of unusual individuals and the larger group that responds to this. Each influences the other and acts on the other in ways that form a necessary part of the social process. I am not simply arguing here for a more carefully considered sociological use of the term charisma, set over against its more popular modern use; the more significant point is that charisma can only be effectively understood in relation to its opposite, which concerns that which is ordinary, routine and frequently found.[10]

According to Dirk Käsler, Weber's intellectual development was strongly influenced by a concern to understand the role of economic and juridical institutions in governing individual freedom and the possibility of individual self-realization in a social setting.[11] This raised the question of the interplay between the authority felt by the individual and that imposed by the group. It is to this issue that the concept of charisma is addressed, and, with it, the clearer grasp of its opposite, which is to be found in that which is routine and everyday. Accordingly, for any change to be brought about by the work of unique individuals in the more lasting and commonplace life of the community, the insights of the charismatic leader need to be 'routinized', i.e. brought to the level of everyday routine. We can let Weber speak:

> The term 'charisma' will be applied to a certain quality of an individual personality by virtue of which he is set apart from ordinary men and treated as endowed with supernatural, superhuman, or at least specifically exceptional powers or qualities. These are such as are not accessible to the ordinary person, but are regarded as of divine origin or as exemplary, and on the basis of them the individual concerned is treated as a leader. In primitive circumstances this peculiar deference is paid to prophets, to people with a reputation for therapeutic or legal wisdom, to leaders in the hunt, and heroes in war... Charismatic authority is thus specifically outside the realm of every-day routine and the profane sphere.[12]

In its pure form charismatic authority has a character specifically foreign to everyday routine structures. The social relationships directly involved are strictly personal, based on the validity and practice of charismatic personal qualities. If this is not to remain a purely transitory phenomenon, but to take

---

10. C. Schäfer-Lichtenberger, *Josua und Salomo: Eine Studie zu Autorität und Legitimität des Nachfolgers im Alten Testament* (Leiden: E.J. Brill, 1995), pp. 24ff.

11. D. Käsler, *Max Weber: An Introduction to his Life and Work* (trans. P. Hurd; Cambridge: Polity Press, 1988), pp. 127-29.

12. Eisenstadt, *Max Weber on Charisma*, pp. 48, 51.

on the character of a permanent relationship forming a stable community of disciples or a band of followers or a party organization, it is necessary for the character of charismatic authority to become radically changed. Indeed in its pure form charismatic authority may be said to exist only in the originating process. It cannot remain stable, but becomes either traditionalized or rationalized, or a combination of both.[13]

Weber contends that charismatic leadership provides a basis of authority which is short-lived and relatively unstable, and this is fully substantiated in the biblical stories about how kingship became a part of Israel's life. It tended to remain an ideal type of authority, intermittently experienced, but which could later be appealed to in support of relatively weak forms of traditional authority.

It is also relevant to note that the most powerful manifestations of charisma may often only be truly identified *after the event*. Stories of how this charisma was displayed and experienced by the larger community may then be told in respect to the changes which the charismatically endowed leader helped to bring about. Appeals to his, or her, great charisma, as exemplified by exceptional feats, are therefore made in order to justify changes which would otherwise be questionable, or even vigorously opposed.

3. *Prophecy and Charisma*

The particular relevance of these remarks to the rather different question concerning how notions of charisma may help towards a better understanding of Israelite prophecy is twofold. On the one hand they show that charismatic authority tended to remain a relatively infrequently experienced and ideal type of authority. On the other hand they show that written records of the major charismatic heroes tended to be utilized in support of more long-lasting patterns of authority vested in institutions. The ideal of divine charisma was appealed to in support of institutions which might otherwise remain weak and insecure. We shall see that this is a relevant point in relation to the need to understand the character and structure of the biblical prophetic writings.

Our immediate concern is with the light that the concept of charisma can shed upon the nature and contribution of prophecy to the development of ancient Israel, and to the formation of a corpus of prophetic writings in the Bible. It is readily apparent that Weber himself, in his important studies of socio-religious development of ancient Judaism, accorded a very prominent place to the activities of the prophets.[14] Not surprisingly therefore biblical

13. Eisenstadt, *Max Weber on Charisma*, p. 54.
14. M. Weber, *Ancient Judaism* (New York: Free Press, 1952); also Weber, *The Sociology of Religion*, pp. xxxiiiff.

scholarship has found itself endeavoring to draw insight and support from these observations. However, the emphases that have accompanied these observations have frequently drawn attention to features that were not those singled out by Weber himself. At the same time, it also needs to be recognized that the critical reconstructions of the development of Israelite prophecy upon which Weber drew have undergone very substantial reappraisals in recent years.[15] Accordingly, several of the features to which Weber devoted special attention should now be regarded in a more critical light.

Several aspects of the activities and achievements of the biblical prophets entitles them to be described properly as charismatic figures. It is also appropriate to suggest that a closer examination of Weber's ideas on the subject outside his specific interest in ancient Judaism serves to illuminate a number of features of prophecy which have hitherto largely been left aside from consideration of their charismatic significance.

We may begin by reconsidering the question of social position and the functioning of a prophet. It is noteworthy that on these issues several studies have placed a surprisingly heavy emphasis upon the psychological aspects of prophetic activity, its alliance with forms of ecstatic religion, and the socially marginal position which the prophet occupied within the life of the community.[16]

When Weber wrote his essays on ancient Judaism this emphasis was readily intelligible on account of the attention that the writings of H. Gunkel and G. Hölscher had drawn to these matters.[17] Yet it remains doubtful whether the many attempts to uncover the psychology of prophecy, which may or may not be valid in their own ways, have much real bearing on the question of its charismatic quality as Weber presented the notion. The fact that a prophet may have behaved in a strange manner, that he, or she, may have come from an economically weak stratum of society, or that such prophecies were uttered in a trance-like state of extreme excitement has little bearing on whether or not this entitles such figures to be classed as charismatic in the sense in which Weber employed the term. Fundamentally, Weber's notion of charisma is to be understood in connection with the qualitative difference of a relatively few outstanding individuals who are capable of initiating major social change. Such a notion belongs, not so much to the unusual behavior displayed by religious functionaries in a

15. C. Schäfer-Lichtenberger, 'The Pariah', *JSOT* 51 (1991), pp. 85-113.

16. R.R. Wilson, *Prophecy and Society in Ancient Israel* (Philadelphia: Fortress Press, 1980), pp. 56-58, 62-64; I.M. Lewis, *Religion in Context: Cults and Charisma* (Cambridge: Cambridge University Press, 1986), pp. 27-30.

17. P.H.A. Neumann, *Das Propheten Verständnis in der Deutschsprachigen Forschung seit Heinrich Ewald* (Darmstadt: Wissenschaftliche Buchgesellschaft, 1979), pp. 109-11.

community, but rather to the highly distinctive attainments of such individuals within the larger group. Also it is a major feature of the argument presented here that the concept of charisma is particularly applicable to the canonical prophets of Israel and Judah on account of the radical positions they adopted towards the major religious and political institutions of their time. The 'charismatic' authority contrasted with the more traditional forms of authority vested in these institutions.

In recognizing the appearance and public popularity of a number of 'false' prophets the biblical record amply warns us against supposing that the enduring significance of prophecy lay in the manner of its public presentation or reception. The fact that only a tiny handful of prophets have ultimately been accorded canonical status indicates that only a few were thought to manifest the true quality of charisma such as Weber described. This charisma manifested itself through its power to initiate change, to elicit recognition for one individual over against the authority of well established institutions, and to exhibit a distinctiveness of authority which lacked any other explanation save that it derived from a special divine gift.

It would be more appropriate to apply Weber's concept of charisma to explain why some prophets were identified as 'true' while others were 'false', than to characterize whole groups of practitioners such as mantic prophets as charismatic figures. At the most we should recognize that the latter, because of their social and behavioral distinctiveness, had the potential for being recognized as charismatic figures in the narrower sense. We should certainly note the tendency to draw special attention to the various manifestations and phenomena associated with ecstatic religion. No doubt this is also related to the way in which prophets frequently emerged in society from small communities that had been forced onto the margins of economic and political life. Nevertheless, such observations have only a partial bearing on their being regarded as charismatic figures in the narrowly defined understanding of charismatic uniqueness with which Weber was concerned.

Consequently all attempts to associate the possession of charisma with the psychological eccentricities of prophets, or with their origins from distinct social groups, has only limited significance for the more unique gifts with which they are credited in the biblical records. The charismatic endowment possessed by specifically named prophetic individuals must be linked more directly to the particular religious and political insights which they displayed and to the fundamental changes in the status of religious institutions that they helped to bring about.

4. *Charisma and Written Testimony*

On the positive side of maintaining the claim that prophets displayed charismatic quality in the sense that Weber regarded as most important, there would appear to be worthwhile insights to be gained. Foremost among these insights are the issues relating to awareness that a gap exists between the existence of a prophetic book, purporting to derive from the prophet, and the original activity of that prophet for which we have effectively no other surviving testimony.[18] The stimulus towards preserving a written record of a prophet's sayings and actions would seem to have arisen out of a sense that he had shown himself to be a uniquely endowed individual; he possessed charisma.

In the biblical canon of prophecy it is not difficult to see why the beginning of the written preservation of the sayings of a number of leading prophetic individuals begins in the eighth century BCE. It is because this was the period when the sister kingdoms of Israel and Judah first fell under the ruinous impact of Assyrian imperial expansion. Accordingly, it is necessary to acknowledge that the preservation of written prophecy was, in the first instance, related to the issues attendant upon this disastrous political experience. So, recognition that an element of charisma attached to the achievements of Amos, Hosea, Isaiah and Micah in the eighth century BCE was inseparably linked to the stance they adopted over these issues. Their threats and warnings were seen as providing some explanation of the political disasters that overtook Israel and Judah. Other features concerning their religious loyalties and moral insights must be regarded as secondary to this, even though they cannot be dismissed as unimportant.

A second issue concerning the value of using the term charisma in connection with the work of the biblical prophets is closely related to this. It concerns the question of the purpose of preserving the prophets' sayings in written form for future generations to read and ponder. Such action can scarcely have been intended simply as a consequence of lasting interest in the immense political and social turmoil brought about by Mesopotamian political incursions from the eighth to sixth centuries BCE. It must have been because the prophets' words provided legitimation for changes which these events brought about.

This further helps to explain the fact that the canonical shape of the prophetic writings bears ample evidence that it was more important to preserve knowledge of the prophet's sayings than to recall a record of his

---

18. R.E. Clements, 'Prophecy as Literature: A Re-Appraisal', in D.G. Miller (ed.), *The Hermeneutical Quest: Essays in Honor of J.L. Mays for his 65th Birthday* (PTMS, 4; Allison Park, PA: Pickwick Press, 1986), repr. *Old Testament Prophecy: From Oracles to Canon* (Louisville, KY: Westminster/John Knox Press, 1996), pp. 203-16.

life. The charisma was not important in itself; it mattered only in relation to the social and religious changes which the charismatic individual brought about. The written prophetic word was looked upon as the authoritative testimony, which served to explain the cessation of major features of Israel's and Judah's national life and their replacement by others. It also provided assurance that a time would come when fundamental institutions of that national life which had foundered, such as the Davidic kingship and the Jerusalem temple, would be restored.

The concern to locate such prophecies within the life and work of specific prophets has arisen precisely because these prophets were believed to have displayed charisma in the full Weberian sense. They had foreseen the coming ruin of Israel and Judah and the great institutions, which had shaped the existence of these kingdoms. Nor is it at all difficult to see how the fact that Judah appeared at first to have survived the ruin that befell the Northern Kingdom in the eighth century produced a strong, but ultimately disappointed, expectation that the survival of the Davidic monarchy and the Jerusalem temple would serve to ensure the political continuance of Judah.

Subsequent events of the sixth century inflicted upon Judah and Jerusalem by Nebuchadrezzar frustrated all such expectations. This fact has meant that a further group of prophecies concerning the fate of both kingship and temple has been given great prominence in the preserved prophetic corpus. Not only have the entire books of Jeremiah and Ezekiel been shaped by this knowledge, but the much older collection of Isaiah's prophecies has been substantially recast and supplemented as a result. The book of Isaiah is a post-587 BCE book, even though it retains older elements.

It may also be argued that the complexity of the tensions inherent in the final shaping of the history of Joshua–2 Kings (the so-called 'Deuteronomistic History') are also a result of the frustration of the hopes that were bound up with the fortunes of the Davidic dynasty and the Jerusalem temple.

Prophecy was vitally important as a medium through which Israel and Judah could interpret, and come to terms with, these tragic events and this fact lies at the very centre of the 'charismatic' authority of the recorded prophets. Their claim to be able to speak directly on behalf of God placed them outside more traditional and established forms of authority linked to religious institutions. They felt no compulsion to submit to them, and did not need to appeal to them for legitimacy.

However, once the catastrophes which had befallen Israel and Judah lay in the past, these communities needed to restore some degree of credibility to these institutions, which provided more fixed and stable forms of authority. This was necessary in order for these communities to cope with the routine of everyday life. It is this process of giving credibility to a greatly revised religious order of life which written prophecy provided. In order to do so it was dependent upon appeal to the original highly respected prophet's words. His special insights and gifts provided the means of substantiating the claims to legitimacy of the new order.

5. *Charisma and the Wider Community*

Clearly, the charismatic leader would have been nothing without the larger group which existed around him, and to which his message was addressed. In considerable measure it is this group—its needs, and its deference to the prophets' words, which marked him out as an especially important figure. This group, therefore, played a necessary role in the identification and affirmation of the charisma displayed by the prophet.[19] The role of this group, however, is qualitatively and functionally different from that of the original charismatic leader. The charismatic leader displays a unique element of authority over the group, whereas the group recognizes itself as having been the recipient and beneficiary of this gift.

An excellent example of this appropriation of the message of a uniquely individual prophet by the concerns and interests of a larger, institutionally related group, is found in the book of the prophet Jeremiah. As is now widely recognized, this prophet's words have been accommodated, in their written form, into an intellectual and religious framework characterized as Deuteronomic, or Deuteronomistic.[20] So far as we can identify its features this was an influential, and centrally based, reform movement that first emerged during the seventh century in the wake of the intrusions into Israel and Judah which had begun a century earlier.

The thesis that the major prophets of the Hebrew Bible were drawn from socially marginal groups appears largely to have arisen in order to fit such figures into a recognizable pattern, rather than on the basis of substantive evidence. The kind of moral and religious offences that the prophets accuse their contemporaries of committing and tolerating, are, for the most part, the kinds of offences which were endemic to Near Eastern society for many centuries. They relate to corruption, abuse of the legal system, greed and oppression, all of which could not have been either newly perceived, or uniquely rampant, problems of Israel and Judah in the eighth to sixth centuries BCE. Thus there is little reason for supposing that opposition to them arose in any very obvious way among the more marginal elements in society.

---

19. Cf. n. 18 above.

20. S. Herrmann, *Jeremia. Der Prophet und das Buch* (Erträge der Forschung; Darmstadt: Wissenschaftliche Buchgesellschaft, 1990), pp. 66-81; R.E. Clements, 'Jeremiah 1–25 and the Deuteronomistic History', in A.G. Auld (ed.), *Understanding Poets and Prophets: Essays in Honour of George Wishart Anderson* (JSOTSup, 152; Sheffield: Sheffield Academic Press, 1993), pp. 93-113.

There would then seem to be little reason for claiming that the major canonical prophets were especially the representatives of marginalized social groups, although we cannot exclude this possibility. Much more important is the point that it was the major central religious and political institutions of Israel and Judah that were threatened with total eclipse as a consequence of the Assyrian and Babylonian interventions and attacks. The words of the major prophets served to provide a basis for renewing and re-asserting the authority of these institutions when their survival was under threat. All the indications are that both Isaiah and Ezekiel came from within a group which stood within the main circles of governmental authority. Even if, as is often argued, such figures as Amos, Hosea and Jeremiah emanated from more peripheral communities, it would appear that their prophecies have been accommodated into the framework of ideas of a more central establishment.

So we can regard much of the prophetic invective as of a relatively conventional nature, even though it was evidently delivered with great intensity and passion. The primary significance of the charismatic insights of the prophets was provided by the broader political scene of the period in which they emerged. This established the need for preserving a written record of their words, rather than as the consequence of a crisis of unprecedented social and moral pressures that their respective communities were experiencing.

If this is a valid observation, then it should lead us to recognize that the charismatic quality of the canonical prophets is primarily to be seen in the connection between their distinctive insights and emphases and the collapse of the political institutions in which they operated. In foretelling the imminent threat of ruin and disaster befalling Israel and Judah the remarkable succession of prophets accurately read the message of their times. Most of their contemporaries failed to do so!

6. Charisma and the Canon of Written Prophecy

Awareness of the nature of the charismatic distinctiveness and individuality of the great prophets is of relevance to the belief that the literary form of prophecy in the Hebrew Bible may be understood as the work of 'schools' of prophets. Such views were at one time advocated by a number of Scandinavian scholars and find one of their strongest expression in Engnell's essay 'Prophets and Prophetism in the Old Testament'.[21]

Engnell rejects the idea that any major distinction can be made between the work of the original prophet and that of his disciples. All prophets are

---

21. I. Engnell, 'Prophets and Prophetism in the Old Testament', in *Critical Essays on the Old Testament* (trans. J.T. Willis; London: SPCK, 1970), pp. 123-79.

regarded as the leaders of schools and the books ascribed to individual prophets are the products of such schools. Engnell regards it as pointless to try to distinguish between the work of the original prophet and that of his followers. I have consistently remained sceptical about this claim to the existence of prophetic schools, and I think that the term can only be helpful in a much modified sense. To a large extent the importance attached to the notion of charisma, as Weber understood it in relation to individual creativity and situations of social change, could not easily be spread too widely.

Individuality and distinctiveness are of the essence of what constitutes charismatic authority. The belief that schools of prophets existed resolves the question of individual and corporate elements in the formation of the prophetic literature by setting aside the individual aspect of the specific prophetic charisma. It may even suggest that such charisma could be passed on from one prophet to another in a transfer of authority analogous to that of a royal dynasty. Yet there is only minimal evidence that this occurred, and clearly the Hebrew Bible contains no attempt to provide authorization for such prophetic schools on the model displayed by the monarchy.

On this particular score Weber's special interest in the question of charismatic authority attaching to prophets appears to be a valuable corrective to several assumptions about prophecy that have otherwise had a powerful influence among biblical scholars. In a real measure they help us to recover a greater sense of the individuality and creativity of the great prophets. For Weber, the sense of the prophet's uniqueness, the awareness that he stood apart from other individuals and perceived truths that were hidden from their eyes, was the essence of his task. The idea that a prophetic 'office' existed of the kind that meant that a continuing succession of figures occupied the same role may have been true in the sense that cultic officials of such a kind existed in ancient Israel; but it fails to accord with the sense of uniqueness accorded to the named figures of classical prophecy. They were somehow different, and it is this difference that the notion of charisma seeks to explain.

In maintaining a scepticism concerning the existence of significant schools of prophets who maintained a distinct religious identity, we must nevertheless recognize that a prophet's words needed to be remembered and appropriated by the groups that came to surround him. This could not occur without that message being elaborated and subjected to some degree of adaptation and modification. In Weber's terminology it needed to be 'routinized'. Religious ideals needed to be spelled out in terms of everyday precepts and rules that could be acted upon in an everyday setting. It was in this respect that the kinds of moral and religious invective, that had served to back up the prophet's threats, provided a useful medium of instruction. They enabled prophecy to become detached from the unique and unrepeatable situations in which it had originated and accommodated into a more lasting literature of admonition and assurance and legitimation.

Similarly, since the great prophets had arisen at a time of threat to the established religious institutions of the nation, it became essential that their teaching should be clarified to show what kind of institutions they did support. Since these charismatically endowed prophets had addressed their sayings to situations which witnessed major upheavals in the life of Israel and Judah, it had to be shown in what manner they had interpreted such upheavals. By offering reasons for calamity they were able to demonstrate that the divine government of Israel remained an intelligible belief.

It is in these reasons for calamity that the strength and originality of the prophetic contribution is to be seen. Such reasons included various features of cultic polemic, but most prominently of all, they included the giving of priority to moral integrity and commitment to righteousness. It was this emphatic priority that marked the enduring feature of prophetic originality. We should not suppose that the prophets perceived a different kind of moral order from that which shaped the thinking of lawmakers and sages. Rather, the moral and social issues on which they focused attention were, in large measure, issues which were endemic to a society experiencing the economic and social changes which coloured ancient Israel's life. Nevertheless, the prophetic invective placed such a weight of importance upon these moral questions that they took on a new significance as factors by which the entire life of the nation could be seen and judged. To a considerable extent, in the prophetic invective, the historical order was itself seen to be subject to moral judgment. In place of arbitrary and uncontrollable forces, history, with its many vicissitudes, was moralized.

The awareness that the insights of the charismatic prophet marked the experience of catastrophe as a transitional, but necessary, aberration of the divine purpose in specific situations shows how the prophetic charisma did not itself represent a permanent form of authority. Like all charismatic authority, it was temporary and unique to one individual. It could only be effective when its demands were modified and adapted to accommodate to the more lasting religious needs of the people.

7. Charisma and Routinization

Charismatic authority needed to be transformed, by the nature of its own unstable character, into a variety of forms of more traditional authority. The spoken word of the original prophet needed to become the meticulously preserved written word of the prophetic book. In the process, considerable additions and changes needed to be made for the work of routinization to be implemented. The unique and transitory situation which the original prophet had encountered had to be set in a perspective that made it possible for the more enduring and practical needs of the community that respected him to be met.

So there is much in Weber's understanding of the nature of charisma which helps to explain the contents and shaping of the prophetic literature of the Hebrew Bible. The necessity for some form of routinization seems to me to assist, at least in part, in understanding why so much additional material has been incorporated into each of the prophetic books. During the nineteenth century this material came to be classed as 'inauthentic' and to be largely set aside in the work of interpretation. However, it is noteworthy that this is not the feature of Weber's interpretation of charisma which has most interested biblical scholars. Instead, certain other aspects attaching to the concept have elicited more attention. I might then suggest that Weber's own insights have actually tended, rather ironically, to be routinized in a manner which has exaggerated certain features at the expense of others. It is then open to suggest that it is these latter features which may prove to be more helpful so far as understanding the prophetic literature is concerned.

In particular the inevitability of the tension that Weber pointed to between the original charismatic authority of the prophetic individual and the ongoing life of religious institutions seems to be a helpful one. It describes very well the various interests that have led to the supplementation and editing of the prophetic sayings to form them into books. For the most part this is not the work of individuals who aspired to setting their own prophecies and teachings alongside that of the great charismatic figures. Rather, it should be seen as a work of interpretation and routinization that endeavored to make the insights and messages of the great prophets applicable to the ongoing needs of a larger world of followers.

Furthermore, it seems apparent that the sayings of prophets have frequently been used to serve as a form of legitimation for major shifts in the operation and control of the cultus in Israel.

Judaism was forced to accommodate profound departures from the original model it had projected of the Mosaic cultus. The earlier conventional tendency to contrast the a-cultic, or anti-cultic, stance of the pre-exilic prophets with the more evident pro-cultic interest of the post-exilic ones is largely misinterpreted. The shaping of the canonical corpus of prophecy has endeavoured to accommodate both features to a common purpose. This work of canonical shaping and collecting drew upon the words of the prophets as a form of authorization for adopting inevitable and unanticipated changes to this original priestly model of cultic life. The notion of the charismatically endowed prophet provided the essential link in the chain of divine command and human appropriation that made such changes acceptable.

To this degree it is arguable that the Hebrew prophetic writings show as much concern about forms of traditional authority as about the exclusively charismatic. Perhaps, more precisely, the essential feature is that the very nature of appeals to charismatic authority required that they should be seen in relation to the ongoing, institutional aspects of religion which they challenged. The older picture of an almost inevitable confrontation between prophet and cultus failed to grasp the point that each could only properly function in relation to the other. It was because the cultus was vulnerable to change and obsolescence that it required to be revised and reinvigorated by the input which only the charismatic prophet could provide. Appeals back to the prophetic word of God of the past served to provide a basis of authority by which the less exciting, but more enduringly necessary, religious institutions of the present could be maintained. In general perspective, therefore, it is arguable that Weber's interest in the limitations and instability of all forms of charismatic authority has much to contribute towards a better understanding of the nature of prophecy.

Chapter 3

ISAIAH: A BOOK WITHOUT AN ENDING?

The answer to the question posed in the title of this essay is, in a purely
formal sense, quite simple. The ending of the book of Isaiah is to be found in
Isa. 66.24 and reads:

> And they shall go out and look at the dead bodies of the people who have
> rebelled against me; for their worm shall not die, their fire shall not be
> quenched, and they shall be an abhorrence to all flesh.

When we read this we are not at all surprised that neither ancient readers nor
modern scholars have been happy to regard this brief verse as the appropriate closure to the book. It is not at all typical of its overall message,
which has earned for it the title of 'The Fifth Gospel'. In any case, from the
point of view of a planned literary structure, this can scarcely be the book's
intended ending with due regard for its overall content. Isaiah 60 is the real
and effective end to it. If you prefer, either ch. 61 or 62 would do but not
quite as well. The claim for Isaiah 60 rests on the fact that it resumes and
summarizes the book's most central theme which concerns Jerusalem and its
destiny.[1] It brings to a resolution problems and issues regarding the city's
place among the nations of the world which occupy a central role in the
book from the beginning. If we are looking for a skilfully planned *inclusio*
of the kind that corresponds with the issues that repeatedly rise and fall
throughout the intervening chapters, then this is very clearly evident
between chs. 5 and 60 (62). It is ch. 60 that conveys what F. Kermode has
called 'the sense of an ending' appropriate to the scroll's beginning in the
first chapter.[2]

1. R.E. Clements, 'A Light to the Nations', in J.W. Watts and P.R. House (eds.),
*Forming Prophetic Literature: Essays on Isaiah and the Twelve in Honour of J.D.W.
Watts* (JSOTSup, 235; Sheffield: Sheffield Academic Press, 1996), pp. 57-69; reprinted
below as Chapter 13.

2. F. Kermode, *The Sense of an Ending: Studies in the Theory of Fiction* (Oxford:
Oxford University Press, 1967).

If there are good reasons for dismissing Isa. 66.24 as the book's planned ending, with a much more suitable one to be found in ch. 60, there are also other comparably suitable passages in the book. The first of these is to be found in 4.2-6, although the more familiar 2.2-4 would serve as well as an ending as it does an introduction. It clearly establishes what the book of Isaiah is all about—the city of Jerusalem! Another ending has been thought to occur in Isa. 12.1-6, which is sometimes classed as 'a Psalm of Thanksgiving'. It is scarcely this, but rather appears less impressively as the last of the sequence of additions which give a radical eschatological colouring to Isa. 11.1–12.6. Other comparable passages are to be found in Isaiah's sixty-six chapters which almost make it a book of beginnings and endings. Attention here will primarily be focused on Isaiah 35, but with some related concern for Isaiah 60. Before we can do that, however, some broader issues have to be addressed.

1. *Isaiah as a Book*

The subject of beginnings and endings confronts us with concerns about the nature of literature and the question: 'What is a Book?' In an essay on the subject,[3] John Barton raises questions regarding the fundamental nature of several of the writings of the Hebrew Bible. In a sense the Pentateuch taken as a whole constitutes a single book, but it is one that is very unlike a modern one, unless we compare it to some of the larger modern anthologies of writings around a particular theme. Moreover, if modern historical-critical explorations into its many sources are even partially correct, its final form is very different from such earlier structural forms that its component parts once possessed.

Similarly, the prophecies of Isaiah in some sense constitute a single book, and much recent writing concerning it has sought to focus on this contention.[4] But what kind of a book is it? Is it, as some defenders would still contend, a collection of prophecies from a single author or group of authors, in which case the presumed authorship provides the missing link between its

3.   J. Barton, 'What Is a Book? Modern Exegesis and the Literary Conventions of Ancient Israel', in J.C. de Moor (ed.), *Intertextuality in Ugarit and Israel* (OTS, 40; Leiden: E.J. Brill, 1998), pp. 1-14; repr. in *The Old Testament: Canon, Literature and Theology: Collected Essays of John Barton* (SOTS Monographs; Aldershot/ Burlington: Ashgate, 2007), pp. 137-48.

4.   C.R. Seitz, 'Isaiah 1–66: Making Sense of the Whole', in C.R. Seitz (ed.), *Reading and Preaching the Book of Isaiah* (Philadelphia: Fortress Press, 1988), pp. 105-26; D. Carr, 'Reaching for Unity in Isaiah', *JSOT* 57 (1993), pp. 61-80; repr. in *The Prophets: A Sheffield Reader* (The Biblical Seminar, 42; Sheffield: Sheffield Academic Press, 1996), pp. 164-83; E.W. Conrad, *Reading Isaiah* (Minneapolis: Fortress Press, 1991).

various parts? Or is it an anthology put together around a number of central themes concerning the fortunes of the royal house of David and the destiny of the city of Jerusalem? In this case the subject matter provides the missing link. Or yet again, are there structuring units that help to give it a framework to hold its parts together? Or is there no such unifying structure so that its final form is merely the residual shape that was left when practical considerations dictated that the scroll could extend no further?

It is to these questions about understanding the final form of the scroll of Isaiah that this article is addressed. I take the internal evidence to show for certain that it was not from a single author. It also seems clear that there are elements of a structural pattern in the final form which has, nonetheless, been disrupted and broken into at various points. If the scroll is the product of a single authorial group, or of a regionally based scribal tradition, then this could explain the bringing together of so much disparate material into one large scroll. It would simply be a 'collection' with some degree of randomness showing through in its make-up!

But are there sufficient signs that it is more than this and that some basic overall structure has contributed to its shape and message? This question amounts to asking whether the book's 'unity', to use the ill-defined noun that has become conventional, is more than the product of some external authorial factor, and whether there are genuine, if half-obscured, inner literary connections and structures which bind the parts into a whole? How did the scroll actually come to be formed, or is this an impossible question to answer? Overall the question of the final form of the scroll and that regarding its overall unity have tended to merge into one another, although they are not quite the same. Several parts read as though they were what a modern book would assign to notes and appendices.

Much of the discussion concerning unity has focused on the observation that throughout the entire scroll there are a surprisingly large number of internal cross-references of the sort that now fall under the general heading of intertextuality. These have been taken, as sufficient in some degree to impart a measure of unity. It is certainly striking in regard to the Isaiah book that one of its features is the widespread occurrence of reinterpretations of key words and themes that occur earlier, adding new messages to a received prophecy and sometimes a whole series of messages.[5] These impose an added dimension of mystery and authority upon the original occurrence. Sometimes they do more than this and contribute a degree of structural shape. At a literary level it is easy to appreciate that when a divine warning is conveyed through metaphors such as those of blindness, darkness, or the

---

5.　K. Nielsen, *There Is Hope for a Tree: The Tree as Metaphor in Isaiah* (JSOTSup, 65; Sheffield: JSOT Press, 1989); K.P. Darr, *Isaiah's Vision and the Family of God* (Louisville, KY: Westminster/John Knox Press, 1994).

felling of a tree, then it is appropriate that the contrasting benefits can be described in terms of recovery of sight, the shining of light, or new growth from the stump of a tree. Isaiah is full of such verbal richness and demonstrates how, even when separated by long stretches of text, a degree of structural interconnectedness can be found. Like the girder framework of a building, cross-references serve to create form and structure.

It is not surprising therefore that, in some instances, we find that the original verbal imagery is later picked up to establish a literary connection even when a significantly different message is conveyed. Besides the possibility of reversing an earlier threat, new purposes could be found for God to send a 'signal to the nations' (5.26; 49.22). Alongside these internal allusions, there are also others which make reference to passages from other prophetic books and parts of the Hebrew Bible,[6] and these also tell us something about the context in which a prophetic book took shape. They show that intertextual allusions do not simply point to unity within one book but reach across to link together a larger canonical collection.

Unity of a different sort is also demonstrable when a particular theme, such as that concerning the destiny of the royal house of David, is taken up and reconsidered in the light of later political developments.[7] In this way a sequential chain of prophecies on a particular subject is established which indicates that, once a particular major issue was focused, then it was natural that further significant developments relating to it should be added on. The connection is sometimes reinforced by consciously alluding back to earlier prophecies on the subject.

Included in these verbal and thematic features, which tend to go under the heading of 'unity', there is also the widely recognized literary technique of establishing an *inclusio*. In one of many expressions of this device a particular threat that foretells the coming of a time of judgment is later rounded off by a reversal of it to give a message of reassurance and hope. In this way structures with beginnings and endings are formed, again often bridging surprisingly large expanses of text.

All of these literary features are properly open to classification as aspects of a book's unity, even though there is no reason to conclude that the same author, or group of authors, have been responsible for them. Rather, they appear as widely used techniques which possessed a special appeal and usefulness for poet-prophets. These usages indicate techniques which reveal a desire to create literary structure.

---

6. B.D. Sommer, *A Prophet Reads Scripture: Allusion in Isaiah 40–66* (Stanford: Stanford University Press, 1998).

7. P.D. Wegner, *An Examination of Kingship and Messianic Expectation in Isaiah 1–35* (Lewiston, NY: Edward Mellen Press, 1992).

Overall, the question of unity leads us to look for evidence of this kind of planned structure with appropriate beginnings and endings. We may also expect to see it further in the presence of hinge-points, or transition pieces, which serve the purpose of holding together different blocks of material. Such indications of a transition enable the reader to recognize where priorities are being established and where, in a given timescale of divine purpose, the reader is placed.

Before going into greater detail about the shape and structure of the present Isaiah scroll, I want to suggest an important preliminary step. Among the many recent attempts to examine critically the book's final structural shape we should note the observations of Marvin Sweeney[8] that chs. 1–4 and 63–66 form a kind of overarching *inclusio*. The themes that appear in 2.6–4.1 reappear in 63.1–66.24. Similarly, within the unit made up of chs. 2–4, the opening promise in 2.2-4 and the concluding one in 4.2-6 form a richly reassuring *inclusio* affirming Jerusalem's future glory. It is the pieces in between that add a note of warning. While Sweeney's points are valid and helpful up to a point, they do not do as much as might have been supposed towards an understanding of the final form of the book. This is because, although wholly appropriate in content, from a literary perspective these chapters (that is, chs. 1–4 and 63–66) stand apart as peripheral to the book as a whole. They form a prologue and epilogue to it and no longer appear as parts of its main body. In reality chs. 2–4 show every sign of having once existed as an independent scroll focused on Jerusalem and its destiny which has been incorporated into the book of Isaiah at a relatively late stage. Similarly the fact that ch. 1 has evidently been designed to form a general introduction to the book in its entirety has been widely recognized. Both these introductory units (1 and 2–4), are linked to the larger work on account of their concern with the city, not on account of other evident links to the Isaiah tradition. Chapters 2–4 and 63–66 do little to bolster the claim for the unity of the book when taken as a whole. This primarily consists of the contents of chs. 5–60 (62). In many respects the distinctiveness of these framework chapters, with their focus on Jerusalem, makes them as much a sign of the book's disorder as of its planned shape.

There are two reasons for this. The first is the widely recognized feature that the present opening chapter of the book serves its purpose as introduction by pointing to Jerusalem, and by establishing its theme as a summons to the city to repent in order to hasten the arrival of its glorious future. The present ending of the book stands somewhat obliquely to this appeal and functions awkwardly as its intended conclusion.

---

8. M.A. Sweeney, *Isaiah 1–4 and the Post-Exilic Understanding of the Isaiah Tradition* (BZAW, 171; Berlin: W. de Gruyter). Cf. also Sweeney, *Isaiah 1–39*, pp. 51-57.

The second point in regard to Sweeney's claim concerns the fact that the historical shape and origin of the book are far more clearly seen by noting its beginning at ch. 5, rather than with the preceding chapters. Chapters 63–66 read as a series of epilogues to the larger whole and the scroll's effective ending comes in ch. 60. Chapters 61 and 62 simply repeat the same message. Chapters 63–66 which follow scarcely provide a suitable ending at all for the book since they undermine the very certainties and finalities that ch. 60 has established. If we are looking for any sort of planned structure to the book as a whole in its present form, then this has to be found between chs. 5 and 62. Chapters 2–4 and 63–66 are only very loosely attached to this. They share a common subject matter, but show no real integration with it. We can then more or less leave aside chs. 1–4 and 63–66 in looking for a clear structural basis for understanding the book as a whole. They simply form a prologue and epilogue to it, affirming that its theme is Jerusalem and its destiny. Had they appeared in a modern book, there would almost certainly have been indications to this effect.

In noting the overall structure of the book of Isaiah in its present form, the major hinge-point comes in the conjunction of chs. 40–55 with the preceding chs. 1–39. What has the so-called 'Second Isaiah' got to do with 'First Isaiah'?[9] Various explanations have been put forward to account for this.[10] The major disagreement surrounds the issue of how early in the book's formation this conjunction was made and how we are to account for the evident allusions, found in chs. 40–55 that hark back to prophecies in the earlier part of the book. How confidently can it be concluded that these sixteen chapters, or at least the major part of them, once formed a separate collection? Certainly in many respects they appear to represent a completely separate and self-contained collection and have frequently been regarded as such. At the same time, in a number of their major themes, their affinity to the earlier collection is strongly evident. These themes focus on the fate of the city of Jerusalem and the royal dynasty of David which had become inseparably linked to it.

All of these perceptions add up to recognition that there remains some sort of structural shape to the book of Isaiah when taken as a whole, but it is a broken and disturbed structure. There is a primary structure to be found in chs. 5–35, which has subsequently been extended as far as ch. 62 where it is re-established by the addition of three more promises in chs. 60–62. These promise the end of Jerusalem's time of trial and a glorious future for the city. The result is that not only ch. 35, but also chs. 55, 60, 61 and 62 all

9.   C.R. Seitz, 'How Is the Prophet Isaiah Present in the Latter Half of the Book? The Logic of Isaiah 40–66 within the Book of Isaiah', *JBL* 115 (1996), pp. 219-40.

10.   H.G.M. Williamson, *The Book Called Isaiah: Deutero-Isaiah's Role in Composition and Redaction* (Oxford: Clarendon Press, 1994).

represent close parallels to one another. They all express 'the sense of an ending' and make Isaiah a book of beginnings and endings. The primary structure to the book is to be seen in chs. 5–35 and several of the components that contribute to this stand out clearly.

The larger goal of my concern is to identify this primary structure and to ask what it implies about the processes which have contributed to the book's composition. This feature is central to the major work by J. Vermeylen[11] examining the origin and editorial history of chs. 5–35. Once this point is established it highlights the further feature that the narrative units that make up chs. 36–39 provide a striking, and inevitably controversial, element within the book when taken as a whole. On the one hand they offer a valuable key to understanding why the two parts of the book belong together since they appear to form a bridge between them. Yet they do so rather obliquely and show sufficient differences from both the preceding and following parts of the book to form an alien element in it. Had they been designed from the outset as a literary and thematic bridge they would surely not have been so allusive and enigmatic in the connections that they reveal.

There is a further point that deserves to be brought into the argument. A significant feature of a narrative ending is that it presents a measure of closure. It is this which accounts for the familiar story-book phrase '…and they lived happily ever after'. Certainly it is this that we should look for in a collection of prophecies in which a 'final' prophecy, even if it does not actually occur at the end of a book, indicates a sense of fulfilment and completion. Nothing more needs to be said after it. It does not invite a sequel. It is just such a note of finality that is present extensively in most of the passages we have noted as constituting 'endings'. Isaiah 60 asserts:

> Violence shall no more be heard in your land,
> nor devastation or destruction within your borders,..,
> Your sun shall no more go down,
> or your moon cease to shine;
> for the LORD will be your enduring light,
> and your days of mourning shall be ended.
> Your people shall all be righteous;
> they shall take possession of the land forever (Isa. 60.18, 20-21).

When we seek any kind of structured shape to the final form of the Isaiah book, then it is within chs. 5–62 that we need to look for it. Even so, the thematic and ideological links within this presumed 'primary scroll' display a number of awkward jumps and transitions. There appear to be several 'books within the book'. The transition from chs. 5–35 and 40–62 leaves

---

11. J. Vermeylen, *Du prophète Isaïe à l'apocalyptique: Isaïe I–XXXV, miroir d'un demi-millénaire d'expérience religieuse en Israël* (EBib; 2 vols.; Paris: J. Gabalda, 1975).

a number of issues unresolved and the narratives of 36–39 achieve such a resolution only by raising further difficulties. There is, nonetheless, a measure of coherence to such a presumed 'primary scroll' of the Isaiah book if we take it to have consisted of chs. 5–62. It begins with threats to Jerusalem's leaders, warning of coming judgment upon the city, and it concludes with assurances of the city's final vindication and glory.

In between is a long sequence of prophetic material, drawn from various ages, all of which show a positive focus on Jerusalem and the royal dynasty of David whose throne was established there. Inseparable from these two themes is a recurrent concern with the divinely ordained unity of Israel, and a related assurance that, under the umbrella of protection provided by the divine commitment to Jerusalem and the royal house of David, Israel can live, and remain secure, among the nations of the world which pose a threat to it. It is then significant to find in Antti Laato's study exploring how ancient Jewish scribes and scholars read the message of the book, that this is how it was understood in an earlier age.[12]

So far as the book's thematic and ideological structure is concerned, Isaiah 62 marks its effective ending. All of this implies very strongly that we need to rethink the past two centuries of research that has persistently asserted that Isaiah really consists of at least two, or more probably three, independent books. Inseparable from any such consideration is the aware-ness that the idea of a book, or scroll, in anything like the sense that such a title conveys to a modern reader may be inappropriate when applied to an ancient collection of prophecies. Evidence of separateness and distinctive-ness, such as identifies a distinct unit, is interwoven with evidence of attempts to bring closure and ending, as well as concern to demonstrate links and connections, which point to a strong literary relationship between the parts. The book of the prophet Isaiah simply cannot be explained by drawing analogies, or supposed parallels, from literature of another kind altogether.

2. *The Legacy of B. Duhm and its Aftermath*

Few scholars have brought a more influential change in Isaiah studies than Bernhard Duhm, whose commentary of 1892 established a benchmark for further research.[13] His well-publicized division of the book into three large units—the 'First Isaiah' of 1–39, the 'Second Isaiah' of 40–55 and the

---

12. A. Laato, *'About Zion I will not be silent': The Book of Isaiah as an Ideological Unity* (CBOT, 44; Stockholm: Almqvist & Wiksell, 1998).

13. B. Duhm, *Das Buch Jesaja übersetzt und erklärt* (HKAT, 3/1; Göttingen: Vandenhoeck & Ruprecht, 1892). For Duhm's work and its contemporary reception see now especially, R. Smend, *From Astruc to Zimmerli* (trans. Margaret Kohl; Tübingen: Mohr Siebeck, 2007), pp. 103-17.

'Third Isaiah' of 56–66—was taken up as effectively making redundant any discussion of how the present sixty-six chapters came together to form a single book. For more than a century the break that is evident between chs. 39 and 40 had become fully accepted in critical studies, but Duhm pressed this division further by researching more closely into the historical background that is reflected in its separate sections.

The desire to move beyond Duhm's pioneering work necessarily reopens the question about the unity and final shape of the book. This does not depend on the dogmatic assumption that the final form is somehow sacrosanct, but rather builds on the recognition that Duhm's threefold division is not the only possible one for understanding the book's present structure. In the first instance it gives rise to a chronological problem through its placing of the 'First', 'Second' and 'Third' Isaiah sections as literary units in a clear historical sequence. This would work well enough were it not for the fact that it runs counter to the recognition that a large part of 'First Isaiah' contains some of the latest prophecies of all. This, all along, has proved to be the Achilles' heel of Duhm's attractive thesis. As a result the primary analogy of the 'growth' of the Isaiah scroll, in which new sections were simply added on, will not do as an explanation of its extant form.

A second problem resulting from Duhm's division is that it takes too little account of the evident attempts to establish literary structures within the book and it is in this regard that the question of apparent beginnings and endings acquires significance. These demand a due measure of attention and require us to consider what they tell us about its structure and what they reveal about how it came to be put together.

A third problem arising from these features of Duhm's three-part analysis is that the presumed historical context for each of the larger units is allowed to explain too much of their essential message. We assume that we know where each part fits into Israel's story and other possible contexts are ruled out. Whatever role any particular unit plays in the book as a whole tends to be disregarded in the interests of interpreting it against its presumed historical setting. What we may call 'out of context' units, of which there are many, are set aside and generally ignored. Yet their place in the literary structure of the book as a whole may be significant. Overall Duhm assumed that the present literary structure of the book, when seen in its broad compass, is not very significant and may be set aside in noting the more probable historical contexts of the three larger units. We may add that much of this task has proved misleading. Sometimes it has been impossible to implement without creating further difficulties. We may therefore proceed to enquire what the presence of several apparent endings reveal about the way in which the book has been put together?

I have already noted that, in the light of Sweeney's contentions regarding chs. 1–4 and 63–66, these chapters cannot be allowed to determine the overall character of the present book. In the wake of his observations, these chapters can be seen to stand at the margins of the main book. There exists, however, yet another dimension to the question of the book's unity. When we look at it on the ideological plane we are presented with a different range of critical perceptions. The over-riding characteristic that now colours it is that of a transition from prophecy to apocalyptic. Perhaps it can best be categorized as a trajectory, or theological mutation. Awareness of it has increasingly coloured the approaches of many scholars and is especially marked in the works of Paul Hanson,[14] J. Vermeylen,[15] Otto Kaiser,[16] and now most recently Uwe Becker.[17] Overall this mutation establishes a dominant feature which is well summarized in the title of Vermeylen's two large volumes: *Du prophète Isaïe à l'apocalyptique*. For those like Paul Hanson who have held closely to the main outlines of Duhm's analysis its development is to be traced in the movement from 'First Isaiah' to 'Third Isaiah'. Yet in fact such analysis highlights still further the difficulties raised by the present structure of the book.

One prominent feature of the trajectory from prophecy to apocalyptic is the taking of metaphors and themes which occur in the given text, such as those of darkness covering the earth (8.2 [9.1]; cf. 60.1-3), a divine signal to the nations (5.26; cf. 11.10, 12; 49.22), a highway from Mesopotamia to Judah (40.3-5; cf. 11.16; 19.23; 35.8), or a great pilgrimage of all nations to Zion (2.2-4; 49.22-23; 60.8-16), and reformulating them on an enlarged scale with dramatic new intensity. The striking feature is that, in this progression, there is a move from addressing real history into a mythical, undefined, future history in which religious principle over-rides any realistic political expectation. So the structure of Isaiah has to accommodate not only a move from judgment to hope, but from a close relationship with actual political events to one in which God alone dictates what happens next. The actual historical and political context becomes hidden and almost irrelevant. We begin with a decadent Jerusalem and end up with a new world order!

---

14. P.D. Hanson, Jr, *The Dawn of Apocalyptic* (Philadelphia: Fortress Press, 1979); *Isaiah 40–66* (Interpretation Commentaries; Louisville, KY: John Knox Press, 1995).

15. Cf. n. 11 above.

16. O. Kaiser, *Der Prophet Jesaja, Kapitel 13–39* (ATD, 18; Göttingen: Vandenhoeck & Ruprecht, 1973); *Isaiah 13–39* (trans. R.A. Wilson; OTL; London: SCM Press. 2nd edn, 1980); *Das Buch des Propheten Jesaja, Kapitel 1–12* (ATD, 17; Göttingen: Vandenhoeck & Ruprecht, 5th edn, 1981); *Isaiah 1–12* (trans. J. Bowden; Old Testament Library; London: SCM Press, rev. edn, 1983).

17. U. Becker, *Jesaja, von der Botschaft zum Buch* (FRLANT, 178; Göttingen: Vandenhoeck & Ruprecht, 1997).

The stage of each new scene appears to become larger and more nations appear upon it. In many passages it becomes hard to distinguish metaphor from intended real event, so it is not surprising that arguments have arisen as to where the transition-point falls which marks the beginning of biblical apocalyptic.

From the point of view of the thematic content of the book as a whole therefore, the shift from addressing a historical crisis to formulating a message about an apocalyptic end-point to world history, is what characterizes it. It is no longer a typical book of prophecy, but an apocalypse. On this point there can be little argument and, disconcertingly, the apocalyptic features appear most prominently in that part of the book where we should least have expected them, namely, the part ascribed to 'First Isaiah'. So, problems arise when we endeavour to correlate this ideological trajectory with the literary shape of the book which we have.

So this shift to apocalyptic from the more familiar kind of prophecy, which is directly addressed to specific historical events, does not fit in at all well with Duhm's threefold division. It has to depend on the claim that the so-called Third Isaiah (chs. 56–66) is the section that first borders on apocalyptic and the other, more overtly apocalyptic, parts of the scroll in chs. 24–27 and 34–35 really fall outside its main scope altogether. They are taken to have been composed independently at a very late time and then retrospectively, and inexplicably, inserted into the earliest division of the Isaiah scroll. Duhm should really have had a 'Fourth Isaiah' in order to explain them!

Awareness of this fact has dominated the last twenty years of Isaiah studies. Moreover, not only have these studies drawn attention to the more neglected chapters of the so-called 'First Isaiah', but it becomes apparent that they concern important aspects regarding the shape and message of the book as a whole. In many of its features the past three decades of Isaiah research have been devoted to researching what the apocalyptic parts of chs. 5–35 imply about the make-up of the book as a whole. How and why did the chronologically late apocalyptic chs. 24–27 and 34–35 come to be incorporated into the book in this unexpected way? What does their presence tell us about the book's structure and development? The search for Duhm's elusive 'Fourth Isaiah' becomes fundamental to making sense of the book as a finished whole. Instead of being an elusive, and independently explicable, part of the book of Isaiah the question of the origin and significance of these six chapters becomes a central feature of the quest for discerning the 'original' book of Isaiah. Certainly if we retain any expectation of being able to 'read Isaiah as a book' we shall need to understand what these sections imply about the book's origin.

3. *The Apocalyptic Isaiah Book*

As the book stands, the apocalyptic dimension pervades it quite extensively. Most scholars have recognized that it becomes explicit in chs. 24–27 and 34–35—often called 'the Isaiah Apocalypse' and 'the Little Isaiah Apocalypse', respectively. What has become more fully evident in the more recent work is the recognition that it effectively colours the whole of chs. 5–35. It does so partly through the phenomenon of *relecture* in which the oldest prophecies are vested with radically fresh meaning by adding fresh comments to them (e.g. the reinterpretations of the 'briers and thorns' from 5.36 in 7.23-25). Further comments then appear in the form of summarizing formulas drawing attention to the wider, universal implications of the older prophecies (cf. esp. 8.9-10; 10.33-34; 14.26-27; 17.12-14; 26.20-21; 27.12-13; 29.5-8; 31.8-9).

These summaries emphasize Mount Zion's unique protection by God (e.g. 14.32) and the triumphant role which it is to play as the focal centre for a pilgrimage by members of all nations. The theme clearly has its origins in the ancient Jerusalem-Davidic ideology familiar from a number of psalms. It is the presence of this ancient cultic mythology which does much to colour Isaiah's prophecies with an apocalyptic brush. All of this adds up to recognition that the present book has been made three-dimensional in a way for which Duhm's analysis did not sufficiently allow.

When, therefore, we re-examine that part of the book which Duhm took to belong to 'First Isaiah', we can see it as a work of a very different, and remarkably complex character. This is not because there are no original, eighth-century elements within it, but because these have subsequently been subsumed into a different kind of book. In spite of its evident literary complexity this structured apocalyptic book displays a coherent framework and plot; it has a clearly marked beginning and ending; it reveals its message by making bold comments to the reader and gives a remarkably far-reaching promise about Jerusalem. Accordingly it bears all the hallmarks of having been constructed to form a coherent book. Moreover, if any one part of the book of Isaiah can be said to display the marks of an overarching unified structure, it is to be found in these chapters.

Admittedly this reconstruction of the literary facts prejudges a major issue which bears directly on such an interpretation of chs. 5–35. It concerns whether chs. 24–27 and 34–35 are meant to be read as independent collections of prophetic material—the so-called 'Isaiah apocalypses'—or whether they have been composed as additions and extensions to the larger collection that now constitutes the book which begins with ch. 5. This must now be regarded as a major issue for Isaiah studies to address and the evidence would certainly appear to favour the latter conclusion. The apocalyptic chapters which have for a long time been widely acknowledged as standing out distinctively within chs. 1–39 seriously disturb the assignment of the first part of the book to an identifiable prophet whom we can continue to call 'First Isaiah'. These chapters cannot simply be lifted out of this part of the book and relegated to the margins as 'secondary' and extraneous to it. On the contrary they have an integral place in the book's present structure. Whether we see this structure beginning with ch. 2 or ch. 5 makes no substantial difference, although the latter is more likely to be the case.

Such a conclusion recognizes the prominent role which the 'foreign nation' prophecies of chs. 13–23 play within it and focuses sharply on the issue of Jerusalem confronted by the hostility of many nations. This is, in reality, its major theme and is well expressed in 14.32:

> What will one answer the messengers of the nation?
> 'The LORD has founded Zion,
> and the afflicted among his people
> will find refuge in her'.

It is the evidence of this structured shape of chs. 5–35, which displays both a recognizable beginning and ending and a consistency of theme that provides the essential key to understanding the extant structure of the book. If any literary unit deserves to be described as the written expression of 'the vision of Isaiah the son of Amoz' (Isa. 1.1), then it is to be found here, between Isaiah 5 and 35. This is not to preclude the possibility that there may not be still later additions embedded within it. Nevertheless, so far as a recognizable literary form is concerned, the structured shape of chs. 5–35 still stands out as clearly identifiable. To this was then later added the separate narrative collection of chs. 36–39. A much briefer unit in 2.2–4.6, with its core made up of strictures on the disobedient in Jerusalem, is essentially parallel in content and is wholly devoted to the destiny of the city. It has been given a memorable introduction, full of promise, in 2.1-4 and a suitably comparable conclusion in 4.2-6. The inclusion of this unit into the Isaiah book appears to have been made a late point in the scroll's compilation, undertaken on account of its obvious relevance to the focus on Jerusalem as the primary subject of the Isaiah book.

A primary concern must therefore build on the evidence for the structured shape that pertains to Isaiah 5–35 and the far-reaching significance this has for understanding the present book. Making sense of this unit marks a major step towards making sense of the book in its larger compass. It rests on the fundamental conviction that, where there are demonstrable beginnings and endings, they represent genuine literary units, or 'booklets' within the book and are not merely editorial 'pauses'.

Belonging to the contention that Isaiah 5–35 once formed a coherent unit is the perception that ch. 35 forms its conclusion. Along with Isaiah 60, which I have already briefly noted, it represents one of the clearest examples of a final summarizing message that the book contains. It quite firmly brings a sense of closure to what has preceded it, rounding out the picture of what Jerusalem's ultimate destiny among the nations will be. It is linked directly to Isa. 6.10 by its reversal of the threat of Israel's blindness and deafness (35.5). In so doing it links up with the earlier reversal of this same threat in 32.3, a passage which Hermann Barth suggested once formed the conclusion to the seventh-century 'Anti-Assyrian' redaction of Isaiah's prophecies.[18]

Yet the role of Isaiah 35 as a unit of closure raises several puzzling questions. Not only does it achieve its note of finality by harking back to the commissioning narrative of Isaiah 6, but it also looks ahead by summarizing major themes from chs. 40–55. The theme of a great highway (35.8) reappears more extensively in the well-known passage in 40.3-5. The promise of streams in the desert (35.6-7) re-appears in 41.5. The summons to 'strengthen the weak hands' has close parallels in 40.29-31. Finally the concluding promise of 35.10 repeats *verbatim* that given in 51.11.

Admittedly, most of these motifs also appear elsewhere in Isaiah, but the case appears indisputable that the promises of ch.35 have been drawn from knowledge of the contents of chs. 40–55. This fact led O.H. Steck to conclude that ch. 35 was specifically composed to form a bridge to these later chapters.[19] In this case the chapter is really not a conclusion at all, but has been designed to link together the edited collection of earlier Isaianic prophecies with the message of the later chapters which it anticipates. Steck proceeded to suggest that ch. 35 was composed at the time when the all-important conjunction was made between the earlier book and chs. 40–55. It forms a bridge to the new prophecies, as much as it is a terminus to the old ones!

Undoubtedly, Steck's observations about the presence of these two-way allusions are fundamental to understanding the chapter. The forward looking allusions are so striking as to be undeniable. Nevertheless the conclusion that Isaiah 35 is simply a transition piece, and not really a true ending, also raises difficulties. In several respects such two-way connections may be held to point in the opposite direction since they clearly show a concern to summarize the message of chs. 40–55 in order to round off and conclude the message of chs. 5–35. Certainly it appears that the prophecies now preserved

18. H. Barth, *Die Jesaja-Worte in der Josiazeit. Israel und Assur als Thema einer produktiven Neuinterpretation der Jesajaüberlieferung* (WMANT, 48; Neukirchen–Vluyn: Neukirchener Verlag, 1977).

19. O.H. Steck, *Bereitete Heimkehr: Jesaja 35 als redaktionelle Brücke zwischen dem Ersten und dem Zweiten Jesaja* (SBS, 121; Stuttgart: Katholisches Bibelwerk, 1985).

in chs. 40–55 were already established as a group before Isaiah 35 summarized them, but, if so, this chapter makes their further unfolding unnecessary. The note of finality in Isaiah 35 regarding Jerusalem's triumphant future is strong, as also is the framing of an *inclusio* by the allusion back to ch. 6. The sombre threat of Israel's blindness and deafness, understood metaphorically, is reversed in a dramatically literal fashion. To a large extent the chapter becomes redundant if it does no more than anticipate what was intended to be more fully declared in the later chapters. Even its reversal of the threat of ch. 6 comes prematurely if this chapter is not a final ending, but merely a transitional piece, acknowledging that a further period of Israel's blindness is still to follow (cf. Isa. 42.19).

In its literary character too Isaiah 35's employment of the imagery of ch. 6 is striking in that the original metaphors are subsumed into a literal promise of the recovery of sight and healing. In much the same way other figures of speech taken from chs. 40–55 are given a new touch of realism. Thereby poetic exaggeration is transformed into apocalyptic vision and the promise is made that the Jerusalem of the future really will be a place where miracles happen daily!

We should note also that an air of finality is strongly present, since the glory of the rebuilt city is to witness a permanent change in the quality of life: 'everlasting joy shall be upon their heads—sorrow and sighing shall flee away' (Isa. 35.10). What is promised in Isaiah 35 displaces any need for the more qualified message that emerges later, since nothing more needed to be said. Accordingly, along with awareness that a coherent apocalyptic message pervades the presently structured Isaiah 5–35, we must also recognize that ch. 35 is clearly its conclusion.

What we find in the preserved form of Isaiah 5–35 points to the recognition that at some unspecified period in the post-587 BCE era the received collection of Isaiah's prophecies was made the subject of a far reaching literary reworking. This reconstructed them as an apocalyptic visionary book which constituted 'the vision of Isaiah son of Amoz' (Isa. 1.1). Nevertheless, O.H. Steck is clearly correct in his observation that ch. 35 makes allusions forward to texts and imagery from Isaiah 40–55. What then are we to make of this fact in regard to the story of the compilation of the book?

The most straightforward explanation would seem to be that, at the time when Isaiah 35 was composed, chs. 40–55 constituted a separate work. On the evidence of the internal structure and coherence of these chapters, this is a reasonable conclusion to draw. The fact that chs. 40–55 make several important allusions back to the older collection of Isaiah's prophecies should not occasion surprise, since they also make reference to prophecies from the book of Jeremiah, as well as drawing heavily upon a number of psalms. We should not then interpret the close literary links with other collections of prophetic texts as necessarily implying that they were all edited together on a single scroll. Rather such a widely evidenced phenomenon points us, in the case of the Isaiah scroll, to some central library archive, in this case almost certainly preserved in close proximity to Jerusalem and most probably in the temple itself.

In this post-exilic era of Israel's literary achievements the phenomenon of intertextuality was a prominent feature. Old texts were re-read and seen in a new perspective; but, alongside this, other comparable texts were providing a fruitful source of parallel imagery and comparison which served to generate fresh, and more complete, pictures of what the future held in store. The fact should not surprise us that Isaiah 35 has drawn major ideas and themes from the prophecies now preserved as chs. 40–55. It has used them in summary form to create a picture of the glorious future that awaits the restored Jerusalem. In many respects the clear intention of summarizing the message of chs. 40–55 points to this separateness, rather than to their running continuity on a single scroll.

It was then only as a subsequent literary move that the recognition that Isaiah 40–55 formed an appropriate sequel to chs. 5–35 led to their being combined onto a single scroll. By the time this occurred the narrative unit of Isaiah 36–39 had been joined to the main book so that chs. 40–55 were split apart from ch. 35. Very plausibly too the unexpected reintroduction of concern with the divine commitment to the Davidic royal house in ch. 55 may itself be a consequence of this joining together of the two main collections. Since the tradition of the royal Davidic covenant figures prominently in chs. 1–35, but is understood in a very different way in chs. 40–54, the need to clarify a contentious issue is evident.

At what further point in this process the introductory chs. 1–4 were prefaced to chs. 5–35 to extend the book further cannot readily be determined, but is not of major importance. The significant feature is that these enlargements did not essentially alter the basic shape or add greatly to the overall message of the book.

4. Conclusions

We arrive at certain useful conclusions regarding the present structure of the book of Isaiah. The first of these is that Isaiah 5–35, with the possible exception of some late additions, was formed into a planned and self-contained whole as an apocalyptic book in the post-exilic age, most probably late in the period of Persian control over Judah, although an earlier time cannot be ruled out.[20] Insofar as any one unit contained within the extant sixty-six

---

20. This is the preferred conclusion of Sweeney, cf. *Isaiah 1–39*, pp. 434-54, who sees a major redefining of the Isaiah tradition in the fifth century BCE.

chapters can be regarded as having formed the 'original' book of the prophet Isaiah, then it is within these thirty-one chapters that it is to be found. It possesses a clear beginning in 5.1-7 and a conclusion in 35.1-10. It quite evidently contains within its compass the evidence of earlier sub-units, or sections, which must themselves be evidence of prior editorial arrangements. We can most plausibly date this major step towards the formation of a comprehensive 'Isaiah scroll', or 'book', to the second half of fourth century BCE when the long-running period of stability for the entire Levantine region under Persian rule was breaking-up. Its central message concerns the sovereign authority of Yahweh, the God of Israel, over the nations of the world. This apocalyptic book incorporated a great deal of earlier written material, being based upon collections of prophecies from the eighth century Isaiah of Jerusalem. There appears little reason to draw the conclusion that all of this earlier material had previously been contained on one single scroll. Such a late unifying step in the formation of the book certainly appears to have introduced further additions to it. Nevertheless it is this post-exilic, apocalyptic work which represents the missing 'Fourth Isaiah' to which Duhm failed to accord a distinct identity and which best deserves the title of 'the vision of Isaiah of Jerusalem'.

The next major step in the formation of the present book of Isaiah was achieved by the joining together of the prophecies of a 'First Isaiah' scroll with a further scroll containing chs. 40–55. This development was made necessary by the failure of the attempts to restore the rule of the Davidic royal house in Jerusalem after its collapse in 587 BCE. By the time that chs. 40–55 were added to the earlier book such hopes of a restoration had clearly been abandoned and the central feature of the re-interpretation of the Davidic royal dynastic promise in these sixteen chapters was a consequence of this. A controlling theme lies in their re-interpretation of the significance of the ancient divine promise to the house of David which is conclusively affirmed in Isa. 55.1-5. This promise is interpreted as a covenant bringing assurance to the scattered remnants of Israel of protection and authority for them among the nations (55.5).

Consequently the joining together of chs. 5–35 with 40–55 was a step which carried with it important religious and political implications for the interpretation of the corpus of canonical prophecy as a whole. It seems unlikely that the further additions now preserved in chs. 56–66 were all made at one time. Quite plausibly chs. 56–60 had already, by this time, already become linked to 40–55. Isaiah 60.1-22 shows every sign of having been composed to establish a firm ending to the questions raised earlier about Jerusalem and its restoration.

By showing the importance of the close connections between Isaiah 1–4 and chs. 63–66, Marvin Sweeney has pointed to the importance of the re-orientation that the political developments of the late sixth, and early fifth, centuries BCE brought for Israel's self-understanding as a people called 'Israel'. They were both a 'remnant' (cf. Isa. 37.32) and yet remained the 'children of the LORD (Yahweh) God' (Isa. 1.2). The unity that forms the book of Isaiah into a connected whole is essentially the continuity of this people as one people under one God. Ultimately the much sought after 'unity' of the book of Isaiah, with all its separate component parts, is less a literary unity than a religious and sociological one. Whoever hears this prophetic word, and finds within its strictures, warnings and promises concerning the truth of his, or her identity, finds that this restores the knowledge and discernment that their ancestors lacked (Isa. 1.3).

The final steps which brought together into one book this great wealth of prophetic material dealing with Israel as the 'vineyard', or 'people' of the LORD (Yahweh) God aimed to address a people scattered among many nations. By hearing the word of the prophet they would re-engage with their past and rediscover their identity.

Chapter 4

WRITTEN PROPHECY:
THE CASE OF THE ISAIAH MEMOIR

Even in a period of scholarship when it was widely accepted that prophets
were essentially preachers and that the transition from speech to a written
text of prophecy marked a departure from the norm, the case for believing
that the prophet Isaiah had left a written memoir (*Denkschrift*) appeared a
strong one. In my commentary of 1980 I expressed strong confidence in the
case for such a conclusion, and I would still defend such a position. The
arguments for and against this have remained divided, and clearly it must
now be conceded that some of the arguments in favour call for closer examination.[1] Nevertheless the belief that Isaiah composed a written memoir and
that parts of it, if not its entirety, are still to be found embedded in the text of
Isaiah 6–8 is firmly defensible. Many of the objections to such a conclusion
can be accommodated by defining the scope of the memoir more narrowly
than was earlier claimed.

The identification of an Isaiah prophetic memoir is illuminating and significant with respect to the question of a transition from orality to literacy in a
socio-religious context. As an aspect of religious activity prophecy was
especially affected by this transition since written prophetic texts, or 'oracles',
made it possible to draw from them a wider range of meanings than was
likely in their older oral form. Semantic ingenuity and versatility took priority over rhetoric and poetic impact. Moreover, recording prophecies in
written form, whatever the medium of preservation, made them available to
address far more extended historical periods than a single spoken address
could reach. Noting this transition provides clues about the circumstances
and interests that encouraged the writing down of prophetic messages in the
first instance. The result is that prophetic books are much more intricate and
complicated artefacts than records of speeches such as a great orator may
leave. In a society in which it was accepted that prophecy, on account of its
divine inspiration with the prophet acting as the very mouth of God, should

---

1. R.E. Clements, *Isaiah 1–39* (New Century Bible; London: Marshall, Morgan &
Scott, 1980), pp. 70-101.

properly be spoken, written prophecy marked an innovation. Accordingly, for sayings of an oracular nature to be given a written form lent to them a fresh potential, beyond that which their original spoken form allowed. This new potential in turn opened up possibilities for new ways of discerning the intentions of God, thereby making written prophecy a far more theologically diverse medium than its earliest form possessed. How this diversity is to be judged is not within the remit of this present examination.

The identification of a written memoir from the prophet Isaiah is most closely associated with the name of Karl Budde, whose monograph of 1928 discerned its presence in Isa. 6.1–9.6.[2] According to him the account of the prophet's call in ch. 6 marked its beginning, and the royal coronation oracle of 9.1-6 formed its conclusion. The note regarding the role of the prophet's sons and their sign-bearing names in 8.17-18 declared the memoir's overall purpose.

In effect the entire memoir is comprised of a record of the prophet's call, the conveying of a sequence of messages to King Ahaz through the sign-bearing names of three children (Shear-jashub, Immanuel, and Maher-shalal-hashbaz) and the declaration of the coming of a new king of the Davidic royal line in 9.1-6. The declaration in 8.17-18 reads like a summarizing con-clusion, suggesting either that it has been misplaced or, as is argued below, that what follows it was added later.

To each of the children's names are added interpretations, thus removing the ambiguity implicit when the bare name was left without fuller expla-nation. These interpretations show each of the names originally to have been positive and reassuring so far as the future of the king and his royal throne were concerned. Not until we are informed of the rejection of the prophet's message in 8.5-8 does the potential ambiguity implicit in the names allow them to be understood differently. What was meant as assurance is now turned into threat. That this is now the message of the completed memoir is expressed openly in 8.11-15. In order to make sense of the memoir there-fore, it is necessary to recognize that the message of the name-interpretations required their revision and reappraisal in light of the rejection of the message they were originally meant to convey.

This is spelled out clearly in the pictorial language typical of prophecy. Clearly some active response on the part of the king was expected to the assurances contained in the names, but no indication is given as to what this action was. Nevertheless, it is the negative and absolute character of the royal rejection which explains the purpose of the memoir. Because God's assurance had been refused, judgment must follow. This word of judgment

---

2.   K. Budde, *Jesajas Erleben: Eine gemeinverständliche Auslegung der Denkschrift des Propheten (Kap. 6,1–9,6)* (Gotha: Leopold Klotz, 1928). Budde's thesis had been outlined by him earlier in 1885.

is then elaborated in warnings of depredations from Assyria in both Israel and Judah (8.7-8). Outside the scope of the original memoir the same message is conveyed incontrovertibly in 5.26-30, although the identity of the enemy is left unclear. Within the compass of the memoir itself the message appears again in 7.18-20, but here it must certainly be regarded as an addition to the original text, as also in the gloss added to 7.17.[3]

The prophet's summary in 8.17-18 provides a conclusion to the memoir by noting that he will await God's future action, which by implication is expected to confirm the correctness of the warnings that God had 'hidden his face' from the house of Jacob. There is an overall chronological and theological coherence in the memoir, once it is recognized as such. The period of time that had elapsed between the giving of the original prophecies through the sign-names and the writing of the memoir is undisclosed but need not have been more than two or three years. Of utmost importance is the conclusion that the purpose of the memoir differs in a number of respects from the purpose of the messages attached to the children's names. It is very much a part of the memoir's *raison d'être* to show how and why this was so. These names had been reassuring and positive, whereas the message of the memoir as a whole is of divine threat. The situation had been changed on account of the rejection of the original assurances given by the prophet to the royal house of David.

It has to be conceded that the essential core of Budde's case does not require that everything that is currently to be found in Isa. 6.1–9.6 was authentic to Isaiah, even though Budde himself was relatively positive on this point. By far the most important of the expansions to the original text is to be found in 9.1-6 (NRSV 9.2-7), which reinterprets the significance and application of the Immanuel prophecy of 7.10-17. As I have dealt with this problem in an earlier essay, there is no need to repeat the arguments here.[4] The mysterious, but highly significant, name was originally applied to Isaiah's soon-to-be-born second child. At a later point in the editing of the memoir this has been secondarily applied to a royal prince who would

3. For the wider issues concerning the written forms of prophecy cf. Susan Niditch, *Oral World and Written Word: Ancient Israelite Literature* (Louisville, KY: Westminster/John Knox Press, 1996). The subject of the presumed 'Isaiah Memoir' is now comprehensively covered in the study by Thomas Wagner, *Gottes Herrschaft: Eine Analyse der Denkschrift (Jes. 6,1–9,6)* (VTSup, 108; Leiden/Boston: E.J. Brill, 2006). Cf. also M. de Jong, *Isaiah among the Ancient Near Eastern Prophets* (VTSup, 117; Leiden/Boston: E.J. Brill, 2007).

4. R.E. Clements, 'The Immanuel Prophecy of Isa 7.10-7 and its Messianic Interpretation', in E. Blum, C. Macholz, and E.E. Stegemann (eds.), *Die hebraische Bibel and ihre zweifache Nachgeschichte: Festschrift R. Rendtorff* (Neukirchen–Vluyn: Neukirchener Verlag, 1990), pp. 225-40; repr. in Clements, *Old Testament Prophecy: From Oracles to Canon* (Louisville, KY: Westminster/John Knox Press, 1996), pp. 65-77.

replace the faithless Ahaz. That this royal prince was identified as Hezekiah may be regarded as assured. In the process of reinterpretation the original situation presupposed by the memoir has been left behind and the assurance of the Immanuel name has then been reapplied in order to meet a new situation. Already in this fact the remarkable flexibility of written prophecy reveals itself. Throughout written prophecy we discover repeatedly that a procedure of *relecture*—re-reading a preserved saying, or text in order to bring out a new meaning, or application—is to be found. This is a feature which is especially marked in the completed Isaiah scroll.

The whole sequence of sayings in 8.19-23, whether taken as one single unit or, more probably, as a series of additions, must be held as later additions, added to provide exegetical reinterpretations of the importance of heeding God's 'instruction' and 'testimony' referred to in 8.16. Yet these additions are of particular interest because v. 16 appears misplaced from an original location after 8.2. The words 'testimony' and 'teaching' originally applied to the name Maher-shalal-hash-baz written on the tablet referred to in 8.1 as the solemn act of legal attestation shows. Yet its relocation to 8.16 strongly suggests that it has been secondarily applied to the written memoir as a whole and has, accordingly, been moved to link with the prophet-author's concluding remark regarding this in 8.17-18.

However 8.20 understands the reference to God's 'teaching and instruc-tion' more widely than this, thus occasioning the warning against the false teachings of v. 19. So a strong case exists for regarding all that occurs between 8.18 and 9.6 as an expansion of the original Isaiah memoir.

However more extensive additions than this can be identified of which the most prominent is to be seen in the expansion of the account of the prophet's commissioning in 6.12-13. This looks ahead beyond the situation of Judah and Jerusalem in the eighth century to contemplate the disasters that occurred in the sixth. Similarly Isa. 7.1, which provides a general historical intro-duction to the circumstances relating to the course of the Syro-Ephraimite war, has undoubtedly been introduced from 2 Kgs 16.5 and serves to clarify the context of the prophecies which follow. So also, the evident gloss in 7.8b and the elaborations detailing how God's judgment will fall in 7.18-25 are later insertions. As a feature of literary significance we should note the unlikelihood, on account of their varied form, content, and historical refer-ence, that these additions were all made at the same time. It seems that we are faced with a sequence of miscellaneous additions made at different times that would, if taken as a single attempt at reinterpretation, be self-contra-dictory.

The key warning in 8.8-9, addressed not to Israel but to unnamed nations who threaten her, must also be regarded as a later addition. It has been located at this point on account of the ideas of God's protection of Jerusalem attached to the promise of the name Immanuel (8.8; cf. 'for God is with us' in 8.10). It stands in line with the more extensive level of editorial redaction in the Isaiah scroll on the same theme. It proclaims a warning to Israel's potential enemies as expressed in Psalms 2, 46, and 48 (cf. Isa. 14.24-27; 17.12-14).

Overall, therefore, there remains a strong case for identifying an Isaiah memoir, subject to the proviso that this has subsequently undergone a considerable amount of expansion. When these additions were made is, for the most part, unclear, but it becomes evident from their varied contents that they were made after the memoir had been incorporated into some larger collection of Isaiah's prophecies. This leaves a memoir which is basically comprised of Isa. 6.1-11, 7.2-17 (apart from 7.8b), and 8.1-8, 11-18. Overall it is relatively brief, has a clear theme, and most importantly has a recognizable and congruent theological purpose. Nor is it unimportant that the memoir relates closely to the situation of the Syro-Ephraimite conflict in which the threat to the royal house in Jerusalem was a paramount issue.

Objections to the claim that Isaiah wrote, or caused to have written, such a memoir of his prophetic interventions with King Ahaz have ranged widely over virtually every part of the text that is included in these three chapters. Some scholars argue that only some parts of the extant text can have emanated in the form of a memoir from the prophet Isaiah, others that virtually none can have done so and that the so-called 'memoir' must be regarded as a fictive construction by a late editor. In the latter case, the memoir no longer offers an authentic autobiographical record from the prophet, nor does it provide reliable evidence relevant to the history of the Syro-Ephraimite conflict. Instead, it has been made to appear so for reasons that arose later regarding concerns over the future of the Davidic royal house. A late author writing after the exile had fresh reasons for presenting a given portrait of an eighth-century BCE prophet and his message, namely in order to account for a state of affairs concerning the future of the Davidic royal house when no such king any longer reigned.

Both Otto Kaiser and Uwe Becker have argued that there are traceable fragments of a memoir that was authentic to Isaiah but that these fragments have been heavily supplemented and added to. Both scholars regard the memoir as primarily found in Isaiah 6, but as having been extensively elaborated and reconstructed in order to address issues far removed from those which concerned the original prophet.[5] By contrast, H.G.M. Williamson, while defending the authenticity to Isaiah of much of the content of Isaiah

---

5. O. Kaiser, *Isaiah 1–12* (trans. John Bowden; OTL; London: SCM Press, 1983), pp. 118ff.; U. Becker, *Jesaja, von der Botschaft zum Buch* (FRLANT, 178; Göttingen: Vandenhoeck & Ruprecht, 1997).

6–9, regards the attempt to reconstruct an original written and independent memoir as unhelpful and unnecessary.[6]

More far-reaching questions have now arisen to challenge Budde's thesis that the main core of material in Isa. 6.1–9.6 once formed an independent memoir, authentic to the eighth-century prophet Isaiah. The form in which Budde originally proposed the reconstruction is scarcely any longer defensible in view of the many additions to it we have noted. Yet, that a core memoir once existed in the scope we have outlined, and that it once formed what is almost certainly the oldest part of the extant Isaiah scroll, is both wholly credible and defensible as a literary hypothesis. If so, then it touches directly on issues concerning how and why prophetic books came into existence at all. The case for identifying a memoir from Isaiah demonstrates that at least some small part of the present book of Isaiah was actually written by the prophet himself in order to function as a piece of prophetic testimony. This was a secondary action, contingent on the fact that the prophet's earlier spoken messages had been rejected. If a good case can be made for the identification of such a written testimony, or 'memoir,' as conventional practice has come rather misleadingly to describe it, then we have an instructive example of written prophecy fulfilling a role significantly different from that of a more conventional spoken message.

There are three main points of criticism and objection raised by Williamson in regard to the identification of such a memoir text. Although his argument is directed in the first instance against Budde's specific hypothesis, he raises issues that relate more widely to whether any case at all can be retained for it, or whether the memoir hypothesis should not now be abandoned. The main criticisms are three in number.

First, chs. 6 and 8.1-18 are couched in the first person, whereas ch. 7 (in vv. 3 and 13) refers to Isaiah in the third person. Probably the reference to Yahweh in v. 10 would also need to be reverted back to the prophetic use of the first person for divine speech. The issue is of additional significance since vv. 10 and 13 occur in the passage (7.10-17) dealing with the sign-name of the second child. If this is a child belonging to the prophet and is to be included among those referred to in 8.18, then we should certainly have expected the first-person form to be retained at this point.

Second, the location of the memoir in 6.1–8.18 disturbs and interrupts the continuity between units that precede and follow it, especially the woe oracles of 5.8-24 and the refrain from 9.8–10.4. Contrastingly 10.1-4a appears more appropriate as a further woe-saying belonging to ch. 5, which deals with the authorities in control in the city of Jerusalem.

---

6. H.G.M. Williamson, *Variations on a Theme: King, Messiah, and Servant in the Book of Isaiah* (Carlisle: Paternoster Press, 1996), pp. 73-79.

Third, the narrative of ch. 6, usually described as the prophet's call narrative, might have been expected to form the opening unit of the present book taken as a whole, as the opening narratives of Ezekiel and Jeremiah do in their respective books. The question has long been raised whether Isaiah 6 really reports the experience of the prophet's call and not another, later experience that rather served as a special act of commissioning in regard to a particular political situation.

Clearly all three objections take note of significant literary facts, but it is not clear that they amount, either individually or taken together, to a case for rejecting the identification of a memoir altogether. They vary in their rela tive impact on the theory as a whole, and it may be convenient to deal with them in a reverse order of their importance. Overall, it must be remarked, the issues are modified by recognition of the presence of expansions and additions to what we regard as the original memoir text.

We may begin with the second of Williamson's points, since it is the least prejudicial to the thesis as a whole. This relates to the fact that the identification of the memoir in 6.1–8.18 disturbs the structure and flow of ideas and reference between 5.8-24 and 9.8–10.4. This point must certainly be acknowledged. But does this tell us anything at all about the memoir? Awareness of the likelihood of a disrupted text explains the dislocation of the refrain of 5.25 which really belongs to 9.8–10.4. However no altogether satisfactory explanation is forthcoming to show why this occurred. In any event, the compositions of 7.8-23 and 9.8-21 look as if they were incompletely preserved, if we assume that they were once uniformly structured poetic units.

The observation that 10.1-4a appears to belong with ch. 5 must certainly be conceded. Similarly, 5.26-30 is a separate, if undoubtedly highly important, addition to ch. 5. But this too, like the so-called memoir, disrupts the expected sequence of the text between chs. 5 and 10, although it is easy to see why it should have been inserted in its present location for thematic reasons. Disruption of the continuity of themes and images, along with the separation of exegetical comments from the texts to which they refer, is a feature that is prominently evident throughout the entire section of Isa. 5.1–10.34. The cause of these apparent disconnections and dislocations is sufficiently unclear to allow that more than one explanation has brought them about. On balance, the theory that the section 6.1–8.18 contains a once-separate memoir text provides a useful, if only partially adequate, explanation as to why there appear to be so many dislocations and disruptions between the units of chs. 5 and 10. Even if it does not wholly explain these, the argument for a memoir that was at one time separate provides a useful starting point for doing so. On what principles prophetic texts were compiled and edited into scrolls still remains much of a mystery throughout the entire Old Testament corpus of written prophecy.

The truth is that in prophecy generally and the prophetic book of Isaiah in particular there are many instances where the identification of units, of possible fragmented texts, and of dislocations and relocations from other contexts need to be considered.

Many identifications of this sort evince a high level of plausibility but hardly ever carry any explicit manuscript support. Evidently the techniques and copying safeguards of the written preservation of prophecy were fraught with limitations that gave rise to problems of this kind. The critic can only seek to suggest possibilities and strive for the best sense available. That preserved written prophecy also shows itself to have been a complex and vulnerable type of material for later scribes and copyists to deal with cannot be denied. The practice of combining copying with redacting and interpreting a given text gave rise to many problems. So we cannot draw too many conclusions one way or another by identifying where probable and possible dislocations occurred as a consequence of these procedures. The surviving piecemeal form in which one can discern the reconstructed Isaiah testimony text is simply one product of a search to trace the earliest stages of the formation of the biblical scroll. Among the biblical writings, the scroll of Isaiah has aroused as much discussion as any because of its evident stages of growth. The substructure still shows!

The third of Williamson's reasons for questioning the attempt to identify a separate Isaianic memoir concerns the role of the narrative of Isaiah 6. I have argued that this originally extended only as far as v. 11. Popularly it has been regarded as Isaiah's call narrative, leading to the expectation that it ought properly to have appeared at the beginning of the book. Yet this is to mistake its proper function as a text recalling the prophet's claim to be the recipient of a divine commissioning. It is the mistake of titling it a call narrative that has made its present location problematic. The opposite is the case, once its proper literary function is granted. Far from weakening the interpretation of the function and nature of Isa. 6.1-11, the memoir hypothesis greatly strengthens it!

The desire to interpret written prophecy 'biographically' has brought about the feeling of difficulty over the present location of Isaiah 6. It is wholly coherent, both from a literary and theological perspective, when it is read as the opening affirmation of the prophet's claim to have been commissioned by God to bring a message to the king. This is how the memoir begins. Since we know nothing of Isaiah's life and activities before this event, nor anything concerning the relationship between his inner psychological experience and the production of this written text, we cannot verify its authenticity. We take it on trust, noting its extensive appeal to traditional imagery concerning the heavenly divine court. We are therefore hardly in a position to comment on the preceding background to this experience of

Isaiah's. For us it is a text that makes excellent sense as a claim that the message following it had a divine origin. That is its purpose, and that is what it achieves.

The desire to regard Isaiah 6 as a call narrative rather than a narrative of commissioning is at best unhelpful. Nothing at all is said or even implied regarding Isaiah's earlier activities. The narrative gains immeasurably in meaning and intelligibility when we link it directly to what follows in ch. 7. In this regard it is a matter of paramount importance that the text includes a very skilfully articulated awareness of anticipated, or more probably already experienced, opposition to the message that is to be the main burden of the prophet's task. It gives a clear intimation that the eventual outcome of events will prove disastrous for the nation. Failure to recognize this feature leaves us confused and baffled by the prophet's inconsistency. Only when we link the warning note sounded in this commissioning to the information provided by chs. 7 and 8, which shows that God's assurances given through the prophet were spurned by the king, is this tension relieved. Only then do we have a credible place for the note of promise attached to the interpretation of the name Shear-jashub in 7.3-9. The warning of 6.11 explicitly anticipates disaster, but only the amplification provided by the unfolding sequence of actions in chs. 7–8 shows why this inevitability of national catastrophe has come about. What Isaiah 6 reveals to us is that, in writing afterwards of his God-given task, Isaiah has anticipated the end result from the beginning. There is a heavy and unmistakable note of irony in his having done this.

There has admittedly been much scholarly discussion over the ambiguities between assurance and threat that Isaiah's preaching reveals. The presence of names, themes, and words of hope and reassurance read strangely against the prophet's claim given in 6.9-11 that his message throughout will be one of unremitting disaster to the nation. The fact that such intimations of hope and reassurance appear in the interpreted names of the children referred to in chs. 7–8 provides the strongest possible reason for coupling Isaiah 6 with the narratives that contain them. Only then does their inclusion within the larger structure of the memoir explain their reversal. This alone explains the circumstances that have turned such glowing promises into bitter warnings. Far from providing an argument against the memoir hypothesis, the presence of Isaiah 6 as a narrative of divine commissioning supports such a hypothesis to the hilt. Seen for what it is, as a narrative of legitimization for the prophet's unwelcome and unfruitful mission, the passage provides one of the strongest reasons for embracing that hypothesis. The separate composition of a written testimony serves, better than any other theory, to resolve the tensions and incongruities latent in Isa. 6.1–8.18.

Throughout these chapters we encounter the prophet's unusual insistence on the truths of divine sovereignty and foreknowledge with a demand for human obedience and responsiveness. Only when rejection of God's word is chosen is there a warning of the inevitability of disaster. The prophet claims, by his exploitation of ironic language and imagery, to know that national disaster will be the outcome of his mission and that this fact was revealed to him at the beginning! Only the unfolding sequence of encounters in the memoir between the prophet and the king uncovers a theologically consistent timetable for this claim. The theology of Isaiah 6 is well explained once the chapter is seen as the beginning of a narrative telling a story of the prophet's experience of rejection.

Seen in this light, the belief that the prophet was responsible for producing a written memoir, composed at an interval of two or three years after his first approach to the king, makes excellent sense. The theory serves to explain the nature of the commissioning narrative, with all its theological and psychological eccentricities, and throws much-needed light on the use of irony to convert images of assurance into threats. The designation of Isaiah 6 as a call narrative ought, then, to be dropped altogether and replaced by recognition of its function as a text of authorization. It does no more than assert the prophet's claim to have experienced an act of divine commissioning for the immediate task in hand. He may have been, and probably was, an established prophetic personality long before this time. Certainly his polished artistic skills warrant such a conclusion.

We must still deal with the first of Williamson's reasons for questioning the usefulness of the memoir hypothesis as a means of interpreting and resolving the difficulties in the text of Isa. 6.1–8.18.[7] This concerns the point that ch. 7 presents the prophet and his message by use of the third-person form, in contrast to the first-person form used in chs. 6 and 8. This objection weighs heavily with many who have considered the memoir hypothesis in the form Budde adumbrated.

To alter the text so as to revert back to a presumed first-person usage in 7.3 and 13, and probably 7.10 also may at first appear to be a rather high-handed action. It looks like a case of adjusting the facts to fit the theory rather than the other way round. Yet it is not a difficult assumption to make, once one takes into account the extent of the many glosses and additions that, on any reckoning, appear in the memoir text. The complex nature of prophetic literature and its literary development into a form of liturgical scripture has to be recognized. It was the very hallmark of prophetic speech in ancient Israel that it employed the otherwise presumptuous idiom of using the first-person speech-form of God addressing the people. Much of the extensive debate concerning the use of divine speech in psalmody and its origin with the so-called 'cult-prophets' has hinged on the distinctive nature

---

7. Williamson, *Variations on a Theme*, pp. 79-84; cf. also his *The Book Called Isaiah* (Oxford: Clarendon Press, 1994), pp. 102-103.

of this form. A subsequent adaptation to a less authoritative, but more familiar, third-person form in the recording of prophetic messages allowed freer citation of prophetic words in public worship. Clearly this is precisely the kind of change that the shift from oral to written prophecy would have encouraged. The phenomenon is well attested in the book of Jeremiah, where the use of the original prophetic first-person form for divine speech is adapted into a third-person form.

Yet this is only part of the general background to the problems present in Isaiah 7. If, as I have argued in my essay already noted,[8] the addition of 9.1-6 as a royal coronation oracle arose in conjunction with a change in the interpretation concerning the identity of the child to be named Immanuel in the prophecy of 7.10-17, then such minor changes are readily explicable. Whether or not Isaiah himself may have been responsible for this shift of reference is another issue altogether, but this appears unlikely. The relatively minor alterations to the presentation of 7.3, 10, and 13, took place either at the same time as this addition or as a consequence of it. Reluctant as any scholar must be to posit unsupported changes to a text, no matter how difficult, the suggestion in this case involves a far less radical change than supposing that later authors deliberately composed additions, making them appear as biographical, or autobiographical, elaborations. Their extraordinary clumsiness in failing to hide their secondary role would be amazing.

Overall the question of the possible change in the personal form of address from the first to the third person in Isaiah 7 has to be considered in relation to the much broader recognition that a number of intelligible interpretive additions have been made to the original memoir text. It is no longer in precisely the compass and shape that the prophet himself gave to it. Once this point is conceded, as it must be, then the change in the form of address becomes a relatively minor point.

In summary, it would appear that the identification of what was apparently a separate written testimony text in Isa. 6.1–8.18* belongs as a hypothesis along with the many plausible explanations for the disorderliness of the written prophetic scrolls. Many complex literary features need to be considered in regard to Isaiah 1–12, when read as a finished unit, and our explanation of 6.1–8.18 remains one of the most plausible of the many hypotheses about the origin and growth of these chapters. Its ultimate claim to recognition must rest on its ability to make better sense of a difficult sequence of prophecies and narratives than the alternative explanations have been able to do. It shows the figure of Isaiah as an accomplished speaker, and probably also author, although the use of a professional scribe should not be ruled out.

---

8. Clements, 'The Immanuel Prophecy'.

Taken as a separate unit the memoir shows how written prophecy could fulfill a function beyond what was possible with oral prophesying. It is best described as a testimony text, since it is not autobiography except in a secondary and accidental manner. Its purpose as a witness to future generations of Israelites and Jews that God is both faithful and just is evident. It ensured that the future generations who were destined to suffer the disasters that Isaiah had foretold would understand why they were doing so and on whom the responsibility for this rested.

Overall, therefore, there remains a good case for identifying a written memoir as the original basis of the text of Isa. 6.1–8.18, as Karl Budde proposed. This memoir has, however, certainly received many subsequent additions, the most plausible of which we have noted. The identification of such a memoir strengthens and supports the case for regarding the child bearing the second of the sign-names, that is, the Immanuel child of 7.14, as a child soon to be born to the prophet in the same way as the first- and third-named children were his.

A further point of interest concerns how far the case for such a piece of literary analysis in the book of Isaiah contributes towards understanding the nature of written prophecy more widely. In this regard, we may suggest the two following points.

Of first importance is the recognition that awareness that the purport of the prophet's message had been rejected by the king, who undoubtedly was regarded as acting on behalf of the people more generally, explains the need to write prophecies down. The act of recording the message in a brief text was not necessarily an action contemporaneous with the original spoken declaration, but a second step, aimed at giving to prophecy an additional, and more lasting significance. It turns prophecy into a theodicy for the downfall of a nation. The record of Jeremiah's action in Jeremiah 36 bears a closely similar stamp. The generally recognized fact that the preserved sayings of pre-exilic prophets are judgmental in their tone is therefore no accident. In essence, the experience of rejection went hand in hand with the belief that by acting in this way the prophet's hearers were themselves responsible for choosing doom rather than deliverance. Such a belief provides a reason for the resort to written preservation. The written text testifies against them. If the present generation does not listen and heed the prophet's message, then future generations will do so under a very different set of circumstances.

Secondly, the written form of prophecy greatly increases the potential for extending its interpretation. The reinterpretation of the sign-names of Isaiah's children provides a classic example of this. So do the expositions of the importance of Isaiah's 'torah-testimony' in 8.19-23 and the many further examples of key names and themes being given new interpretations in other parts of the book. It is a feature relevant to our study of the literary intricacies and frequent disorderliness of the prophetic books that they display such complexities. In the book of Isaiah, expositions of key words and images occur out of conjunction with the texts from which they originate, as the exposition in 10.20-23 of the name of Shear-jashub from 7.3 shows. Similarly, and certainly of direct relevance to the memoir hypothesis, is the presence in 7.23-25 of thematic expositions of the subject of 'briers and thorns' relating to 5.6.

Once committed to a scroll the needs and exigencies of writing imposed constraints on how and where additions could be made to a specific passage. The whole phenomenon of intertextuality opened up a rich vein of enlarged interpretations in which the accepted authority of a given text could be utilized to create further messages. So a certain kind of sensitivity was required in reading a prophetic text, since it was seldom possible for it to maintain the type of poetic or literary structure that other formal texts required. Neither chronology, nor poetic structure and balance, nor even consistency of theme and subject matter could give a single overriding shape to any prophetic scroll. Disturbances and out-of-sequence intrusions abound, dooming any attempt to present an all-encompassing 'message' of a book.

A final point of theological significance may be noted. By its very nature written prophecy was a different proposition from what its origins in oral prophesying had been. It could seek to defeat the tyranny of time by giving future generations the chance to hear messages from the past that had failed to enjoy the response their authors sought. More especially it could hope to counter the despair engendered by the seemingly irreversible nature of past follies. Disasters that had become inevitable as a result of past mistakes could serve as lessons and warnings so that future generations might not suffer the same fate as their forebears. The search to find meaning in a hostile and unpromising history could then hope to build a new future on the ruins of the past.

PART II

ISAIAH AND JERUSALEM'S DELIVERANCE IN 701 BCE

Chapter 5

THE POLITICS OF BLASPHEMY:
ZION'S GOD AND THE THREAT OF IMPERIALISM

The story of how Jerusalem was saved from destruction by the armies of Sennacherib in 701 BCE has exercised the minds and attentions of scholars since earliest times. It presents a paradigm of divine intervention and providential protection which many would wish to be true, but which most of history belies. For more than a century and a half it has appeared primarily to pose a historical question as to the veracity of the facts in the light of a very different picture of events painted by the Assyrian record. There is a certain irony in the fact that the Sennacherib Chronicle which describes the events of that momentous year was one of the earliest of the major historical texts to come to light with the rise of Mesopotamian archaeology in the first half of the nineteenth century.[1] Yet, for all its considerable detail, rather than confirming and clarifying the biblical record of those events, it has served to raise fresh questions about them which have defied clear explanation.

If, when the conditions are right, God is able to intervene directly through angelic forces to destroy whole armies when they threaten the chosen people, then the entire notion of providence must be shaped to take account of such an experience. On the other hand, if the same events can give rise to two contrasting, and essentially incompatible, interpretations of their religious significance, then it is this contrast of perspectives which must primarily engage our interest. To this extent the problems of interpretation relating to the events of 701 BCE serve as something of a paradigm of wider questions of interpretation regarding the historical nature of the Bible. The purpose of this study is not to offer another attempt at a solution to the historical and literary questions which relate to the biblical account of Jerusalem's deliverance in 701 BCE. Rather it is to reiterate, and if possible to clarify more fully in the light of recent discussion, some essential points

---

1. According to A.R. Millard modern knowledge of the Sennacherib Chronicle dates from 1851 when Sir Henry Rawlinson published a translation of it in *The Athenaeum* 1243 (23 August 1851), pp. 902-903. Cf. A.R. Millard, 'Sennacherib's Attack on Hezekiah', *TynBul* 36 (1985), pp. 61-67.

that were made in my short essay on the subject published in 1980.[2] A great
deal has been written on the issue in the past decade and, in the profusion of
revisions and reassessments which have been put forward, some very perti-
nent insights have been obtained, while a number of essential points appear
to me to have been too readily ignored.

Our primary concern is straightforward: the narrative of 2 Kgs 18.17–
19.37 // Isa. 36.1–37.36 can best be classed as a disputation narrative, a point
that arises clearly enough from the study by B.S. Childs at an early stage of
the current discussion.[3] Although it possesses a historical narrative form, the
evident purpose of this story is to demonstrate that the king of Assyria has
been guilty of blasphemy against the God of Israel. He must be punished
accordingly. The entire narrative is not merely coloured by this ideological
feature, but has clearly been constructed in order to assert it. The blasphemy
is openly expressed to the people of Jerusalem and its ruler through the
Assyrian ruler's representative, who is titled the Rabshakeh. All Jerusalem's
citizens are said to have heard the offensive claims made by this official and
the prophet Isaiah defines the charge, in a quasi-legal fashion, as one of
blasphemy.

The offence requires a response in a twofold sequence. First it must be
proved, and the Assyrian ruler must be shown the outrageous nature of his
claim to be superior in power to Israel's God. Thereby the charge of blasphemy will be confirmed. This is achieved by a brief recounting of the
events of the year 701 BCE in which the Assyrian ruler made no direct
military attack upon and conquest of, Jerusalem. This escape particularly
contrasts with the more fearful fate that had befallen Samaria less than a
quarter of a century earlier (2 Kgs 18.34).

The circumstances which led to Jerusalem's being spared a horrific siege
and destruction have caused much argument, but that it was so spared must
be conceded. So far as historical events are concerned this represents the
central point of the entire discussion. The biblical record describes a

2.   R.E. Clements, *Isaiah and the Deliverance of Jerusalem: A Study of the Inter-
pretation of Prophecy in the Old Testament* (JSOTSup, 13; Sheffield: JSOT Press, 1980).
More extensive studies are to be found in F.J. Gonçalves, *L'expédition de Sennachérib en
Palestine dans la littérature hébraïque ancienne* (EBib, NS, 7; Louvain: Université
Catholique de Louvain, 1986), pp. 441-87; C.R. Seitz, *Zion's Final Destiny: The Devel-
opment of the Book of Isaiah—A Re-assessment of Isaiah 36–39* (Minneapolis; Fortress
Press, 1991); C. Hardmeier, *Prophetie im Streit vor dem Untergang Judas. Erzählkom-
munikative Studien zur Entstehungssituation der Jesaja- und Jeremiaerzählungen in II
Reg 18–20 und Jer 37–40* (BZAW, 187; Berlin: W. de Gruyter, 1990); E. Vogt, *Der
Aufstand Hiskias und die Belagerung Jerusalems 701 v.Chr* (ed. L. Alonso Schökel;
AnBib, 106; Rome: Biblical Institute Press, 1986), pp. 24-59.

3.   B.S. Childs, *Isaiah and the Assyrian Crisis* (SBT 2/3; London: SCM Press, 1967),
especially pp. 78-93.

remarkable divine intervention accomplished by 'the angel of the LORD'. Those scholars who seek an essentially unique historical explanation for the ideology of the narrative do so on the understanding that this reference to the actions of the special divine messenger must be interpreted as indicative of an event not reported in 2 Kgs 18.14-16 which compelled the Assyrian forces to withdraw prematurely. At the heart of the narrative, therefore, lies the question of how language concerning such an angelic intervention is to be understood. Secondly, as a suitable expression of personal punishment, a report is given of the circumstances of Sennacherib's untimely death (2 Kgs 19.37), providing explicit confirmation that the God of Israel had punished his blasphemy.

1. *The Attempts at a Historical Solution*

In his study *Isaiah and the Assyrian Crisis*, B.S. Childs ends his summary of the attempts to achieve a clear cut historical solution to the question of what actually happened: 'The historical problems have not been solved; in fact greater complexity calls for even greater caution'.[4] Several scholars have continued to claim that the problem of the narrative is essentially a historical one, and that, when carefully scrutinized, the Assyrian records provide hints that something untoward happened outside Jerusalem in 701 BCE which gave rise to the remarkable theological colour of the biblical narrative.[5] Others retain the contention that a second campaign, unrelated to that reported in 2 Kgs 18.14-16, must explain the narrative.[6] Thereby it is argued that the problem is a historical one in which the interpreter must reconcile the different perspectives which appear in the varied accounts relating to the events of 701 BCE. Virtually all recent discussion has taken it as probable, that, because the Sennacherib Chronicle is bombastic in tone, it unduly magnifies the scale of the Assyrian ruler's success, so that its information should be regarded as historically suspect.[7] It is possible therefore that it hides the evidence of reverses which would corroborate the biblical record of a humiliation suffered by Sennacherib outside Jerusalem.

---

4. Childs, *Isaiah and the Assyrian Crisis*, p. 120.
5. So especially Millard, 'Sennacherib's Attack'; also P.E. Dion, 'Sennacherib's Expedition to Palestine', *EglTh* 20 (1989), pp. 5-25, is more cautious: 'It is safe enough to assume that Sennacherib's unusual restraint was caused by some setback, but we do not know what really happened' (p. 23).
6. Cf. W.H. Shea, 'Sennacherib's Second Palestinian Campaign', *JBL* 104 (1985), pp. 401-18.
7. J. Geyer, '2 Kings xviii 14-16 and the Annals of Sennacherib', *VT* 21 (1971), pp. 604-606; Cf. also C.R. Seitz, 'Account A and the Annals of Sennacherib: A Re-assessment', *JSOT* 58 (1993), pp. 47-57.

C.R. Seitz even goes so far as to suggest that the very existence of the arrogant tone of the Sennacherib Chronicle shows that there was something to hide![8] In consequence of this he concludes that, although the story of 2 Kgs 18.17–19.37 (Account B) is not a simple piece of contemporary Judean reporting on the events of 701 BCE, nevertheless it retains a reliable historical memory which serves as explanation for its existence. His argument is significant because of its hesitancy: 'It is most likely that behind this narrative lies an extended oral legend, going back to the miraculous events of 701 themselves'.[9] In the interests of defending the ideological stance of the story we are forced to claim that some event, unreported in either the parallel biblical narrative of 2 Kgs 18.14-16 or the Sennacherib Chronicle, must have occurred. Yet this is to remain content with a speculative, and narrowly historicist approach to resolving the problem. We have to posit the existence of 'an extended oral legend' in order to explain the unique character of the Judean interpretation of what happened. P.E. Dion is more cautious.[10]

Our concern is not to deny that there may have been a number of unexpected factors which influenced the tactical and strategic decisions of Sennacherib in 701. In mounting campaigns at such a long distance from his capital city, this ruler, like all similar military commanders, had many problems, both commonplace and unforeseen, to contend with. The so-called 'miraculous' element would therefore have to lie in the scale of the unforeseen circumstances and the timing at which they occurred. However, our primary point is that it is essential that we should first clarify the theological and political features of the story, which give to it its distinctive ideology, before resorting to historical speculations in order to account for them.

The issue is essentially one concerning how we are to account for a narrative with a distinctive ideology which affirms that the king of Assyria had committed a serious blasphemy against the God of Israel and was punished for it. Because of the blasphemy, the angel of God intervened to spare Jerusalem and to bring the Assyrian ruler to an ignominious end.

Before looking in more detail at the structure of the narrative of Account B in 2 Kgs 18.17–19.37 we may note questions that have arisen concerning the much shorter narrative in 2 Kgs 18.14-16 which constitutes Account A. This report has usually been regarded as substantially in agreement with the information given in the Sennacherib Chronicle, as more original to the text

---

8. Seitz, 'Account A', p. 53. He suggests that the Chronicle was written to mollify Sennacherib's offended pride at not having captured Jerusalem.

9. Seitz, *Zion's Final Destiny*, p. 95

10. Dion, 'Sennacherib's Expedition', p. 25: 'This study has led me to discard the historical reliability of B2 altogether, and to put many strictures on the documentary value of B1 itself'.

of 2 Kings than the Account B and probably drawn from an authentic state archive.[11] Some of the points raised in criticism of these conclusions are noteworthy, especially those which note that the information given in 2 Kgs 18.14-16 regarding when Hezekiah surrendered and when he paid tribute, are not easily reconciled with what is reported in the Sennacherib Chronicle.

Yet, in spite of these obscurities, their presence does not change the fact that the information provided by the Judean Account A can be reconciled with that of the Sennacherib Chronicle. 2 Kings 18.14 is agreeable to the archaeological and Assyrian evidence that the siege and capture of the fortified city of Lachish was the outstanding conflict of the entire campaign.[12] This was where the major battle was fought and, after its capture, it would seem extremely unlikely that Hezekiah had either the military resources or the will to continue further resistance. Whether preparations for a siege of Jerusalem had begun by the time Hezekiah surrendered is not now clear. It seems likely that, after the fall of Lachish, further Judean resistance was impossible. The substantive point must remain that it is the different evaluations placed upon the fact that Sennacherib did not fight against, and capture, Jerusalem in 701 BCE which constitutes the central point at issue regarding Account B. The biblical record regards this as an act of preservation by angelic intervention, whereas the Sennacherib Chronicle ignores the possibility as irrelevant to the campaign.

What is remarkable is that there is surprisingly little clear historical and military information contained in Account B which could establish a more detailed picture of the course of the campaign. Attention is given to the circumstances of Sennacherib's death (2 Kgs 19.37) and there is a prophetic warning that the Assyrian king will 'hear a rumour' (2 Kgs 19.7). It is affirmed and that he will not enter Jerusalem (2 Kgs 19.32) and we might wish to add to these the hint from Isa. 10.16 that the Assyrian forces will be stricken with a 'wasting sickness' (Heb. *rāzôn*). Yet finally the reference to the destructive angelic intervention is all that we have to go on to establish a reason for Jerusalem's deliverance (2 Kgs 37.35).

Where the Account A bears all the marks of having been an original part of the text of the Deuteronomistic History,[13] it seems virtually certain that this biblical Account B, together with the two narratives concerning Hezekiah which follow it in 2 Kings 20, were added later. The historical uncertainties that remain unresolved regarding what happened in 701 BCE do not change the literary conclusion that Account A was original to the text of 2 Kings, and that Account B had a separate origin and has introduced a significantly different perspective on the events of that year.

11. Seitz, 'Account A', pp. 50-53.
12. Cf. D. Ussishkin, 'Lachish', in *ABD*, IV, pp. 114-26.
13. Seitz, 'Account A', pp. 56-57.

This is really the heart of the entire problem: can this perspective given by the biblical record of Account B best be accounted for by concluding that Sennacherib was thwarted by some imperfectly known historical upturn of events in his attempt to achieve his intended goal of capturing Jerusalem in 701 BCE. The narrative would then have arisen on the basis that a recollection of these events, interpreted as a visitation by the angel of the LORD, had been kept in Judah. Both the biblical Account A and the Sennacherib Chronicle could then be regarded as neglecting, or even hiding, details of this frustration of the Assyrian intentions from us. Our contention is that such a supposition regarding the existence of a separate oral legend is not necessary. The twin facts, that Jerusalem had not fallen to an Assyrian siege in 701 BCE and that Hezekiah had retained his throne after his surrender, were facts which, in themselves, were sufficiently important for the perspective given in Account B to have arisen. Particularly was this so when the survival of Judah was contrasted with the fall of Samaria in 722 BCE and the collapse of the native monarchy in the northern sister kingdom of Israel. Even more remarkable did such an event appear after the catastrophes of 598 and 587 BCE.

In many respects the strongest argument in favour of the view that Sennacherib was acting under some form of unexpected duress in departing from Judah in 701 BCE without entering Jerusalem is the fact that Hezekiah was allowed to retain his throne. It might well have been expected that sterner measures would be taken against him. The highlighting of his humiliation in the Sennacherib Chronicle could then be some mark of compensation for this leniency.

Yet even this is to argue on a rather speculative basis. If Assyrian imperialist goals were to be met it is evident that, when distances over which control was to be maintained were great, the administration had no alternative except to work through firmly established vassal-rulers who could be made compliant to their demands. The frenetic harshness that reverberates through the vassal-treaties of Esarhaddon fully illustrates this point.[14] It is wholly understandable therefore that the imperial administrators of Assyria, typified in the narrative by the figure of the Rabshakeh as adopting an arrogant tone and a threatening manner, were well aware of their limited powers of authority. They would have been fully alive to the fact that, in order to exercise control over Judah they could best operate through a recognized ruler of the Davidic dynasty who would be forced into compliance with their demands.

---

14. Cf. P.J. Calderone, *Dynastic Oracle and Suzerainty Treaty* (Manila: Loyola House of Studies, 1966), pp. 14-40.

The complex and brutal arrangements introduced into Samaria after its collapse provide ample evidence of the extreme measures to which an imperial power could be driven in an effort to maintain control over a region, once its internal administrative structure had been overthrown (2 Kgs 17.24-34). If there was an element of leniency in allowing Hezekiah to keep his throne in Jerusalem in 701 BCE, it is more likely to have been the result of long term administrative necessity than of the Assyrian king's hasty and forced departure from Judah in that year. However, both factors could have played a part.

We must certainly admit that the Sennacherib Chronicle contains a degree of arrogant bluster and may very well also include exaggerated claims of military achievement. If it were otherwise the Chronicle is hardly likely to have been composed. Official histories have always maintained a biased view of historical events from the eighth century BCE to the present day! Yet it is to press this point too far, and in too speculative a direction, to claim that this characteristic of the Chronicle is present in order to hide some unfortunate reverse which was dishonouring to Sennacherib. The most we can say is that, if there were such circumstances which put duress upon the Assyrian forces when planning to press their assault upon Jerusalem, it would not have found a place in the official record of the campaign.

When all the facts are taken into consideration the most likely explanation of what happened to Hezekiah and Jerusalem in 701 BCE is that, after the fearful and disastrous siege of Lachish had been concluded, further resistance against Sennacherib was hopeless and Hezekiah surrendered.

The conclusion from this review of the historical reliability and literary significance of what is presented in 2 Kgs 18.14-16 and in the Sennacherib Chronicle is that they do not, in themselves, help us to explain the distinctive ideological perspective contained in Account B. Yet neither do they indicate that some other event, or some other campaign, than the one they report on which occurred in 701 BCE, is being referred to in Account B.

2. *The Literary Character of the Biblical Account B*

Since our concern is primarily to understand and interpret the biblical story of the confrontation between Hezekiah and Sennacherib contained in 2 Kgs 18.17–19.37 (Account B) we need to define its essential form and character. From a purely literary point of view we may note that it contains a great deal of unevenness and signs of repetition. Some of this may be accounted for as indicative of a literary desire to reinforce certain confrontational aspects of what is narrated by repeating what is essentially the same point a second time. However, it has more usually been taken to be a mark of parallel sources having been woven together. For long the division into B1 and B2, advocated by B. Stade, drew to itself a wide following.[15] More recent criticism of this would appear to reveal the weaknesses of such a simple two-part analysis to deserve serious attention.[16] Even so, the various alternative proposals for a division into separate literary strands, or sources, cannot be regarded as more than provisional. A process of enlargement and expansion of an original narrative has clearly taken place by supplementation. Some of this material shows indications of deriving from a narrative with a closely parallel structure, whereas other parts undoubtedly add new features to an original core text.[17] This is particularly evident in regard to two of the three prophecies ascribed to the prophet Isaiah (2 Kgs 19.21-34) where the original narrative sequence required only one.[18]

Whatever conclusions are reached regarding the literary origins of the materials which now go to make up the final form of Account B its essential plot and formal characteristics remain clear and are inwardly consistent and coherent. There is little to support the contention therefore, that a literary-critical analysis of the story can assist towards uncovering a more basic historical core which could help to identify some oral legend about particular historical events.

This inner coherence is markedly evident in regard to the overall ideological stance adopted by the narrative. The Assyrian ruler has committed a blasphemy, demonstrated by his imperialist claims, and must be punished accordingly. In its final form it is essentially a didactic disputation narrative in which two primary figures, the Assyrian Rabshakeh and the Judean prophet Isaiah make formal speeches. Each is in reality acting on behalf of other figures who lie in the background of what is reported, but are in fact the central protagonists. These are the king of Assyria, for whom the Rabshakeh speaks, and the God of Israel, for whom the prophet Isaiah speaks. In between these major contestants stands Hezekiah, the king of

---

15. B. Stade, 'Miscellen', *ZAW* 4 (1884), pp. 250-77; cf. Childs. *Isaiah and the Assyrian Crisis*, pp. 73-103; Clements, *Isaiah*, pp. 53-68; K.A.D. Smelik has most sharply criticized this undue dependence upon Stade's literary-critical conclusions.

16. K.A.D. Smelik, 'Distortion of Old Testament Prophecy: The Purpose of Isaiah xxxvi and xxxvii', in *Crises and Perspectives: Studies in Ancient Near Eastern Polytheism, Biblical Theology, Palestinian Archaeology and Intertestamental Literature* (OTS, 24; Leiden: E.J. Brill, 1986), pp. 70-93; 'King Hezekiah Advocates True Prophecy: Remarks on Isaiah xxxvi and xxxviii / II Kings xviii and xix', in Smelik, *Converting the Past: Studies in Ancient Israelite and Moabite Historiography* (OTS, 28; Leiden: E.J. Brill, 1992), pp. 93-128.

17. Smelik, 'King Hezekiah', pp. 105-109.

18. Cf. my treatment of these in 'The Prophecies of Isaiah to Hezekiah Concerning Sennacherib: 2 Kings 19.21-34//Isa.37.22-35', in R. Liwak and S. Wagner (eds.), *Prophetie und geschichtliche Wirklichkeit im alten Israel. Festschrift für Siegfried Herrmann zum 65. Geburtstag* (Stuttgart: Kohlhammer, 1991), pp. 65-78.

Judah, and Jerusalem the city where this king's throne is established and where the temple of the God of Israel is situated. The action comprising the historical events which the narrative reports are in reality only a small part of it. They amount to no more than the action of the angel of the LORD and the sentence of an untimely death being carried out upon the Assyrian king (2 Kgs 19.35-37), in very much the same manner as a court-room verdict is carried into immediate effect once it has been reached.

Although other potential historical eventualities, which might help to clarify the nature of the intervention by the angel of the LORD, are alluded to in an oblique manner, they form no part of the conclusion. Overall we can see that the narrative focuses upon the speech and letter of the Rabshakeh and the prophetic response to them. Certainly it relates to a major military and political event, but there is no firm indication that this was other than what has been described in 2 Kgs 18.14-16. It overlooks the element of personal humiliation in Hezekiah's surrender and contrastingly sees the protection of Jerusalem and the preservation of the Davidic throne as great victories.

The element of historicity is important to the narrative, since it serves to validate the rightness of the sentence passed on 'the king of Assyria' for having perpetrated a blasphemy, and therefore cannot be ignored. However, this leaves us with the very substantial question of how the language regarding the angelic action is to be understood and whether it needs to be translated into terms of a military setback which lay outside what is otherwise recorded concerning the events of 701 BCE in the Judean and Assyrian records.

The overall form of this Account B may be compared to a report of proceedings in a court-room and it may well have been loosely modelled on reports of actual legal proceedings. However this is essentially a literary device to establish a theological point concerning the blasphemous nature of the Assyrian claims to rule over Jerusalem. The untidy literary make-up, often ascribed to the author's use of a combination of separate, and partly parallel, sources obscures the court-room form. The 'case' is a charge that the king of Assyria has perpetrated a blasphemy, clearly understood to amount to a capital offence, and undoubtedly having strong political overtones regarding Mesopotamian imperialist demands. The evidence for this charge is that the king has claimed to exercise jurisdiction and power over Jerusalem, and that Yahweh, the God of Jerusalem, has no power there.

For making such excessive and outrageous claims, which are spelled out with significantly stylized detail, the king of Assyria must be punished and this punishment is eventually seen to be carried out. This action then provides the conclusion to the narrative, being important to its quasi-legal structure. Insistence that the king of Assyria has no power over Jerusalem is asserted firmly by the prophet Isaiah and proof that this is so is demonstrated by the Assyrian failure to capture the city as the Rabshakeh had claimed to be able to do. A feature incidental to this, which appears in the Rabshakeh's speech, is the contrasting of Jerusalem's protection by Yahweh with the fate that had befallen Samaria (2 Kgs 18.34).

Evaluation of the form of the story is important since it brings to light its major features and characteristics. It is notable that it does not make use of the typical 'royal chronicle' form and not even the prophetic speeches ascribed to Isaiah are typically prophetic in their character. Nor can it be said to present a particularly favourable estimate of Hezekiah, who simply accepts Isaiah's message, but concentrates instead on the importance of the Davidic dynasty. There is a threefold sequence of fulfilment: a sign (19.29) demonstrates the rightness of Isaiah's prophetic message; the remarkable deliverance of Jerusalem then fulfils the reassuring element of this (2 Kgs 19.35) and finally the circumstances surrounding the death of Sennacherib prove the charge of blasphemy (2 Kgs 19.37). This introduction of a 'sign' probably indicates an awareness that 'signs' played a significant role in Isaiah's prophecies (cf. Isa. 7.11, 14; 8.18; 19.20; 20.3).

It is difficult to see why the narrative can be thought to provide evidence, either for a later second campaign led by Sennacherib when something untoward took place, or for a carefully preserved oral legend about circumstances in 701 BCE, unreported in either the Sennacherib Chronicle or 2 Kgs 18.14-16. At the most the narrator has drawn broadly upon knowledge of difficulties that beset all ancient military commanders.

The heart of the story lies in the great claims made for the king of Assyria by the Rabshakeh and their rebuttal by Isaiah. The historical events provide proof of guilt and serve as a sentence. As to the historicity of the Rabshakeh's visit and letter we may adopt a reasonably positive attitude since they appear to be typical, if somewhat stylised, expressions of Assyrian imperialist measures. When they took place for Jerusalem we cannot know, but they remain wholly plausible.

Overall it is the theological element which provides the structure and purpose of the narrative labelled Account B. The question of historicity then comes down to one of whether Sennacherib mounted a second attack upon Jerusalem after Hezekiah's initial act of submission, either in 701 BCE, or later. I would hold to my claim set out in *Isaiah and the Deliverance of Jerusalem* that we do not need to posit any such second campaign, or second attempt on Jerusalem, to understand the so-called Account B. It is not a question of whether the narrative is historical, or otherwise, but whether it reports a different overall situation from that briefly summarised in the Account A. It does not. The claim of A.R. Millard is mistaken therefore that, according to my view: 'What we read in 2 Kings 18.17–19.37 is, in effect, no more than a theologian's fairy-tale, an interweaving of an old story with theological theory to produce a narrative which is unhistorical'.[19] The events of 701 BCE are certainly historical, as the combination of evidence well attests. The issue is whether what the Bible describes as the intervention of the angel of the LORD in the events of the year 701 BCE, which provide the basis for Account B, requires us to postulate that some otherwise unknown happening took place in order to account for this distinctive biblical perspective concerning a blasphemy and its punishment. Our contention remains that it does not.

3. *Imperialism and its Ideology*

So far the chief focus of interest has been to identify the essential character of the story of Jerusalem's remarkable deliverance in 701 BCE and to note the theological issues on which it focuses. To attempt to explain these issues as the chance result of some otherwise imperfectly known circumstance that affected Sennacherib's actions in 701 BCE marks a failure to perceive their central importance. These issues are basically twofold: Israel is not like other nations because Yahweh its God, is not powerless like other gods; secondly the imperialist claims of the king of Assyria constitute a blasphemy which must be punished. The events of 701 BCE provide proof of the former point and the manner of Sennacherib's eventual death proves the latter charge. All of this leads us to recognize the great extent to which the theological ideology of this narrative is rooted in Israel's experience of Mesopotamian imperialism. If we are to indulge in speculations at all, it may be in order to suggest that the author(s) of the narrative must have witnessed, and been incensed by, the brash and arrogant claims of Assyrian victory inscriptions. The very proud claims evident in the Sennacherib Chronicle are precisely the kind of claims that the narrative is designed to rebut.

We can therefore quite briefly list the prominent ideological features that are to be found in it: (1) the Assyrian ruler has blasphemed Yahweh, the God of Israel, by his claim to exercise control over Judah and Jerusalem. (2) Jerusalem is not like other nations, nor even like Samaria, whose deities do not have power to protect their citizens. (3) Yahweh's honour is bound up with the fate of his people and their city and he is able to act directly to defend it. In achieving this, he does not need the assistance of other nations who may seek to act together in mutual defence treaties. Such treaties do not work, and are positively misleading. (4) In acting to defend his honour Yahweh will not be acting solely for his own sake, but also with regard for the Davidic dynasty, which represents a chosen agency of divine government (2 Kgs 19.34).

---

19. Millard, 'Sennacherib's Attack', p. 73.

Taken as a whole we are forced to recognize that, in order to understand the story, we must seek to evaluate and locate this ideology, rather than endeavour to find an underlying oral legend. It is the ideology that has made use of the events of 701 BCE as proof of its own validity. Ehud Ben Zvi has usefully drawn attention to the many features which show this ideology to have arisen at some significant distance in time from the event which provides it with its claim to truth.[20] In view of the existence of the so-called 'Zion tradition' preserved in such psalms as 46 and 48, it could be argued that, as Mowinckel long ago suggested,[21] all that was needed was to apply the psalmic tradition of Zion's assurance of divine protection and victory to a particular situation.

Yet this is very inadequate and represents so limited and incomplete a part of the ideology demonstrated in the narrative as to provide no sufficient explanation of its origin. What we are faced with is not simply a narrative tinged with psalm-like assurances. Too many other features are present for this to be the case. Most noticeable is the evidence of the harsh consequences of Assyrian imperialist control—probably already experienced over some substantial interval of time. C.R. Seitz's suggestion[22] of an origin in the dark years of Manasseh's long reign is the very earliest we could reasonably posit such a strong anti-imperialist sentiment. Yet even this is to place the story to a very early period. More plausible is the suggestion of H. Barth that the anti-Assyrian ideology of Josiah's reign, beginning to flourish at a time when the ending of the dark century of Assyrian imperialism was at last in sight, marks a probable time for the origin of the narrative.[23] Yet this carries the rather contradictory feature that, to have claimed that Assyrian power was already humiliated and defeated in Sennacherib's time in 701 BCE leaves unexplained why Judah had suffered so much, and for so long, after that event took place. Why had Manasseh's reign been so terrible, and Josiah's marked such a new dawning, if Sennacherib's humiliation and defeat had already occurred in 701 BCE?

This brings us clearly to the conclusion that the very nature of the story about how the angel of the LORD protected Jerusalem and inflicted a humiliating defeat upon Sennacherib in 701 BCE points to a time of origin when those events were already a distant memory. The earliest that such an interpretation of an event could reasonably be thought to have arisen is during

---

20. E. Ben Zvi, 'Who Wrote the Speech of the Rabshakeh and When?', *JBL* 109 (1990), pp. 79-92.

21. S. Mowinckel, *Psalmenstudien II* (Kristiania: J. Dybwad, 1921), p. 65.

22. Seitz, *Zion's Final Destiny*, pp. 100-102, 140.

23. H. Barth, *Die Jesaja-Worte in der Josiazeit: Israel und Assur als Thema einer produktiven Neuinterpretation der Jesajaüberlieferung* (WMANT, 48; Neukirchen–Vluyn: Neukirchener Verlag, 1977), pp. 239-65.

Josiah's reign, when the weakness and crumbling authority of Assyrian control had become evident in Jerusalem. Even this poses some difficulties, but it is understandable that, in opposition to what was regarded as the 'quietist' and submissive policy which had prevailed in Judah under Manasseh a strong anti-defeatist party had emerged. It is feasible that it was just such a party that fostered the new directions undertaken by Josiah, and the court-circle which supported his throne.

Such a view offers considerable encouragement for the arguments of C. Hardmeier that the story formed a central platform of policy, based on an interpretation of past events in Judah, which misled Zedekiah into rebellion against Babylon in 589–87 BCE.[24] In doing so the protagonists of such a policy became the main opponents of Jeremiah. Such an interpretation has considerable merits and draws attention to some prominent characteristics of the narrative. It fully recognizes that, however much the language of a strongly formulated Zion-tradition as revealed in Psalms 46 and 48 may have bolstered the ideology of the narrative, this cannot have been its primary source. It is an out and out politically motivated narrative affirming a strong anti-imperialist sentiment based on a concept of blasphemy as an offence punishable by death. Moreover, even allowing for the inconclusiveness of the attempts at a straightforward two-source literary analysis of the narrative (B1 and B2), there is strong evidence of supplementation and growth in its composition over an extended period of time.

We must conclude therefore that the underlying ideological feature that has shaped the narrative, viz. that Mesopotamian imperialism represents a blasphemous denial of the power and authority of Yahweh over Judah and Jerusalem, was its most fundamental building block. The various components of the narrative can then be seen to have developed as elaborations and highlighted illustrations of this. Such would appear to be in line with the conclusions reached by Ehud Ben Zvi regarding the origin of the Rabshakeh speech and letter.[25] In the light of this it appears unlikely that we can arrive at a precise date for the narrative in each of its features. The most convincing explanation is that it took shape over an extended period of time, beginning no earlier than the latter period of Josiah's reign and continuing through into the reigns of Jehoiakim and Zedekiah. In its final completed form, however, there are other considerations to be borne in mind which concern its literary context.

From our overall review of some of the recent discussion concerning the many problems, historical, literary and theological, relating to the biblical record of the events of 701 BCE nothing substantial emerges to suggest that the widely adopted conclusions, reflected in my earlier work, are not

24. Hardmeier, *Prophetie im Streit vor dem Untergang Judas*, pp. 95-169.
25. Ben Zvi, 'Who Wrote the Speech of the Rabshakeh?', pp. 91-92.

basically on the right lines. Account A (2 Kgs 18.14-16) formed part of the original text of the narrative of 2 Kings, generally taken to be a constitutive part of the Deuteronomistic History, in spite of its unfavourable implications for the reputation of Hezekiah. Account B (2 Kgs 18.17–19.37), however, was incorporated later, almost certainly when this composite narrative was in its extant form, and in conjunction with the two narratives that follow it in 2 Kings 20.

The question remains whether the final version of this Account B was made after the disastrous events of 587 BCE had taken place, and in full cognizance of all that these later events implied for the status of Jerusalem and the threat posed by Mesopotamian imperialism. In my earlier work I thought that this was not so, and that it raised uncomfortable questions if such a late time of origin was conceded.[26] However, I believe that this was mistaken and that this concern to magnify the theological importance of Jerusalem, and with that the need to shift the balance and orientation of the larger historical narrative in which it now resides, were all finally felt most acutely in the wake of the disastrous events of 587 BCE.[27] There is a conscious concern to contrast what happened to Jerusalem in 701 with what took place later in 587 BCE. Thereby knowledge was upheld of the greatness of Israel's God, and the sovereign power with which this deity challenged and overruled the blasphemy of all human imperialism. God was not mocked!

---

26. Clements, *Isaiah*, pp. 90-108.

27. Cf. R.E. Clements, 'Isaiah 14,22-27: A Central Passage Reconsidered', in J. Vermeylen (ed.), *Le livre d'Isaïe* (BEThL, 81; Leuven: Leuven University Press, 1989), pp. 260-61 (reprinted as Chapter 11, below, pp. 163-72).

Chapter 6

ISAIAH'S PROPHECIES AND HEZEKIAH'S ALLIANCE
WITH EGYPT: ISAIAH 28.1–31.9

The present collection of prophecies in Isaiah 5–35 shows evidence of having been grouped in relation to two major political crises which overtook Jerusalem in the last half of the eighth century BCE. During both of these upheavals the prophet is presented as proclaiming a relevant message, addressed to the king, but as representative of the people of Judah. These events are, first the Syro-Ephraimite crisis of 735–732 BCE which took place during the reign of King Ahaz. The prophetic legacy of this is to be found in the 'Isaiah Memoir', as discussed above. A second group of prophecies is centred on the political crisis which belonged to the years 705–701 BCE. By this time King Ahaz was dead and Hezekiah was on the throne of Jerusalem.

The prophecies relating to this second period of crisis are widely recognized to be contained in the unit Isa. 28.1–32.8. However the interpretation of Isaiah's message in respect of both of these periods of crisis is made difficult for the modern reader because a great deal of additional material has been woven into the present literary deposits. Original prophecies from the eighth century have been added to with a view to giving them a fuller perspective in the light of what eventually happened and to draw from them wider messages applicable to a later age.

Insofar as chs. 28–32 are concerned, the task of the interpreter is made particularly difficult since sharp warnings against trusting in the power of Egypt to protect Jerusalem and its king are interspersed with positive assurances of a glorious future for the city. These condemnations finish up unequivocally with pronouncements of doom. On the other hand the messages of assurance which accompany these warnings promise unprecedented divine intervention to protect the city should any nation threaten it. A number of these promises are constructed on the basis of citations and allusions to recorded prophecies retained in earlier parts of the Isaiah book. They all use strongly poetic metaphorical imagery to describe God's action.

The most straightforward explanation for this feature of conflicting messages of threat and assurance is that, in the light of subsequent interpretations of what happened in 701 BCE, additional material has been introduced into the present section of text anticipating a favourable outcome for the situation. No prophecies are present which unmistakeably refer to the fearful disaster suffered by the citizens of Lachish, although, to a considerable extent, the warnings against trusting in the power of Egypt to protect Judah may be taken to apply to the entire kingdom ruled by Hezekiah. The critic's task is that of unearthing how much of what is preserved in these chapters properly reflects contemporary prophecies from Isaiah, delivered prior to the dramatic events of 701 BCE, and how much has been added later to take account of the enlarged, more favourable, interpretation of those events.

1. The Literary Structure of Isaiah 28.1–33.24

The search for a convincing interpretation of Isaiah's message must start by noting the distinctive forms of the oracles that are preserved. Overall they consist of relatively short sayings which vary in form and character. Certainly the overall range of the theme concerning Jerusalem's protection supports the view that these chapters at one time formed a relatively self-contained literary unit.[1] This however supports the conclusion that a substantial amount of editing has brought together material from different periods and woven it into a unit around the general theme. With its beginning in 28.1-4, the unit concludes in 32.1-8 with the portrayal of a king who will bring justice and peace. The sections in 32.9–33.24 and 34.1–35.10 appear then to have been added later as supplements to this. Seen in this light, as W.A.M. Beuken notes,[2] the thematic thread which holds together the whole unit is focused on the Davidic royal house and relates the destiny of the city of Jerusalem to this. Overall the destiny of the city is the feature that dominates and the kingship theme is secondary to this. The supplements to the basic unit elaborate still more grandiose assurances about the future of the city and nothing further is said in regard to kingship.

There is however, an element of connection between the city of Jerusalem and the royal house of David in the woe oracle of Isa. 29.1-4. This alludes back to King David's historic capture of the city, but, far from supporting belief in the city's inviolability, the allusion to this event affirms the city's vulnerability.

---

1. For this section the modern critic is especially indebted to M.A. Sweeney, *Isaiah 1–39 with an Introduction to Prophetic Literature* (FOTL, 16; Grand Rapids: Eerdmans, 1996), pp. 353-433; W.H. Irwin, *Isaiah 28–33: Translation and Philological Notes* (Bibliotheca orientalis, 30; Rome: Biblical Institute Press, 1977); W.A.M. Beuken, *Isaiah*. II. *Isaiah 28–39* (Historical Commentary on the Old Testament; Leuven: Peeters, 2000); B.S. Childs, *Isaiah* (OTL; Louisville, KY: Westminster/John Knox Press, 2001), pp. 199-242; M.J. de Jong, *Isaiah among the Ancient Near Eastern Prophets* (VTSup, 117; Leiden/Boston: E.J. Brill, 2007), pp. 83-123.

2. Beuken, *Isaiah 28–39*, pp. 207-21.

The order in which the prophecies appear is haphazard and seems to lack any identifiable chronological structure. The major themes regarding kingship and the city of Jerusalem are linked by the contrast between Hezekiah's trust in his alliance with Egypt and the divine promise that Jerusalem will be protected by the power of Yahweh.

The basic historical facts regarding Sennacherib's campaign have been repeatedly examined and evaluated. They are described in the Assyrian chronicle which requires separate consideration in relation to the reports that are favourable to Hezekiah and Jerusalem in Isaiah 36–37. Overall, both the Assyrian and Judean accounts are in agreement that a rebellion of several of the minor kingdoms of the region of the Levant took place after the death of Sargon II in 705 BCE. This rebellion was punished with devastating consequences for the region generally, including Judah. The worst disaster for Hezekiah was the horrifying siege and destruction of Lachish in 702–701 BCE which was later celebrated in a series of Assyrian wall reliefs. The fall of this fortified city must have marked the end of Hezekiah's resistance and inevitably left Jerusalem open to a similar act of destruction which was only averted when Hezekiah surrendered.

The prophecies which condemn the alliance which initiated the Assyrian campaign are relatively few in number and are easily distinguished from the more numerous messages giving assurance of protection for Jerusalem. As a step towards recovering the content of this message therefore the first line of evidence lies with the sayings which condemn Hezekiah's joining the rebellious alliance and foretelling its disastrous outcome. These take the form of five woe-oracles. The question that the reader is then left with is whether, if these woe-oracles convey the authentic message of the prophet, did the contrasting words of assurance about Jerusalem's protection also originate with him? Either these assurances arose in relation to a different event, or more plausibly, were composed after 701 BCE when the events of that momentous year were seen in a wider context.

2. *The Oracles of Woe*

The series of five woe-oracles warn against reliance on support from Egypt and unhesitatingly declare that the end-result of the rebellion will be disastrous for all its participants. The oracles focus primarily on the point that the alliance can only succeed if Egypt, the prime backer of the rebellion, makes good its promise to defend the signatories. This it cannot, and will not, succeed in doing. The content of these warnings is entirely relevant to the situation that existed prior to the destruction of Lachish. In respect of formal presentation, they stand out as a distinctive mode of prophetic address by the introductory 'woe to...' formula with which they each begin.

This form of prophetic speech has been subjected to extensive examination on account of its easily recognized structural pattern. It combines strong disapproval of actions and attitudes that are specified with a concluding pronouncement regarding the disastrous consequences that they will bring. Such speech units are self-contained and relatively brief, but the collection together of several such woe-utterances intensifies the note of prophetic urgency. Such passionate outbursts condemn the action that is highlighted and foretell its ruinous consequences. The association of the form with similar cries of 'woe' (Heb *hôy*) in a context of lament for the dead does not, by itself, imply an imminent death. The prophetic formula conveys intense anger whereas the use of *hôy* as a mourning cry more consistently expresses grief and sorrow. The most satisfactory explanation for this is that the term *hôy* was simply a basic onomatopoeic expression conveying strong emotion, sometimes of anger, and sometimes of grief or alarm. The different contexts in which it is used define the wider message. The underlying emotional mood made clear this particular meaning. There is no necessity therefore to comprehend all uses of the formula under the same heading and to suppose that they always conveyed a sense of impending death, whether deserved or not.

In the case of the five woe cries in Isa. 28.1–31.9 there is no hindrance to assigning them to the period of Hezekiah's rebellion against Sennacherib. They express anger about a risky political venture rather than sorrow. They also presuppose that the final details of the alliance were in process of negotiation and its ruinous consequences had not yet come to fruition. The possibility that some of them actually originated still earlier than the year 705 BCE cannot be ruled out. Hezekiah's policy appears, on more than one occasion, to have looked to Egypt for support. Nevertheless they fit very well the period of intense political activity that led up to the Assyrian destruction of Lachish in 702–701 BCE.

These five woe-oracles express hostility and rejection of a policy that was almost inevitably bound to involve Judah in conflict. The events that followed are recorded in the complex narrative sequence of Isaiah 36–37, which requires separate examination. In these narratives there are included a number of prophecies ascribed to the prophet Isaiah, none of which relate directly to the theme and content of these woe-oracles. Accordingly the question of their origin and place in the narratives needs to be considered as a separate issue.

So far as a search for the message of the prophet Isaiah prior to the story of the threatened siege of Jerusalem is concerned the five woe-oracles contained in Isaiah 28–32 are the surest pointer to it. They address a message to Hezekiah which is in line with similar messages attributed to Isaiah that appear earlier in the book.

(i) *The First Woe-Oracle: Isaiah 28.1-4*

The individual woe-cries are given no specific time-reference, and the negotiations with Egypt which they describe may have been spread at intervals over a period of time. The first is addressed to a group of revellers of the Northern kingdom of Ephraim. This 'two-kingdom' setting may have been deliberately chosen in order to emphasize Hezekiah's engagement in a regional action which embraced many cities and kingdoms of the area, or it may simply be the result of a desire on the part of an editor to show that both Judah and Ephraim, which had at one time constituted Israel, were involved in the disaster that the conflict brought:

> Woe to the proud garland of the drunkards of Ephraim,
>> And the withered flower of its rich beauty,
> On the head of those bloated with festive delights
>> And those overcome with wine!
> Look, Yahweh has summoned (a servant) who is mighty and strong,
>> Like a hailstorm, a raging tempest;
> Like a torrent of mighty overwhelming waters.
>> With his hand he will hurl them to the ground.
> The proud garland of Ephraim's drunkards will be trampled underfoot,
>> Along with the withered flower of its ornate beauty,
>> Adorning the head of those sated with festive delights,
> It will be like a first-ripe fig before the summer;
>> Whoever sees it eats it the moment it comes to hand (Isa. 28.1-4).

Surprisingly this warning of impending disaster is followed immediately by a short prophecy of hope and re-assurance outlining the glory and beauty that will enrich the lives of 'the remnant of his people—in that day':

> In that day Yahweh of hosts will be a garland of glory
>> And an ornament of beauty to the remnant of his people;
> And a spirit of justice to the one
>> Who sits in judgment,
> And strength to those
>> Who defend at the gate (Isa. 28.5).

Precisely when this time of peace would be realized and this new age of happiness enjoyed is not made clear. The use of the formula—'in that day'—indicates an underlying assumption that this new era of peace and contentment had become an established and well known theme of future hope, but only after great hurt had befallen Israel, which would be reduced to 'a remnant'.

(ii) *The Second Woe-Oracle: Isaiah 29.1-4*

A second woe-oracle occurs in Isa. 29.1-4:

> Woe, Ariel, Ariel,
>   The city where David set up camp.
> Add one year to another.
>   Let the feasts run their round.
> I will again distress Ariel,
>   And there will be moaning and lamentation.
>   And she will again be to me like an altar hearth (Ariel).
> For I will encamp against you round about,
>   And besiege you with a mound.
>   And I will raise ramparts against you.
> Then, lying prostrate you will speak from the earth.
>   From low on the ground your speech shall come.
> Your voice shall be like a ghost's from the earth
>   And your speech shall whisper from the dust (Isa. 29.1-4).

The picture that is described is of a city under siege, which is here given the name Ariel (altar-hearth) in a harsh word-play on the presence of the sacred altar in Jerusalem. The location, with its holy fire, is likened to the burning and destruction consequent on a hostile military assault. As the founder of Judah's dynasty of kings David had, in the distant past, laid siege to the city to capture it, so, yet again God (the 'I' of the prophecy) will prepare a siege of the city. The point is significant that no unique measure of divine protection is ascribed to Jerusalem as a city, or fortress. Rather the contrary is explicitly implied. Just as David had, in the distant past, besieged and captured Jerusalem, so once again it would be besieged and would fall to a foreign attacker. The concluding v. 4 vividly portrays a defeated ruler's abject humiliation and plea for mercy, so terror-stricken as scarcely able to frame the words to speak.

The striking feature, which has already become evident after the first woe-oracle, is that this strong warning of impending threat and destruction for Jerusalem and its ruler is immediately followed by a prophecy which describes in lavish terms a remarkable victory wrought by Yahweh against the 'multitude of foes' who threaten the city:

> But the multitude of your foes shall be like small dust.
>   And the crowd of tyrants like flying chaff.
> In an instant, suddenly,
>   You will be visited by Yahweh of Hosts
> With thunder and earthquake and great noise,
>   With whirlwind and tempest,
>   And the flame of a consuming fire (Isa. 28.5-6).

This remarkable assurance, wrought by a victory accomplished directly by divine intervention from heaven to defend Jerusalem, is then elaborated upon still further in the following two verses (vv. 7-8):

> And the multitude of all the nations that fight against Ariel,
>> All those that fight against her and her stronghold, and who distress her,
>>> Shall be like a dream, a vision of the night.
> Just as when a hungry person dreams of eating
>> And wakes up hungry,
>>> Or a thirsty person dreams of drinking
> And wakes up faint, still thirsty,
> So shall the multitude of all the nations be
>> That fight against Mount Zion (Isa. 28.7-8).

(iii) *The Third Woe-Oracle: Isaiah 29.15-16*

The third of the five woe-oracles occurs in Isa. 29.15-16:

> Woe to those who hide their policy (lit. counsel) from Yahweh!
>> Their deeds are wrapped in darkness,
>>> And they say: 'Who sees us? Who knows what we are doing?'
> You turn things upside down!
>> Shall the potter be regarded as the clay?
> Truly, can something made say of its maker:
>> 'He did not make me';
>>> Or can a pot formed of clay say of the one who fashioned it:
>>> 'You have no understanding?' (Isa. 29.15-16).

This threat is followed immediately in vv. 17-21 by an extensive prophecy giving assurance that the entire region of the Levant, from as far north as Lebanon (v. 17) will, at an unspecified future time ('On that day...' v. 18), enjoy peace and prosperity because the age of 'the tyrant' shall be no more (v. 20). This v. 18 contains allusions back to the threat that was incorporated into the story of Isaiah's commission as a prophet (cf. Isa. 6.10). Once again this allusion to a written 'source' text points to the hand of a later scribe.

(iv) *The Fourth Woe-Oracle: Isaiah 30.1-5*

A fourth woe oracle is preserved in Isa. 30.1-5. Those addressed are accused of pursuing a policy that is contrary to the one approved by Yahweh:

> Woe to the rebellious children, is the oracle of Yahweh,
>> Who carry out a plan that is not mine.
>>> Who make an alliance, but without my spirit.
> So they add folly to folly.
> They journey down to Egypt
>> Without seeking my approval,
> To find refuge in the protection of Pharaoh,
>> And shelter in the shadow of Egypt.

Yet the protection of Pharaoh shall become your shame,
  And shelter in the shadow of Egypt your humiliation.
For though his emissaries are at Zoan
  And his envoys reach Hanes,
They all come to shame
  On account of a people that cannot profit them,
That brings neither help nor profit
  But humiliation and ruin (Isa. 30.1-5).

Like the other woe-sayings of this section, this oracle as it stands is complete in itself. It comprises a sharp condemnation of the national policy of joining the alliance backed by Egypt aimed at rebellion against Assyria. The policy is alluded to by the description of the Jerusalem envoys making their way to Egypt. The prophetic condemnation is strengthened by declaring its inevitable consequence in failure and humiliation. The message of the concluding judgment (NRSV 'Shame and disgrace', v. 5) foretells a consequence far more serious than 'loss of face' and implies ultimate failure and ruin.

Unlike the three preceding woe-oracles, this one is not immediately followed by a sharp reversal expressing assurance of Yahweh's protection for Jerusalem. Instead it leads into a series of similar prophecies of reproof couched in comparable terms of rebuke. Not until vv. 18-26 does this perspective change, when a series of miscellaneous assurances of Yahweh's favour and of Judah's renewed prosperity emerge.

The entire section of vv. 29-33 is a pastiche of allusions to passages in narratives and other prophecies, many of them from other parts of the book of Isaiah, which elaborate upon familiar themes of fire and judgement. The sequence culminates in vv. 31-33 with a declaration that 'Assyria' will be terror-stricken and utterly destroyed. This last pronouncement uses words that draw directly on metaphors and imagery from the royal 'coronation' oracle of Isa. 9.2-7. Once again the time-scale has shifted from that of the eighth century and the threat posed by Assyria in that period is enlarged to become a cover title for the 'multitude of nations that fight against Mount Zion' (cf. 29.8).

(v) *The Fifth Woe-Oracle: Isaiah 31.1-3*

A fifth and final woe-oracle is to be found in Isa. 31.1-3 and follows closely the form and thematic content of those that precede it:

Woe to those who go down to Egypt for help,
  And rely on horses.
Who trust in chariots because they are many,
  And in horsemen because they are very strong;
But do not look to the holy one of Israel
  Or consult Yahweh!

Yet he is wise and brings misfortune,
  He does not withdraw his words.
So he will rise against the house of the wrongdoers,
  And against the help of those who bring disaster.
The Egyptians are men, and not God,
  And their horses are flesh and not spirit.
When Yahweh stretches out his hand;
  The helper will stumble, and the one who is helped will fall,
  And they will all perish together (Isa. 31.1-3).

In this, the last of the five woe-oracles, both the form and content of the previous four are followed closely. M. de Jong questions whether this one can be set alongside the others as authentic to the pre-701 BCE preaching of Isaiah on account of its several allusions back to earlier prophecies.[3] Such a point must be considered and carries weight. Nevertheless the message and general tenor of what is proclaimed is in line with the other comparable warnings. The central feature is the insistence that reliance on help from Egypt is worthless, as is all dependence on human aid. It is contrary to the plan and purpose of Yahweh.

Although this amounts to a typical, and readily intelligible, prophetic message, its reasoning is more reflective than the earlier examples, as de Jong argues. Whatever its origin it undoubtedly expresses a summary of the consistent message of Isaiah regarding the Egyptian link which fostered Hezekiah's choice of rebellion. It conveys an appropriate condemnation of the king's willingness to join the alliance that rejected Assyrian hegemony in the region. Throughout these condemnatory oracles there is a consistent prophetic warning by Isaiah that dependence on Egyptian military support would prove to be fatally misplaced and would lead to a disastrous result (cf. 'they will all perish together', 31.3). Yet the leadership of Egypt—the only really major military force in the region—formed the central plank of the widely supported regional plan of resistance to Assyrian control.

In this instance, as in the case of the first three woe-oracles, the warning of the disastrously misplaced confidence in reliance on Egypt for military protection is followed immediately by an assurance that Yahweh will act dramatically to protect Jerusalem and will deliver the city from its attackers:

Truly Yahweh has said to me:
'As a lion growls,
  or a young lion over his prey;
When a band of shepherds is summoned against him—
    He is not afraid of their shouting
    Nor frightened by their noise;

---

3. De Jong, *Isaiah among the Ancient Near Eastern Prophets*, pp. 94-97.

so Yahweh of hosts will come down
  to fight upon Mount Zion and upon its hill.
Like birds hovering,
  So Yahweh of hosts will protect Jerusalem.
He will protect and deliver it;
  He will repel and rescue it.
Turn back to the One from whom you have greatly strayed,
  O people of Israel (Isa. 31. 4-6).

3. *The Significance of the Oracles of Woe*

The overall theme that dominates the message ascribed to Isaiah is that reliance on military support from Egypt would prove to be a vain and worthless illusion. Such a message is entirely relevant to the situation that arose in the years 705–701 BCE and a comparable prophecy preserved in Isa. 20.1-6 shows that Isaiah had earlier warned against similar proposals for rebellion against Assyrian suzerainty in 720 BCE. At that time Assyrian forces captured and sacked the Philistine city of Ashdod. Evidently, and understandably, the successive Jerusalem rulers, Ahaz and Hezekiah, had toyed with the possibility of rebellion much earlier than 705 BCE. The various intrigues and conflicts involving the Philistine cities of the region help further to fill in the course of this prolonged interplay of regional diplomacy. The intrigues and complications introduced by rivalries between all the minor city-kingdoms provide an informative background to the separate alliances and factions which Assyrian intervention in the area had initiated.

That the prophet Isaiah should have warned against complicity in rebellion against Assyria carries a convincing ring of authenticity. It reveals a prophetic attitude of awareness that all such intrigues, however tempting, were likely to bring ruin upon the region generally. Resistance to Assyria depended on confidence that Egyptian military strength would suffice to protect the lesser kingdoms and peoples of the Levant. Assyria and Egypt were the two 'superpowers' that hemmed in the entire area between the desert and the Mediterranean Sea and the minor kingdoms looked to one side or the other. Confidence that Egypt would bring protection was alluring, but repeatedly unjustified in the light of events.

Such a potentially 'isolationist' attitude on the part of Isaiah is in line with the assurance expressed in the 'Isaiah Memoir' that it was Yahweh who was in sovereign control of Israel's history. Such a message is brilliantly encapsulated in the words of Isa. 30.15:

In returning and rest you shall be saved;
  In quietness and in trust shall be your strength (Isa. 30.15).

4. *The Prophecies of Assurance and Hope*

The conclusion that emerges from these woe-oracles is that, in the period prior to Hezekiah's act of surrender in 701 BCE the prophet Isaiah warned in the strongest possible terms, that the rebellion against Assyria, backed by Egypt, would prove to be disastrous. By betraying his oath of allegiance to the king of Assyria Hezekiah would pay dearly for his rashness. In the light of the decisiveness of these warnings it is difficult to understand how they could have been accompanied by messages of assurance which contrasted with this. Several factors point overwhelmingly to the view that this cannot have been the case.

In the first instance, if the prophet Isaiah had backed up his condemnation of the alliance with Egypt with bold words of assurance, this could only have bolstered the king's willingness to take part in the rebellion. He would have had nothing to lose! All the more would this have been the case if there were already in existence a popularly accepted tradition that Yahweh's support for the Davidic line of kings was absolute and guaranteed the current king in Jerusalem divine protection (cf. Ps. 91.1-13)! Prophets would command little respect if they delivered such a confusing message!

A second point is also relevant. Lachish had already been destroyed by the time Jerusalem was threatened in 701 BCE. How could Yahweh's guarantee to Hezekiah have abandoned the citizens of that unfortunate city to their fate? If 'the Angel of Yahweh' could save Jerusalem for the sake of its royal head, why did this not apply to Lachish where the king chose to make his major military stand?

Taken together these factors point to the conclusion that, in the period prior to the threat to Jerusalem when Hezekiah surrendered, Isaiah had given no unqualified assurance to Hezekiah that, if he embarked on his policy of joining the rebellion against Assyria he and his city would be spared from disaster. On the contrary he openly declared that such a venture would prove disastrous for him and his kingdom. Isaiah's repeated warnings to Hezekiah openly declared that he was playing with a fire that would consume him. Such an outcome proved to be the case, save for the unexpected feature that, when all was lost, Hezekiah surrendered and made a desperate plea for mercy. It was then a matter of the greatest surprise that he was allowed to keep his throne. The Sennacherib Chronicle leaves no doubt that Hezekiah's position had become hopeless after the fall of Lachish and that the payment exacted from him by his conquerors was regarded as a great prize and retribution for treachery.

The reader must therefore be faced in Isaiah 28–32 with a sequence of prophecies which originated in different periods of time. Some of them bear the hallmarks of having originated quite authentically from the prophet

Isaiah before the events of the years 702–701 BCE occurred. They show with all due seriousness that Isaiah opposed the alliance with the many rebel kingdoms backed by Egypt and foretold that it would have a terrible outcome. The only way in which prophecies by Isaiah which appear to present a very different message can be understood is to conclude that they either refer to a second threat which took place a short time later, or, even more implausibly at a still later unknown time when history came close to repeating itself. The former conclusion is drawn by several scholars who have argued that, after Hezekiah's initial act of submission, some further action by Sennacherib was taken against Jerusalem which was frustrated for some reason that is not certainly known. Most probably some action by Egypt is postulated. This second, failed, attempt on Jerusalem was the subject of a more detailed report which then underlies the extended version of this in Isa. 36.1–37.35. The reasons that occasioned this second threat to Jerusalem were quite possibly never fully known and gave rise to the belief that it was an act of the 'Angel of Yahweh'.

There is however no indication in the detailed Assyrian report of the campaign that any such further action took place after Hezekiah's initial surrender—a feature on which both Assyrian and Jerusalem records agree. No adequately convincing evidence has been forthcoming from extra-biblical sources to support the case for a second threat to Jerusalem in the period of Hezekiah's reign, although it has been extensively searched for. What is required in the first instance is a close study of the content of the prophecies that are convincingly authentic to Isaiah in the time prior to 701 BCE to see whether they are in any kind of agreement with those that are included as part of the narrative sequence which tells of the angelic visitation. These appear to present a retrospective interpretation of the reason why Jerusalem was spared the fate of Lachish and belong to the wider context of interpretation that belongs to the Deliverance Narrative of Isa. 36.1–39.8. They focus on the power of Yahweh as God, the divine justice in punishing the arrogance of Sennacherib and they look ahead to the future of Jerusalem and Judah.

As is the case with all the prophecies of the book of Isaiah there is ample evidence that the section of Isaiah 28–32 has been subjected to a considerable degree of shaping and development at the hands of scribal editors. The questions of when this was done, and the reasons for it, are matters for further consideration. Allusions to earlier prophecies are frequent and the reinterpretation of metaphors drawn from earlier prophecies is prevalent. Nevertheless Isa. 28.1–32.8 forms a coherent unit and throughout is presented as dealing with themes and events relating to the events of 705-701 BCE. The subsequent addition of further longer units in 32.9-33.24 develops these prophecies and appears intended to assist in adapting them for inclusion as part of a larger book. Isaiah 33 provides an important concluding link by portraying a joyous and prosperous future era of peace for the city of Jerusalem. This message is then further elaborated with still more euphoric expectation in 34.1–35.10.

The presence of these subsequent additions points to a literary expansion of this section that continued well into the post-exilic (Persian) age when Jerusalem began to recover influence and prestige as a regional city of importance. Overall the unit of Isa. 28.1–32.8, when viewed as an entity appears to have existed at one time as a small collection of prophecies with its central focus on the interpretation of Jerusalem's deliverance in 701 BCE. It celebrates the city's role as a unique 'Protectorate' of Yahweh, the God worshipped in the city's temple. The extensions to this unit focus on the city rather than its line of kings. From being a city rendered important and famous on account of its king, it is elevated to becoming one that was unique as the city 'where Yahweh has chosen to set his Name' (cf. Deut. 12.5, 13-14). The traditional motif of the divine protection of a kingly figure—in this case a scion of the lineage of King David—is extended to apply to the city that was uniquely associated with this royal house.

The most striking feature of these prophecies is the level of literary dependence on passages recorded in Isaiah 5–12. Although the extent of this can be variously assessed, since many are in the nature of allusions rather than explicit citations, this feature points to a carefully developed and ideologically significant work of editorial development. It was undoubtedly the product of a distinctive group of scribal interpreters. Bernhard Gosse describes them as a 'wisdom' school, since their skills and techniques presume a distinctive literary and scribal methodology.[4] This technique fastens on established metaphors and invests them with new meanings and displays a disconcertingly literary dimension, markedly different from the powerful rhetoric and aural impact of prophetic speech.

Nevertheless, for all its prominence as a feature of the Isaiah book and its heavy use of preserved prophetic texts and sayings, this scribal process of developmental interpretation represents a major shift from prophecy in its original form. It recognizes a 'distance' between the original recorded prophetic sayings and their later development; as such it is a distinctively literary, rather than oral, form of communication. In this new literary form it was free to display an ideological leap from the historical realities and contingencies of experienced warfare (siege, famine, etc.) to the more specifically religious and legendary image of a miraculous intervention by the mysterious angel of Yahweh. In short, it interprets real events as a historical paradigm of events that are held still to lie in the future.

4.   See above, p. 11 n. 14.

Throughout the section this time-scale is very difficult to define with precision since past event and future fulfilment are linked in a sort of timeless trajectory. Modern attempts to re-construct an original underlying natural event that took place after Hezekiah's surrender to Sennacherib's forces in order to explain the exuberant language of this narrative development fail to address this point. Certainly the unit in Isa. 33.1-24 appears as a structured summarising conclusion, which is yet further extended by the additions of Isaiah 34–35 setting out, even more comprehensively, a message about the future of Jerusalem supported with the backing of other prophecies.[5] This chapter both breathes an air of finality, appropriate for an entire book, while at the same time anticipating several significant themes from chs. 40–55.

In general the surviving evidence regarding the collecting and editing of the prophecies of Isa. 28.1–35.10 shows this to have been a work that was progressively carried out over a prolonged period of time by a series of additions and re-workings of a central text. It was not completed at a single stroke nor can it have been brought about simply by adding prophecies onto one single scroll. It is a structured and refined accomplishment. If Isaiah 28–32 at one time existed as a separate 'booklet', as is argued here, then it seems highly probable that most, if not all, of these additions were made to it before it was incorporated as part of the larger scroll.

The arguments in favour of recognizing that there existed at one period an 'Isaiah Memoir' gain in strength when the numerous citations from it that are to be traced in Isaiah 28–32 are taken into account. In my earlier study I followed the widely adopted proposal of Hermann Barth to posit the existence of an important written collection of Isaiah's prophecies in the period of King Josiah's reign in the second half of the seventh century BCE. This is the view adopted by Marvin A. Sweeney, and there is no doubt that a strong resurgence of Judean nationalism under King Josiah would find admirable support from the kind of forceful pro-Davidic, pro-Jerusalem ideology that appears in the story of Jerusalem's deliverance by the 'Angel of Yahweh' in 701 BCE. There are, however, strong reasons for caution about assigning such a date to the story as it now appears. In line with this a similar caution is needed in positing a comprehensive and carefully edited collection of Isaiah's prophecies as early the seventh century BCE.

Evidently some early written record of Isaiah's prophecies was made during his own lifetime, but to call this a 'book' may be to exaggerate the extent of its literary character. Nevertheless, as argued above, there is reason to uphold the conclusion that an authentic eighth-century nucleus of prophetic material existed in the form of an 'Isaiah Memoir' of Isa. 6.1–8.16

---

5. Cf. O.H. Steck, *Bereitete Heimkehr: Jesaja 35 als redaktionelle Brücke zwischen dem Ersten und dem Zweiten Jesaja* (SBS, 121; Stuttgart: Katholisches Bibelwerk, 1985).

and, Although this original written nucleus has then been significantly added to and revised in the light of later events, it appears that it provided some basis from which significant citations were drawn in Isaiah 28–32.

A message declaring that Yahweh would intervene directly to defend Jerusalem from the threat of all hostile armies, whether of Assyria or other kingdoms, cannot have formed part of the original condemnatory prophecy concerned with the rebellion against Assyrian control over Judah in Hezekiah's time. As noted below in regard to Isa. 14.24-27 this message was elaborated to become a comprehensive assurance that applied to 'the multitude of all the nations' (cf. Isa. 29.5, 7) that threatened Mount Zion. The purported defeat of Sennacherib's army is made into an exemplary paradigm applicable to the world of nations. In this recasting of a prophetic theme the timescale envisaged is radically shifted from that which had placed Hezekiah's throne and kingdom in peril to one that, from the reader's perspective, was regarded as still future. In its extant form it lacks any identifiable military or political context. The divine protection that was believed to have saved Jerusalem in 701 BCE has been enlarged to a wider, historically unspecified, one in which many nations may be involved. Jerusalem (Mount Zion) is elevated to become the subject of a remarkable divine umbrella of security. Although the message is similar to that ascribed to the prophet Isaiah in the narrative report of the events of 701 BCE, it is now explicitly a promise for a future age. The presumption must be that this future age is directly related to the undefined 'in that day' of Isa. 28.7.

5. The Origin of the Prophecies Concerning the Defeat of the Nations

From the overall perspective of identifying prophecies that relate to the events that led up to Hezekiah's surrender in 701 BCE it must be considered wholly improbable that a message expressing an assurance of this kind can have originated on the lips of the prophet Isaiah in the period prior to Hezekiah's surrender in 701 BCE. Had that been the case, Isaiah would have been a very dangerous and deceptive kind of prophet, offering assurance when danger threatened. Moreover the 'Woe oracles' leave no doubt as to what Isaiah thought the consequence would be of Hezekiah's joining the rebel states. What has happened is that, since Jerusalem was not actually destroyed in that fateful year this reprieve has been elevated in significance. An inevitable act of surrender on the part of a king whose army had been destroyed is celebrated as a triumphant vindication of Yahweh's power and the prophet Isaiah's message! The record has been adjusted and elaborated to take this outcome into the reckoning. In spite of initial warnings and expectations, Yahweh's sovereign control over all human plans and expectations—the central focus of the Isaiah Memoir—was believed to have been marvellously demonstrated by Jerusalem's survival.

Already in the preceding chapter the point was noted that a similar process of elaborated interpretation in the light of events has occurred in the composition of the narrative accounts of Jerusalem's deliverance in 701 BCE. Shorter records have subsequently been edited and combined to form the composite record of Isa. 36.1–37.39. This has then been further expanded in Isaiah 38–39 (// 2 Kgs 19–20) by the addition of stories about Hezekiah which illustrate his change of heart. At some still later point of time this extended Deliverance Narrative was joined to a collection of Isaiah's prophecies. In this the accentuation of the message of Yahweh's sovereignty and the worthlessness of human plans which form a central feature of Isaiah's prophetic tradition has served as a starting-point for further prophecies. Isaiah's repudiation of Hezekiah's trust in the military strength of Egypt has led to an elaboration of the theme—itself something of a truism—that divine help is of greater worth than human aid. The conventional aphoristic contrast between divine and human strength has been given a larger significance in the light of the unexpected nature of events! There can be no doubt that this desire to emphasise the reality of divine help has strongly encouraged the claim that Jerusalem's deliverance was accomplished by a supernatural act of divine intervention.

The inclusion of this scattered group of re-assuring prophecies in Isaiah 28–31, in some instances added on to the authentic warnings threatening the failure of the alliance with Egypt, adds a unique level of expectation of supernatural divine intervention on behalf of Jerusalem. They introduce a revised time-scale regarding the sequence of events and extend it to remain a valid assurance to the benefit of the reader. The situation of the eighth century with the threat to Jerusalem posed by Sennacherib has been enlarged into a timeless assurance regarding a threat to Jerusalem posed by 'a multitude of nations'. Although the Assyrian threat belonged to the past, the assurance of Jerusalem's protection which it revealed has been projected forward into an undefined future. Fresh prophecies address a later situation which was still not resolved so that the timescale of such future threats to Jerusalem is left open. The use of the key phrase 'in that day' (Isa. 28.5) draws attention to this uncertainty. Prophecies that originally addressed a situation that was historically well-defined have been refocused and expanded in the direction of foretelling a wider final apocalyptic *dénouement* to a prolonged period of domination by major world powers.

From the perspective of the theological interpretation of what happened in 701 BCE the entire unexpected outcome of the campaign leading up to Jerusalem's survival is declared to have been part of a divine plan, conceived by Yahweh, Israel's God, in the far distant past. Such at least is the interpretation given in one of the prophecies attributed to Isaiah in response to Sennacherib's arrogance. Yahweh had brought Sennacherib to power and authority, only to bring him to nothing:

> Have you not heard
>   That I determined it long ago?
> I planned from days of old
>   What now I bring to pass.
> That you should make fortified cities
>   Crash into heaps of ruins,
> While their inhabitants, robbed of strength,
>   Are dismayed and confounded.
> They have become like wild flowers
>   And like tender grass,
> Like grass on the housetops,
>   Blighted before it is grown (Isa. 37.26-27).

This is, in its substance, a straightforward elaboration of the message of the absolute sovereignty of Yahweh, God of Jerusalem, as set out in the Isaiah Memoir. The narrative reports of Isaiah 36–39 use the figure of the prophet Isaiah, and an outline summary of his reassuring message to Hezekiah, as a way of interpreting the events of 701 BCE as a demonstration of the divine protection of Jerusalem and the Davidic royal house and the role these institutions were destined to play 'among the nations'. This summary of Isaiah's message shows very close links with the re-assuring prophecies set out in Isaiah 28–31. Awareness of the warnings of the authentic woe oracles against trusting the alliance with Egypt is recast as a basis for urging absolute trust in Yahweh as God. The consequence is that, although no explicit mention is made of these oracles among those attributed to Isaiah in the Deliverance Narratives, the substance of their emphasis on the sovereignty of Yahweh is implied.

This is also true of the speech ascribed to the Assyrian spokesman—the Rabshakeh in Isa. 36.4-10. Overall the developed narrative summarises Isaiah's message as an assurance that Yahweh is in control of history, and no human plan can overthrow or frustrate this. The central message of the woe-oracles—Do not trust the promises of Egyptian help—is thereby recast as a call for the necessity of trusting in Yahweh as God and not trusting in any form of human help—least of all that proffered by Egypt! The original political message becomes a wider appeal for trust in Yahweh alone, in line with the oracular affirmation of Isa. 7.9. In this way a strained, but still recognizable, link with the authentic prophecies of Isaiah is given a wider significance. As a result of this considerable emphasis is placed on the claim that Jerusalem's deliverance from destruction—when it occurred—was solely the work of God. No human helper was required.

It is worthy of reflection in this regard that several of the attempts to uncover some inadequately reported event as the historical basis for the story of Jerusalem's miraculous deliverance in 701 BCE have done so by claiming that military action on the part of Egypt was in the end responsible for Sennacherib's withdrawal. Quite evidently the biblical reporting of the events of that year knew of no such human action and strongly discounted its possibility. Isaiah had correctly perceived the situation: Egypt's promised help was worthless.

Chapter 7

SENNACHERIB AND HEZEKIAH (1):
THE SAVING OF JERUSALEM—ISAIAH 36–37

In my study entitled *Isaiah and the Deliverance of Jerusalem*,[1] I argued that the problems of explaining the biblical reporting of the threat to Jerusalem that occurred in the reign of King Hezekiah have been misled by seeking to find a historical solution to a problem that is, in the first instance, literary and theological in its character. Undoubtedly there are historical, as well as literary and theological, factors involved in piecing together what exactly happened in that momentous year of crisis. Nevertheless failure to give adequate weight to the striking theological aspects of the story, and to understand their origin and purpose, has continued to make the event itself a problem for the modern reader.

1. *The Story of Jerusalem's Deliverance in 701 BCE as a Literary Problem*

In reviewing the substantial range of literary evidence there is little by way of a strictly historical problem in reconstructing the course of events that occurred in Jerusalem in the year 701 BCE.[2] Both the biblical and Assyrian records are in agreement that Hezekiah, king of Jerusalem, surrendered to the Assyrian king and was compelled to pay a large indemnity for his action in having rebelled. If any feature stands out as strange and unexpected it is

---

1. R.E. Clements, *Isaiah and the Deliverance of Jerusalem: A Study of the Interpretation of Prophecy in the Old Testament* (JSOTSup, 13; Sheffield: JSOT Press, 1980).

2. The literature on the subject continues to multiply with extraordinary rapidity. The essays in the volume edited by L.L. Grabbe present a review of recent work. L.L. Grabbe (ed.), *'Like a Bird in a Cage': The Invasion of Sennacherib in 701 BCE* (JSOTSup, 363; Sheffield: Sheffield Academic Press, 2003). Cf. also the study by H.T. Aubin, *The Rescue of Jerusalem: The Alliance between Hebrews and Africans in 701 BC* (New York: Soho Press, 2002). The major issues are also dealt with in M.J. de Jong, *Isaiah among the Ancient Near Eastern Prophets* (VTSup, 117; Leiden/Boston: E.J. Brill, 2007), where an extensive bibliography is set out.

that King Hezekiah retained his throne in a situation where most such rebels would have paid with their lives. The problems of the biblical account are to be found in the first instance at a literary and ideological level in asking how it was acceptable to the ancient biblical scribe to include mention of the devastating destruction of the towns of Judah (Isa. 36.1), but nevertheless to omit details of King Hezekiah's humiliating surrender and payment of an indemnity (2 Kgs 18.14-16). Then to follow this with a long report of the deliverance of Jerusalem (Isa. 36.2–37.38) wrought miraculously by the intervention of the Angel of Yahweh. The contrast between the initial devastation of most of Judah and the subsequent protection of Jerusalem serves to highlight the different levels of the divine willingness to act. Yet, read as a whole, the narrative fails to explain why this was so, until the reader moves ahead to the following chapter to read about the king's pious submission to the will of Yahweh after he became seriously ill.

The reader is made very much aware of the fact that there are tensions, even to the point of a seeming contradiction, within the overall sequence of stories. Why did God appear to undergo a change mind in protecting Jerusalem and its king? Nor is it hard to see that it is not simply the modern reader who feels this tension, since, in reading the group of stories which follow the account of Jerusalem's escape from destruction, it is evident that the story of King Hezekiah's sickness and recovery in Isaiah 38 is intended as an explanation. The point is effectively spelt out in Isa. 38.4-6 which connects the saving of Jerusalem from Sennacherib with the king's recovery from sickness.

Since the initial pioneering essay of Bernhard Stade in 1886 it has been made clear that more than one ancient source was called upon to produce the present narrative sequence. One source, labelled Source A, tells the story of the king's surrender while a second source, labelled Source B, gives a different picture of the saving of the city. The detail of this division of sources has been extensively reviewed and commented upon, with minor variations being put forward. It is evident that the problem is not simply that the timescale of events is not spelled out, but that God appears to act differently in the two stories. So strong are the tensions that one radical solution that has been proposed has been to argue that two similar, but quite distinct, events have been conflated. However, not only is there no evidence that this was the case, but the startlingly different outcome of the two is sufficiently marked to leave the reader with a justifiable feeling that God is inconsistent.[3]

---

3.   Important ideological and historiographic factors are clearly present in the biblical narrative. Cf. H. Graf Reventlow and Y. Hoffman (eds.), *Religious Responses to Political Crises in Jewish and Christian Tradition* (LHBOTS, 444; New York/London: T. & T. Clark, 2008), especially pp. 36-51; A. van der Deijl, *Protest or Propaganda: War in the Old Testament Book of Kings and in Contemporaneous Ancient Near Eastern Texts* (Studia semitica neerlandica, 51; Leiden/New York: E.J. Brill, 2008).

Moreover the sequence of the stories clearly does not presuppose any significant interval. On the contrary, by the subsequent inclusion of the story of the king's sickness and recovery the ancient editor evidently sought to provide an explanation for this apparent inconsistency.

2. *The Two Accounts of Jerusalem's Deliverance*

The first requirement for understanding the narratives in their present shape is to examine closely the evidence regarding their literary origin before drawing any conclusions as to which of their separate components presents a coherent and credible story. It is also essential to consider the question whether they are describing an unbroken sequence of events or are conflating two different threats. In particular it is essential to note carefully the strong political and religious motifs which are present in one of the narratives, which are absent in the other. The fact of the theological and nationalistic differences between the stories must be accounted for before an attempt is made at reconstructing the presumed historical events they are describing. These motifs are in themselves highly controversial and concern prominent and well known features of the royal ideology linking Jerusalem with the dynasty-founder—King David. The claim made explicit in Isa. 37.35 that it was on account of this divine commitment that Jerusalem was spared in 701 BCE highlights an element of royal propaganda that cannot be ignored. Furthermore, because of the presence of these exceptional motifs, the connection with Isaiah's prophecies is undermined to some degree if, in reality, it was in the event Egyptian intervention that ultimately saved the day for Hezekiah and Jerusalem. Yet this is precisely what the suggestions of a number of scholars imply.[4] The most forthright and authoritative prophecies that are ascribed to Isaiah condemn wholeheartedly the king's willingness to put his trust in Egypt for military support (Isa. 30.1-5, 6-17; 31.1-3).[5]

There is, in any case, an awkward anomaly in several recent explanations of Jerusalem's escape from disaster on the basis of some unexpected setback or military intervention that forced Sennacherib to withdraw his threat. These all imply a 'natural' (i.e. military, political or logistical) setback whereas the biblical record is at pains to assert that the means of deliverance was not of this order at all. According to these accounts the 'Angel of Yahweh' accomplished the slaughter of 185,000 of the besieging forces of Assyria *in a single night* (Isa. 37.36). It is quite evident that this was meant to indicate something of a different order from a natural disaster

---

4. So, most recently Aubin, *The Rescue of Jerusalem*, pp. 97-206; P.S. Evans, *The Invasion of Sennacherib in the Book of Kings: A Source-Critical and Rhetorical Study of 2 Kings 18–19* (VTSup, 125; Leiden/Boston: E.J. Brill, 2009), pp. 139-65.

5. Cf. the material reviewed in the previous chapter.

or an act of military intervention from some unexpected quarter. It therefore appears mistaken for the many scholars who have addressed the problems surrounding this event in recent years to have concentrated most attention on unknown, or little regarded, historical factors, in the face of the primary need to understand the character of the biblical record.

These highly distinctive accounts, with their bold literary and ideological claims, must first be taken into the reckoning. It is of little help to search for some undervalued, but vital, item of historical evidence when the central problem lies in the unusual features of the narrator's ideology. This point becomes all the more demanding of attention when there is wide agreement that the story of what happened appears clearly to be a revised version of two closely similar earlier accounts of what happened. In total many scholars have postulated three earlier versions of events in Isaiah 36–37, although none are precisely in their original form and one of them, labelled Account A (Isa. 36.1), is greatly abbreviated in the Isaianic version.

For all the various attempts to recover some unreported, or little reported, action to explain the belief in an exceptional military, or logistical, reason for Sennacherib's departure and Jerusalem's survival in 701 BCE the fact remains that no such event has convincingly been shown to have occurred. The concern to look for an explanation of the biblical record by finding an unexpected setback suffered by Sennacherib's forces which the official Assyrian campaign archivist might understandably have left out of his campaign record can only be sustained by presuming an ancient 'cover-up'! This is looking in the wrong direction.

The biblical story is perplexing on any scale of reckoning since prophecy, although regularly employing the language of direct divine action (e.g. 'I will rise up…'; cf. Amos 3.1 etc.), does not anticipate that this will occur through angelic mediation. It is a prophetic idiom referring to divine purposes achieved through human actions. Similarly in the history of 1 and 2 Kings angelic intervention is a rare, although not entirely absent, mode of divine action and those reports that report it are usually classed with older folk-saga collections. Ascriptions of sudden angelic visitation to achieve military victory are therefore highly distinctive. The fact remains that, in the mainstream of reported history in the books of Samuel and Kings, the explicit affirmation of a sudden angelic visitation to slaughter enemy armies is highly unusual.

In any case close attention must be focused on other religious and political factors which colour the accounts. These were evidently a basic aspect of the purpose behind their composition. The extended literary coverage in the Old Testament of what happened in Jerusalem in 701 BCE shows that what happened then was of such importance that it led to the revising and interweaving of several reports of it. It was recognized as of so unusual a nature, and so significant in its consequences that more than one explanation was current, as to why it occurred. Later generations were not slow to realise that it had far-reaching political consequences and these consequences could be given a religiously advantageous explanation. As sometimes occurs in history, events which at the time were initially greeted with unreserved relief appeared in a more distant retrospect to possess a very special significance. 701 BCE was not simply an occasion which saved the citizens of Jerusalem from a cruel fate, but one which highlighted the prestige of a remarkable dynasty of kings, and, of a unique city.

Like several other contemporary treatments of the subject my own earlier study of the biblical narrative aimed to build on identification of the separate literary strata which are evident in it, and to highlight the ideologies that lie behind them. This literary analysis was first proposed by B. Stade,[6] and has, with minor modifications, been the basis for all subsequent critical re-assessments. The report of what happened in Stade's Account B is not a straightforward near-contemporary record of unusual happenings. As it now exists it is a re-assuring piece of propaganda, part religious in favour of the god worshipped in Jerusalem and part political in praise of the dynasty of kings who ruled there. Only when we are clear about the kind of stories we are dealing with can we be in a position to draw conclusions about their reliability as a factual reporting of a series of events.

The narrative of 2 Kings 13–16 records that after Hezekiah's forces had been defeated at Lachish, the cities of Judah were plundered and ravaged and the king surrendered and paid an indemnity for his rebellion. This is labelled Account A by B. Stade and there is no reason to doubt that it is reliable in its content and was probably based on an official court record. However, the verses which mention the king's surrender and payment of an indemnity are omitted in the version in Isaiah 36 which is reduced to the single verse Isa. 36.1 (= 2 Kgs 18.13). This leaves it simply as a report of the devastation and capture of the cities of Judah. Various explanations have been put forward to account for the divergence, but by far the most convincing is that the author in the Isaianic version abbreviated the longer version since mention of the king's surrender would have appeared strange in view of his subsequent vindication by events.[7]

Reports of the capture of the cities of Judah and Hezekiah's surrender are in general agreement with the information presented in the Assyrian Chronicle.[8] By this action Jerusalem's king avoided total disaster. The city was spared the horrors of siege, rape and destruction that overtook the city of Lachish, as Sennacherib's royal chronicler boastfully publicised; similar

6. B. Stade, 'Miscellen. Anmerkungen zu 2 Kö. 15–21', *ZAW* 6 (1886), pp. 156-92.

7. So H. Wildberger, *Isaiah 24–39* (Minneapolis: Fortress Press, 2002), pp. 363-64.

8. Cf. J.B. Pritchard, *Ancient Near Eastern Texts Relating to the Old Testament* (Princeton, NJ: Princeton University Press, 3rd edn, 1969), pp. 287-88.

destruction was inflicted on other cities of the region. A similar fate must then have been imminently feared by the citizens of Jerusalem.

The question of whether the reporting of these events in 2 Kgs 18.13-20.19 is a more original location than that in Isaiah 36–39 has been much discussed and can be considered after another look at Stade's analysis of Account B.

3. *The Origin of the B1 and B2 Accounts*

B. Stade's analysis of the story of Jerusalem's deliverance in 701 BCE has remained a primary point of reference for all later studies. His Account A (2 Kgs 18.13-16 [= Isa. 36.1*]) is a credible historical record which points to its likely origin in an official royal court chronicle. Its near-contemporary time of origin and its historical reliability are not in question. The more significant feature of Stade's analysis is that the longer Account B can be further divided into two closely parallel reports of the event which are then labelled Accounts B1 and B2.

In the first of these (B1 = Isa. 36.1–37.9a // 2 Kgs 18.17–19.9a), a bombastic, and rather dramatic speech addressed to the citizens of Jerusalem by the Assyrian negotiator called the Rabshakeh is refuted by Isaiah. In the second of the sequences (B2 = Isa. 37.9b-36//2 Kgs 19.9b-35) a similar plot unfolds only this time the Assyrian claims and demands are expressed in a letter to the king of Jerusalem. Isaiah the prophet learns of these demands and refutes them by presenting a series of prophecies (Isa. 37.22-29// 2 Kgs 19.21-28). These not only reject the Assyrian demands, but foretell the protection of Jerusalem and an ignominious end for Sennacherib.[9]

It has already been noted that Account A does not present a historical problem. It provides an effective, and entirely credible, conclusion to the events of the Assyrian campaign. Isaiah's version (i.e. the version of events as reported in the Isaiah book) is an abbreviation of the longer version of Account A in 2 Kings. It reports the capture of the cities of Judah but omits any mention of Hezekiah's surrender. The 2 Kings version is factual and can be regarded as in basic agreement with the summary of Sennacherib's conquests in the region contained in the Assyrian Chronicle.[10] The shorter

---

9.   These prophecies provide important clues to the history and literary structure of the B2 narrative. Cf. my essay, 'The Prophecies of Isaiah to Hezekiah Concerning Sennacherib', in *Old Testament Prophecy from Oracles to Canon* (Louisville, KY: Westminster/John Knox Press, 1996), pp. 35-48, originally published in R. Liwak and S. Wagner (eds.), *Prophetie und geschichtliche Wirklichkeit im Alten Israel. Festschrift für Siegfried Herrmann zum 65. Geburtstag* (Stuttgart: W. Kohlhammer, 1991), pp. 65-78.

10.   D.D. Luckenbill, *The Annals of Sennacherib* (Oriental Institute Publications, 2; Chicago: University of Chicago Press, 1924); Pritchard (ed.), *Ancient Near Eastern Texts* (3rd edn), pp. 287-88.

Isaianic report is just sufficient to serve as an introduction to Account B which appears to be its intended purpose. The present Account B, however, is altogether longer and repetitive, and is ideologically coloured and explanatory, which Account A is not. It is concerned with why events happened as they did, and not simply with recording them.

A fitting conclusion to the enlarged combined report is then set out in Isa. 37.37-38 (= 2 Kgs 19.36-37) which tells of the inglorious end of the arrogant Sennacherib. His murder is seen as punishment for the accusation levelled at him in Isaiah's prophecy that he had committed a blasphemy by presuming to be more powerful that Yahweh, God of Jerusalem. The manner of his death as the result of a palace plot must have occurred some time after 701 BCE, although no extra-biblical evidence is available to confirm when this was and the treacherous manner of its occurrence.

Overall the narratives of Isaiah 36–37, when read as a coherent and continuous sequence, imply that other prophecies ascribed to Isaiah regarding the protection of Jerusalem by the hand of Yahweh are fulfilled. The sovereignty of Yahweh is a major theme throughout the prophecies and the narratives and is contrasted with the worthlessness of human promises of protection. Nevertheless this motif overall is pushed into second place behind the more directly personal accusation that Sennacherib, through his spokesman (the Rabshakeh) and his letter had offended Yahweh, God of Jerusalem. He was therefore suitably punished. Since the major pronouncement of the prophecies is that Sennacherib would return home 'by the way which he came'; i.e. empty of victory (Isa. 37.29 = 2 Kgs 19.28); the slaughter of his army by the Angel of Yahweh (37.36//2 Kgs 19.35) and the fact that this happened 'for the sake of Yahweh's servant David' (Isa. 39.35// 2 Kgs 19.34) introduce new, and unexpected features relating to 701 BCE. The outcome of events represents something of overkill when contrasted with the warnings given in the prophecies.

In reviewing the overall scope of the present account it is evident that several motifs are brought into play: Sennacherib will not destroy Jerusalem like the other cities of Judah; he had offended Yahweh by claiming that his power was superior to that of a god; most surprisingly the protection of Jerusalem is assured because Yahweh will act 'for his own sake and the sake of his servant David' (Isa. 37.35). The defence of the city is then achieved as a result of the intervention of the Angel of Yahweh, proving that Isaiah's warnings that human help would be of no avail are shown to be entirely correct. The motif of direct divine action appears in this way to be linked with the warnings by Isaiah to Hezekiah not to trust in Egypt for protection. There is therefore evidence that the author of the narrative was familiar with a collection of Isaiah's prophecies which contain this warning, even though these are not cited explicitly. The surprising feature is that this warning, which conveys a relatively broad message, is understood in a very literal and precise sense in order to establish the point that the protection of the city was accomplished by the Angel of Yahweh.

The concluding element of the prophecies ascribed to Isaiah is set out in Isa. 37.35 and draws attention to the special status of the Davidic royal family, although this is not a feature which has featured earlier in the narratives. Both this and the closely related mention of the action of the Angel of Yahweh appear to be details of the final edition of the report which were introduced very late into its literary structure. Not only is the angelic intervention not anticipated in Isaiah's prophecies, where the central plot is simply that Yahweh had been blasphemed by Sennacherib and was suitably punished in a very personal manner. Clearly several themes and motifs have been woven into the finished account at different periods of its growth and the most extravagant of the claims has only entered at the latest stage.

The message that is conveyed by the assertions made in Account B can be summarised: (1) Yahweh is superior to the gods of surrounding cities and peoples; (2) Yahweh is superior to Sennacherib, who is a mere human, but who claimed to have power over Jerusalem; (3) Hezekiah is a ruler directly descended from King David, to whom Yahweh had promised eternal support 'over the nations'. (4) Jerusalem is uniquely the city of David and is therefore protected by Yahweh. The last two themes regarding the unique status of Jerusalem's king and the exceptional means that Yahweh employed to protect his royal city are new features added to a collection of stories recalling a remarkable event. More traditional religious themes regarding Sennacherib's blasphemous claim and its punishment and the insignificance of human beings compared with a god are submerged beneath this larger concern with the uniqueness of Jerusalem and its Davidic dynasty of kings.

By the introduction of these features the editor of the final combined version in Isaiah 36–37 has linked the saving of Jerusalem from disaster in 701 BCE to the much older claim regarding the unique status of Jerusalem's royal dynasty. This was an ancient motif that is widely attested in the ancient Near East. The importance of the dynastic principle was part of the broad claim that the royal incumbent was a 'son of god', which prevailed across much of the ancient world. Although such a claim appears to have had an early place in Israel's political ideology, it has been introduced into the story of the events of 701 BCE, because Judah's sister kingdom in the north fared far less well under Assyria's domination, than did Jerusalem. Political capital is made out of a situation in which an entire region was devastated in the wake of Assyrian ambitions in the region; Egyptian plans to establish a barrier of fortress-cities to hold off the power of Assyria from its own frontier had failed. Nevertheless one city—the city of David—had been unexpectedly spared from the destruction which was the fate of many others.

For thirty years the longstanding rivalry between the sister kingdoms of Judah and Ephraim (Israel) had suffered stresses and tensions as a result of these intrusions of Assyria in the region. The death of Uzziah marked the beginning of Judah's deeper involvement in the tensions and conflicts of the region, re-awakening the old rivalry between Israel and Judah. This, in turn, drew Assyria more deeply into the tensions and regional rivalries, and was the occasion for the special commissioning of the prophet Isaiah, as recorded in Isa. 6.1-13. Overall it marked the commencement of a prolonged period of tension between Mesopotamia and the Levant; changing loyalties, confused strategies of containment and cruel destruction and population movements were the inevitable consequences.

In the final version of the story of Jerusalem's survival in 701 BCE this event is ascribed to the special relationship which bound together Yahweh, the city and its dynasty of kings.[11] By introducing these additional features wider issues were brought into consideration beyond those implicit either in the Rabshakeh's speech or the letter which charged Sennacherib with having insulted Yahweh, the God of Jerusalem.

The use of the opening part of Account A (= Isa. 36.1 // 2 Kgs 18.13) as an introduction to the story of 701 BCE and of the report of Sennacherib's death to form its conclusion in Isa. 37.36-38 (= 2 Kgs 19.35-37) provides the enlarged version of Isaiah 36–37 (Stade's Account A+B) with a fitting beginning and ending. It reshapes it into a well constructed and coherent literary whole. Whatever earlier versions were used in its formation it now exists as one continuous and coherent narrative. The element of repetition and parallel actions is not so prominent that the finished version does not read smoothly. In fact the repetition serves to provide emphasis. Similarly the part of Account A that is used makes this also an intrinsic part of the combined whole. The result is that the sequence of episodes now possesses a coherence and consistency in spite of the duplication of the Assyrian claims in speech and letter. Stade's dismemberment into separate, roughly parallel, sources is useful up to a point, but it over-emphasises the distinctiveness and discontinuity between the presumed sources. The narrator of the final version clearly aimed at describing a connected sequence of events, not summaries of two separate campaigns.

These features enable K.A.D. Smelik[12] to argue for the coherence and consistency of the entire narrative of Isaiah 36–37. The earlier versions of

---

11. The importance of the theme of the promise of Yahweh to King David is a major one in the prophecies of Isa. 5–35. Cf. my essay, 'The Davidic Covenant in the Isaiah Tradition', in A.D. Mayes and R.B. Salters (eds.), *Covenant in Context* (Oxford: Oxford University Press, 2003), pp. 39-69.

12. K.A.D. Smelik, 'Distortion of Old Testament Prophecy: The Purpose of Isaiah xxxvi and xxxvii', in Smelik, *Crises and Perspectives: Studies in Ancient Near Eastern*

these remarkable events that were called upon have been skilfully woven together to make a consistent story. Moreover Smelik argues, over against many critics, that the location in Isaiah is more original than that of 2 Kings. This does not refute the notion that, at one time, two loosely parallel earlier forms of the story existed. Nevertheless their separate identities have been woven into one in a revised version. At the same time some important new features have been added. Only by reconstructing their presumed original shape does it become fully evident that several theological and political points are presented in the final version. Primary theological points regarding Yahweh's superior power are anticipated by the Rabshakeh's speech and the Assyrian letter and these are then reinforced in the prophecies ascribed to Isaiah. Nevertheless, even these do not anticipate that the city would ultimately be saved by the direct intervention of Yahweh's angel. Overall several claims are made which are shown to be confirmed by events.

The broad scope of Smelik's argument is followed here, since it brings out several important features, but with the proviso that it must be extended further to include Isaiah 38–39. Of first importance among them is recognition that the present narrative sequence, which ultimately extends as far as Isa. 39.8, had a literary history of its own. It was not composed as part of either the Isaiah collection of prophecies or the history of 2 Kings. It existed as a document in its own right and is focused on the status of Yahweh as God and the Davidic royal house as rulers of Israel. Accordingly the stories of Isa. 36.1–39.8 appear as a documentary unity with a proper beginning and ending; older literary elements have been drawn upon in its composition but these have been skilfully combined and woven together to form the present single narrative. This literary unity has important consequences for assessing its time of origin. Its component parts link together the emphasis on Yahweh's power over other gods of the region with his power over Assyria. They uphold the accusation that Sennacherib had perpetrated a blasphemy; they then proceed to imply that his failure to destroy Jerusalem and his subsequent death were an appropriate divine punishment. Only at the stage when these multiple accusations were combined into the enlarged single narrative were the further features of Isa. 37.35-36 introduced which tell of the promise of protection for the Davidic dynasty and the intervention of the Angel of Yahweh.

Before the question of the place of this narrative in the larger context of the Isaiah book can be considered it is necessary to take into account the

Polytheism, Biblical Theology, Palestinian Archaeology and Intertestamental Literature (OTS, 24; Leiden: E.J. Brill, 1986), pp. 70-93; Smelik, 'King Hezekiah Advocates True Prophecy: Remarks on Isaiah xxxvi and xxxviii / II Kings xviii and xix', in Smelik, *Converting the Past: Studies in Ancient Israelite and Moabite Historiography* (OTS, 28; Leiden: E.J. Brill, 1992), pp. 93-128.

question of its relationship to the stories which follow in chs. 38–39 dealing with Hezekiah. These add further information about his piety and look ahead in Isaiah 39 to the disasters that overtook Jerusalem in the early sixth century. Both from the point of view of content and literary form the entire group of stories belong together so that Isa. 36–37 and 38–39 form a coherent literary unit. The information given in Isaiah 38 provides an explanation for the deliverance recounted in the previous chapters, while the incident of Isaiah 39 looks ahead to events that took place a century later. The whole collection of stories once constituted an independent and self-contained 'booklet'. It has a proper beginning and ending, a connected theme and message and, in its ending it addresses a later situation which challenged this message. In consequence the question of the priority of location in either 2 Kings or Isaiah loses much of its significance. Only secondarily was this collected sequence of stories incorporated, with variations, into either of the two larger works in which it is now located. However, before dealing with these literary issues, it is useful to consider how the message about Jerusalem and its unique assurance of divine protection relates to prophecies retained in the Isaiah collection.

4. *The Narrative of Isaiah 36.1–37.38: The Saving of the City*

It might at first appear possible that, since the prophet Isaiah plays an important role in the narrative sequence alongside King Hezekiah, then these narratives were composed from the outset by loyal court scribes of Jerusalem with the intention of forming a kind of supplement to Isaiah's prophecies in whatever form they existed at that time. Such a viewpoint, however, quickly runs into difficulties. There are admittedly a significant number of verbal links between the two compositions. These especially concern the prophecies of Isaiah 28–31 which relate to the period 705–701 BCE.[13] However none of the specific prophecies ascribed to Isaiah in the narratives are among them. Nevertheless intermingled in the prophecies of this period there are several which appear to anticipate that the confrontation between Sennacherib and Jerusalem would lead to a unique demonstration of Yahweh's power. Did the prophet change his mind and settle for the belief that Yahweh would, in the last resort intervene directly to rescue Hezekiah and Jerusalem from imminent death and destruction?

This issue has already been dealt with above in Chapter 6 and any such change of mind on the part of the prophet must be ruled out. Evidently what has happened is that, in the light of the fact that Jerusalem eventually escaped destruction after Hezekiah's surrender, prophecies that anticipate

13. Cf. Chapter 6, above.

such a dramatic outcome and its angelic manifestation have been introduced into Isaiah 28–31. They convey a message in line with belief in this source of Jerusalem's rescue. So far as the political and religious background to such an inclusion is concerned then the narrative of Isaiah 39 provides the essential important clue. It was not the political situation that arose in the immediate aftermath of 701 BCE that demanded this forceful affirmation of the commitment of Yahweh to the Davidic dynasty. Rather it was the events of the early sixth century BCE which were far less favourable to that royal house.

The point should not be overlooked, however, that a significant level of editorial harmonisation and influence has matched the message of the narrative sequence of Isaiah 36–39 with that contained in the collection of Isaiah's prophecies from the period 705–701 BCE. Whether this took place when the narrative sequence of Isaiah 36–39 was joined as a literary unit to the collection of Isaiah's prophecies cannot be determined. Most probably it was already a significant feature of both literary units. The date when this occurred cannot have been earlier than the late sixth century BCE, and was possibly early in the following century. Overall the conclusion cannot be ignored that the interpretation of 701 BCE contained in the extended narratives that record what happened is directly related to the interpretation of Hezekiah's sickness and recovery which follows it in the following chapter. This is then supplemented still further by the story of Isaiah 39 which looks ahead to the disasters of the early sixth century which had a very different outcome. The episodes belong together and, in its final version, the entire sequence is unmistakeably a piece of theological and political propaganda.[14] It turns the interpretation of a remarkable event into a lesson in politics!

---

14. The use of royal propaganda motifs as a theme in Old Testament prophecy is noted by R. Mason, *Propaganda and Subversion in the Old Testament* (London: SPCK, 1997), pp. 22-65, and now more extensively by van der Deijl, *Protest or Propaganda.*

Chapter 8

SENNACHERIB AND HEZEKIAH (2):
THE SAVING OF THE KING—ISAIAH 38.1–39.8

From the evidence of Isa. 36.1–39.8 (// 2 Kgs 18.13–20.19) the earliest accounts of the story concerning the threat to Jerusalem by the army of Sennacherib ascribed only a minor role to the presence of the reigning king Hezekiah. Instead the confrontation is presented as essentially between Yahweh, the God of Israel, and Sennacherib, the mighty ruler of the great Mesopotamian Power, Assyria who has perpetrated a blasphemy. Only in the combined and revised (Stade's combined B1 + B2) version of the preserved account is the role of Jerusalem's king magnified to the extent that his presence provides a reason why Sennacherib was frustrated in his attempt to capture and destroy the city. Even then it is not the king in person, but more precisely the promise made by Yahweh to the ancestral founder of the royal dynasty that is put forward as the reason why Jerusalem was unique and the subject of unique providential protection. This claim is introduced as the last of the prophecies ascribed to Isaiah in the narratives (Isa. 37.35 // 2 Kgs 19.34).[1]

The stories which follow the account of Jerusalem's deliverance focus further attention on the royal presence of Hezekiah in support of this claim that the city was saved for the sake of Yahweh's promise to King David (Isa. 38.6 // 2 Kgs 20.6). They also confirm indirectly the point that the survival of the king was unexpected after his fate had appeared to be sealed. These stories fall into three episodes: (1) an account of a sickness that befell Hezekiah; (2) a mysterious sign of the king's recovery from this sickness which becomes a further 'sign' that Jerusalem will be delivered from Assyria; (3) a visit by emissaries from Babylon which heralds bad news of future trouble.

---

1. Cf. my essay, 'The Prophecies of Isaiah to Hezekiah Concerning Sennacherib', in *Old Testament Prophecy from Oracles to Canon* (Louisville, KY: Westminster/John Knox Press, 1996), pp. 35-48 (48), originally published in R. Liwak and S. Wagner (eds.), *Prophetie und geschichtliche Wirklichkeit im Alten Israel. Festschrift für S. Herrmann zum 65. Geburtstag* (Stuttgart: W. Kohlhammer, 1991), pp. 65-78.

Already the combined account (B1 + B2) of how the city was saved focuses attention on the contrast between the saving of Jerusalem and the destruction of other cities of Judah and the region generally (Isa. 36.1; 37.12-13 // 2 Kgs 19.12-13).[2] This motif becomes significant in seeking some understanding of the context in which the narrative sequence was put together. It shows why the events of 701 BCE were interpreted in a number of directions as a demonstration of the unique status of Jerusalem. It was 'the city of David'. Accordingly the stories highlight both the events themselves and the significance of Hezekiah as an heir of this promise of Yahweh to the ancestral King David. In pursuing this goal they emphasise the king's absolute trust in the word of Yahweh.

1. *Isaiah 38.1-22: Hezekiah's Sickness and Recovery*

The first of the additional narratives concerning Hezekiah recounts a sickness that afflicted him. This initially provided the reason for the prophet Isaiah to visit him and to respond to his enquiry concerning its outcome by declaring that it would prove fatal. The king reacts to this devastating news with humility, offering an urgent plea to God to remember his godly manner of life; he then relapses into bitter tears, accepting the prophetic verdict as inescapable. His acceptance of the word of God through the prophet is unquestioned. Isaiah then responds to this display of piety with a further prophecy, specifically describing God as 'The God of your ancestor David' and affirming that God had relented and would heal the king, adding fifteen years to his life. Surprisingly this assurance is then further amplified by the assurance: 'I will deliver you and this city out of the hand of the king of Assyria, and defend this city' (Isa. 38.5). Not only is it implied that the sickness was contemporaneous with the threat to Jerusalem, but, in a typological manner the sickness actually relates to this threat and symbolises it. The healing of Hezekiah from the life threatening illness becomes a sign that Yahweh will deliver him and his city from the power of the king of Assyria (Isa. 38.6 // 2 Kgs 20.6). The healing signifies the coming deliverance, implying that the sickness also in some fashion symbolises the military threat.

   Like the entire sequence of 'Deliverance' stories the report of the king's sickness is repeated in 2 Kgs 20.1-11, although more briefly without the psalm celebrating Hezekiah's recovery. A further significant variant in the 2 Kings version is the inclusion of the comment (2 Kgs 20.6) that God will act 'for the sake of my servant David' which does not appear in the Isaiah

   2.   Cf. Ehud Ben Zvi, 'Who Wrote the Speech of Rabshakeh and When?', *JBL* 109 (1990), pp. 79-92; D. Rudman, 'Is the Rabshakeh Also among the Prophets? A Rhetorical Study of 2 Kings xviii 17-35', *VT* 50 (2000), pp. 100-10.

version. It would seem more likely that this was added in the 2 Kings version of the event because it gives further emphasis to a central feature regarding its purpose. The claim is, in any case, an implicit element of the narrative in which the tradition of the promise to King David plays a central role; the editor of the Isaiah version may have regarded the point as sufficiently prominent as to need no further mention.

More generally the assigning of a clear literary priority between the 2 Kings and the Isaiah versions on the grounds of their respective contents has remained a controversial issue and cannot be conclusive. It requires to be dealt with as a separate issue in examining the role that the account of Jerusalem's deliverance in 701 BCE plays in these wider literary settings. The point argued here is that, just as the sequence of stories in Isaiah 36–39 at one time represented an independent composition, so the addition to them of these stories regarding Hezekiah and the future of the royal dynasty belonged originally to this expanded narrative block. Taken as a carefully structured unit these stories formed a 'Deliverance Narrative', which embraced the entire section of Isa. 36.1–39.8 (// 2 Kgs 18.13–20.19). That it should have been current in variant versions is no objection to this, but rather supports such a claim.

The involvement of the prophet Isaiah in the story of the king's sickness provides opportunity to emphasise that the initial forecast regarding the outcome of the sickness was that it would prove fatal. The prophet's presence was necessary as a way of introducing the divine involvement in the king's fate since Isaiah was not only able to tell the king what the outcome of his sickness would be, but also to hint at its wider meaning regarding the fate of Jerusalem. This point becomes highly significant when the reader is made aware that the sickness symbolises this greater threat (Isa. 38.6 // 2 Kgs 20.6). After hearing the verdict of the fatal consequence of the disease, the king's submissive acquiescence in Yahweh's will leads to a reversal of the original negative message. Fifteen years are added to his life and the point is then made clear that the illness is, in fact, a sign to the king and to Jerusalem, regarding the threat posed by the king of Assyria (vv. 5-6).

Yahweh's change of mind becomes meaningful in regard to this wider interpretation of the illness. Belief in the possibility of a change of mind on God's part is in no way out of place in Old Testament portrayals of divine actions. In this case the change takes account of the fact that the prophet Isaiah, as shown by several recorded prophecies, had been consistently condemnatory of Hezekiah for joining the anti-Assyrian alliance and for trusting in promises of protection from Egypt.[3] This trust in human military aid is regarded as a failure to trust Yahweh's power as God. On both counts

---

3. Cf. Chapter 7 above.

Hezekiah is accused of being unmindful of the assurance of Yahweh's promise to protect the dynasty of David (cf. Isa. 7.2); this was why, according to Isaiah, he had left himself open to disaster. Belief in the all-sufficiency of divine power appears to be a recurrent motif of Isaiah's prophecies, which was already set at the centre of Isaiah's earlier assurance to Ahaz (cf. Isa. 7.9). On account of this promise Jerusalem was spared the fate of Lachish, but what the developed narrative has added to such a straightforward account is the intervention by the 'Angel of Yahweh'.[4]

Even without specific reference to the tradition of Isaiah's prophecies the change of mind regarding the outcome of the sickness mirrors closely Hezekiah's actions with regard to Sennacherib. He had joined a rebel faction, trusting that it had the strength to defend him and his city, and Isaiah had condemned this policy. In the outcome the king's actions proved disastrous and the prophet's judgment was shown to be correct. In consequence Hezekiah had no other choice than to throw himself on the mercy of Sennacherib, no doubt pleading that he, and his predecessor, had previously been loyal vassals.

Seen in this light the message of the sickness episode, with its turnaround from a forecast of death to one of recovery and life, mirrors exactly the situation of Hezekiah in 701 BCE. By surrendering, pleading the cause of his previous loyalty and paying a huge indemnity Hezekiah succeeded in saving Jerusalem from destruction and prolonging the rule of the Davidic kingship. This interpretation of events by the biblical author was undoubtedly putting

---

4.   R.W.L. Moberly, *Prophecy and Discernment* (Cambridge Studies in Christian Doctrine; Cambridge: Cambridge University Press, 2006), pp. 1-99, raises the important issue of the quality of 'discernment' in the gift of prophecy in the Old Testament. Moberly's study focuses attention most directly on the prophecies of Jeremiah where a complex contemporary political crisis is addressed by the prophet and subsequently reflected upon in an extensive editorial development. Many of the points discussed by Moberly apply to the prophecies of Isaiah (cf. Isa. 29.14), but wider issues are raised in the even more complex literary development of the Book of Isaiah. Prophecy, both in its leading figures and in its preservation and editorial elaboration, evidently sought to ascertain some understanding of the divine 'plan' for human history. It was not a 'historically focused' interest in past failures, except as a tool for understanding the present and still unresolved future. Accordingly it strove to reach some ideological understanding of the purpose of God for Jerusalem, for Israel and for the nations of the world. Imperialism, and the exploitation and destruction that it brought, are viewed as opposing this purpose. Isaiah's political standpoint appears in tension between a 'Quietist' acquiescence in submission to an oppressive regime (so especially Isa. 30.15), and belief in the divine power to overthrow it by direct action (Isa. 31.8-9). The action of the 'Angel of Yahweh' is presented as the divine answer to this tension and cannot be dismissed by presuming it to be a coded way of describing action by Egyptian (or Ethiopian) forces. Discernment is certainly a highly valuable quality, but requires to be defined by what truths are discerned.

the best case for explaining an act of national humiliation. In his surrender to Sennacherib Hezekiah had experienced a close encounter with death and disaster, but had somehow saved both the kingship and the city. Taken by itself as a historical record the story does not need the visit of 'the Angel of Yahweh' to explain why Jerusalem was saved. Hezekiah's plea for mercy and payment of an indemnity had proved to be sufficient. Sennacherib's response to this was a reprieve for the citizens of Jerusalem.

The inclusion of this story of sickness and unexpected recovery seems to reflect an understandable feeling of surprise that a rebel king like Hezekiah had been allowed to retain his throne. It was an unexpected reprieve for a long-surviving royal dynasty. To what extent Isaiah's condemnation of Hezekiah's policy indicates that joining the group of rebel kingdoms was unpopular is not made clear. Citizens of any ancient city were at the mercy of the decisions and choices of their rulers. It is entirely conceivable that there had been strong popular pressure to join such a rebellion, since the demands made by Assyria as a suzerain power over Judah may have become intolerable. Nevertheless joining the rebel faction brought with it inevitable risks of defeat and further slaughter. The price of failure is well illustrated by the fate of Lachish!

The earlier incident reporting Assyrian activity in the region recorded in Isaiah 20 shows that Isaiah had already earlier challenged similar political pressures in King Ahaz's time when this ruler had been tempted to succumb to Egypt's exhortations.[5] Hezekiah's willingness to risk his kingdom, and the lives of its citizens, by joining a rebel faction would certainly have provoked deep alarm among the people. They knew that they would be the ones who would pay the price for his actions, as the citizens of Lachish tragically learnt. We can understand therefore that Hezekiah's vacillating political engagement with Egypt, as well as with the rulers of the Philistine pentapolis, would have aroused considerable popular alarm. The king had indeed courted disaster but his enforced submission saved him and the citizens of Jerusalem from a cruel fate.

3. *The Sign of the Reversed Movement of the Sun:*
Isaiah 38.7-8, 21-22

Linked to the report of the king's illness and recovery is mention of a sign which was offered as an assurance of healing. This is wholly remarkable in its character. The shadow cast by the declining sun on the dial of Ahaz is to

---

5.   M.A. Sweeney links the unexplained portrayal of a hostile advance against Jerusalem in Isa. 10.27-32 to an earlier threat to Jerusalem by Assyrian forces. They eventually bypassed the city and left it unmolested. See M.A. Sweeney, 'Sargon's Threat against Jerusalem in Isaiah 10,27-32', *Biblica* 75 (1994), pp. 457-70.

turn back ten steps (Isa. 38.8). The initial request for this sign in the healing sequence has now become displaced to v. 22 from its appropriate place before v. 7. However, since the entire story about the sickness constitutes a 'sign' it is not surprising that this request has further become associated, somewhat confusingly, with the remedy (apparently a poultice of figs) which is applied to the source of the royal infection (a 'boil', v. 21). The reason for the apparent displacement of the two verses (vv. 21-22) referring to the sign is not readily evident. Since both contain relatively incidental information there may have been some confusion over what precisely constituted the 'sign'. The sickness was a sign, but so also was the remedy prescribed, and so also was the miraculous 'sign' which is then described. In any event this minor textual disarray does not affect the message of the story. A greater difficulty lies in the nature of the sign itself, which has made it a problem passage.

The occurrence which constitutes the sign is linked to the 'dial of Ahaz' which was apparently a series of steps, forming a kind of sun-clock. Its title points to Hezekiah's predecessor having introduced it and it is tempting to speculate on a possible link with the altar described as having been introduced into Jerusalem by Ahaz from one seen in Damascus (2 Kgs 16.10-16).

As a general background to the mention of a sign the practice of giving such a sign through some more immediate action appears common. When a prophet or priest was consulted about an illness, a worshipper would be given some visible assurance of help or recovery which would serve to boost confidence. The particular sign that is mentioned on this occasion has generally defied conventional rationalising explanations since it involved a reversal of the movement of a shadow caused by the sun. How could this have occurred?

Commentators have focused attention on the possibility that some form of visual illusion may have given rise to the episode—refraction of sunlight from polished stone or similar—since otherwise only a cosmic disaster of impossible proportions could have occasioned it.[6] However, such explanations approach the problem from a mistaken set of presuppositions. Just as the 'illness' of Hezekiah is presented as a type of the deliverance of Jerusalem, so the author has sought for confirmation of the miraculous nature of that deliverance by introducing a sign which makes allusion to a scriptural parallel.

The most direct instance of the reversal of a shadow caused by the sun, or more specifically in the original story of the sun standing still, is recounted in Josh. 10.12-14. It tells how the sun 'stood still' to bring victory to Joshua in the battle against the Amorites at Gibeon. Commentators readily point out

---

6. Cf. G.A. Smith, *The Book of Isaiah* (The Expositor's Bible; London: Hodder & Stoughton, 1892), II, pp. 375-85.

that the origin of this particular story rests with a rhetorical battle-cry being reinterpreted as a literal event. The biblical author's summing up of that occasion is sufficient to see why it was thought to be apposite to Hezekiah's situation. 'There has been no day like it before or since, when the Yahweh heeded a human voice, for Yahweh fought for Israel' (Josh. 10.14).

It is arguable that the point of implying that the sign given to Hezekiah was like that given to Joshua was to show that the victory that was granted to Hezekiah was of the same order as that afforded to the hero of the conquest of the land. The connection becomes all the stronger when it is noted that Joshua's earlier victory at Jericho was one that was accomplished by 'the commander of the army of Yahweh' who is an angelic figure and who appeared to Joshua on the eve of that battle (Josh. 5.13-15). The claim that the deliverance of Jerusalem in 701 BCE was accomplished through the sudden slaughter by 'the angel of Yahweh' of 185,000 Assyrian soldiers in a single night (Isa. 37.36) shows it to have been of the same order as Joshua's victories. The sign and the means of achieving a victory are closely similar. The 'sign' alerts the two respective commanders that God was about to act in a decisive fashion for the future of Israel.

Whether the story about the 'sign' of the reversal of the shadow of the sun, or the belief that Jerusalem was saved by the intervention of 'the Angel of Yahweh', was the more original element in building up the legendary portrayal of Jerusalem's protection in 701 BCE is impossible to determine. The question of priority is of no great consequence. It remains a significant feature that the bulk of the narrative components and their included prophecies in Isaiah 36–37 (// 2 Kgs 18.16–19.37) do not anticipate events beyond conventional military uncertainties (cf. especially Isa. 37.29, 33).

What we are presented with in the Hezekiah narratives is the linking together of two features in such a way that each helps the other to appear credible. A remarkable deliverance was anticipated by an equally remarkable 'sign'. The significant fact is that the author of the Hezekiah stories was familiar with the history of Joshua's campaign and expected his readers to be similarly well informed. The mysterious nature of the 'sign' which heralded Hezekiah's recovery from illness (i.e. that he and his city would be saved from destruction) can then be explained, not by conjecturing some visual illusion or trick of the light, but by noting the intertextual scriptural allusions that the story contains.

Throughout the Hezekiah 'miscellanies' there is a consistent concern to associate the king with aspects of Israel's historical tradition which serve to cast a uniquely favourable light on him and to emphasise his role in saving Jerusalem. Because Hezekiah was a king of the line of David, he is shown to be the subject of a unique providence which brought protection to Jerusalem. It should also be borne in mind that the actual unexpected fact of Hezekiah's retention of his throne after 701 BCE may well have owed something to Assyrian respect for an influential, and long-lived, dynasty of kings.

4. *The Visit of Envoys from Babylon: Isaiah 39.1-8*

The final episode in the series of three stories associated with Hezekiah reports the visit of envoys from Babylon whom the king greets warmly and with pride (Isa. 39.1-8). He expresses his warm hospitality for such a deputation by showing them all his treasures and the contents of his storehouses so that they can admire his wealth and marvel at his elevated status. He leaves out nothing in an effort to impress: 'There was nothing in his house or in his entire realm that Hezekiah did not show them' (Isa. 39.2). When news of the arrival of the envoys from Babylon reached the prophet Isaiah it was met with reserve and condemnation. After the king's admission of what he had done was forced from his lips, and the fact of his enthusiastic welcome for his foreign guests was fully confessed to the prophet, these actions were roundly condemned.

Then Isaiah said to Hezekiah, 'Hear the word of Yahweh of hosts. Days are coming when all that is in your house, and that which your ancestors have stored up until this day, shall be carried to Babylon, nothing shall be left says Yahweh. Some of your own sons who are born to you shall be taken away; they shall be eunuchs in the palace of the king of Babylon' (Isa. 39.5-7). Hezekiah acquiesces in this judgement and, in a concluding comment, appears to accept that the verdict is just, and is thankful that it is not even more disastrous for him personally: For he thought, 'There will be peace and security in my days' (Isa. 39.8).

It is not surprising that the report of the visit of these envoys from Babylon has elicited some bewilderment on the part of commentators. Why should Hezekiah appear so accepting of such a grim forewarning? It is obvious that the author was aware that these later events had already occurred, but why has he wanted to present Hezekiah as so accepting of them—especially since the offence appears so unintended? I have suggested above that the historical connection for this episode may be traced to some record preserved in the royal archives about a deputation from Babylon, but even this may not be certain. Quite clearly the primary historical interest in the report of the visit of the envoys is knowledge of events that occurred a century after Hezekiah's time when Jehoiakim rebelled against Babylonian suzerainty and his successor, the young, newly crowned Jehoiachin, became king. He inherited the ruinous consequences of his father's rebellion against Nebuchadrezzar, so that the disastrous penalties that Isaiah had foretold were fulfilled. These are reported in 2 Kgs 24.8-17—information that was clearly known to the author of this story which completes the sequence of Hezekiah narratives.

All three episodes—sickness, sign and inappropriate hospitality to emissaries from Babylon—were composed as appended commentary to the story of how Jerusalem was spared in 701 BCE. They amplify the message expressed in the claim that Jerusalem was saved 'for the sake of Yahweh's servant David'. They therefore belong indisputably to the narrative sequence of Isaiah 36–37 (// 2 Kgs 18.13–20.19) on which they are in some measure dependant. Nor is there any difficulty in recognizing that the entire sequence of stories at one time formed a self-contained and coherent literary unit. It was the work of a later editor to join this unit as an appendix to the prophetic collection of Isaiah 5–35 and 2 Kings 18. In this latter instance it was intruded into a much longer narrative. In the case of the book of Isaiah there is little reason to doubt that it was added at a time when Isaiah 5–35 still formed a separate literary unit.[7]

The author was conscious of the need to offer some explanation for the fact that the miraculous divine protection of Jerusalem which saved Hezekiah and the city in 701 BCE did not save Jehoiachin when faced with a similar situation a century later. Surely this king could have hoped for divine protection similar to that shown to his famous predecessor. After all, the divine promise had been made to King David, and this remained valid. He would surely have been at least as deserving of doing so, but was instead forced to pay a high price for his father's actions and, according to this narrative, for Hezekiah's foolish welcome to an untrustworthy imperialist power. Although Jehoiachin's life was spared, both he and his entire palace circle were taken to Babylon where he was left to reflect on his misfortune for thirty-seven years (cf. 2 Kgs 25.27-30).

Both the similarities and contrasts between Jehoiachin's fate and that of Hezekiah were sufficient for some explanation to be essential, if credibility was to be maintained in the claim that God had acted in 701 BCE 'for the sake of his servant David'. Why did God not act similarly, and for the same reason, in 598 BCE, and then again in 587 BCE? It is certainly possible that the information available to the author of this story was no more than that which is preserved in 2 Kings 24–25. Merodach-baladan's name would simply have been known as a ruler contemporary with Hezekiah. In this case the need to establish a Babylonian connection in order to explain the events of 598 BCE was sufficient for the author to have introduced this detail. It seems evident also from elements reported about the events of 598 BCE that there were close parallels in the political background of the events of 701

---

7. In this case the argument of K.A.D. Smelik, *Converting the Past: Studies in Ancient Israelite and Moabite Historiography* (OTS, 28; Leiden: E.J. Brill, 1992), pp. 123-25, that the unit of Isa. 36–39 was inserted between 'First' and 'Second' (Isa. 40–55) Isaiah is unnecessary. At the time that the later chapters were added to the Isaiah book the unit of Isa. 36–39 had already been added to ch. 35.

and 598 BCE. Egypt promised help to protect Judah and this failed to materialise. Consistently through two centuries of intrigue and diplomacy Egyptian promises of aid for Judah and its neighbouring kingdoms proved illusory (2 Kgs 24.7).

The story in Isaiah 39 focuses on the disaster that overtook Jerusalem's royal family in the events of 598 BCE. No mention is made of the far worse catastrophe that, in 587 BCE, overtook Jehoiachin's successor as king, Zedekiah, after he too rebelled against Babylon. At this time the city was destroyed and the king was forced to witness the killing of his sons, before being blinded and taken to Babylon. Thereafter the Davidic dynasty ceased to reign in Jerusalem.

In an earlier essay I drew attention to the strange silence in Isaiah 39 about these events of 587 BCE, which were obviously much worse for Hezekiah's descendants than what happened in 598 BCE. I suggested at that time that this may have been because the author was writing in the interval between the two catastrophes. Yet this cannot have been the case, since the narrative clearly shows from its concern with Jehoiachin that it was composed at a time when both events had become part of history. Neither is it possible to suppose that there was an implicit intention on the part of the author of this story to regard the second event, which marked the end of the occupancy of the throne by the Davidic dynasty, as in some way integral with the first and therefore not worth mentioning separately. From both personal and political standpoints the difference in magnitude of the catastrophic nature of the two events is immense, with the first simply removing one branch of a royal family from occupying a throne and the second effectively wiping the immediate family out and destroying its prospects completely. The contrast between the two is so marked that the decision to note only the former event must have been intentional.

When examined closely, and bearing in mind the interest shown by each of the Hezekiah narratives in the fate of the Davidic dynasty, the reason why the setback of 598 BCE is mentioned in detail, while that of 587 BCE is not mentioned at all, becomes evident. From the author's perspective the consequences of the former event were still present and active through the descendants of Jehoiachin. In contrast the consequences of the event of 587 BCE involving Zedekiah spelt closure.

The visit by emissaries from Babylon enables the author to look ahead to the rise of Babylonian power replacing that of Assyria, and provides a valuable clue to the historical context in which this reflective rewriting of the story of 701 BCE was made. It provides opportunity to relate the prophecies of Isaiah to these later misfortunes which embraced Jerusalem and the royal house of David. The treasures that Hezekiah had so proudly shown off to the envoys from Babylon were taken from his heirs and successors who themselves suffered exile and humiliation in Babylon. As Jerusalem's escape from disaster in 701 BCE had confirmed that a unique divine providence governed the destiny of the Davidic royal house so these later events shed further light on that destiny.

These painful events inevitably carried a wide significance for Israel as a whole and, from a reader's perspective raised many questions about culpability, punishment for the sin of pride, as well as about punishing sons for the sins of their ancestors. These questions are left unanswered. The final words with which Hezekiah submits to the consequences of his action (Isa. 39.8 // 2 Kgs 20.19) appear strange and enigmatic. Understood in their least complacent sense, they express relief that not everything would be lost. Yet, in reality, no specific moral or legal difficulties appear to have troubled the ancient scribe. His concern was evidently to look for an understanding of historical events which had already occurred by the time he was writing. His concern is to relate these events to earlier explanations regarding the special significance of the ancient promise to David for Jerusalem.

To what extent the author of these 'Hezekiah narratives' was in possession of factual information available in a court archive cannot be known. It appears highly probable that some further information about events in Hezekiah's reign was available. However, their primary purpose is fully evident. It rests on awareness that the disasters of the sixth century BCE, when Jerusalem was twice besieged and captured by Nebuchadrezzar King of Babylon, contrasted with claims about the unique impact of the ancestral promise of Yahweh to David on the events of 701 BCE. The need to explain these contrasting outcomes to Jerusalem's fortunes provides the background to the condemnation made by Isaiah of Hezekiah's actions.

These stories about Hezekiah's role in the story of the saving of Jerusalem in Isa. 36.1–37.38 (// 2 Kgs 18.13–19.37), must be regarded as a series of later supplements which amplifies the claim that the city was saved 'for the sake of the ancestral promise to David'. They are in effect an elaborate commentary on this claim, designed to uphold its chief feature. As such they belong inseparably to the developed (B1 + B2) version of that account. I noted earlier the point made by K.A.D. Smelik[8] that the narrative of Isaiah 36–37 (// 2 Kgs 18.36–19.37) is a well-constructed and connected unit. The claim can now be made that it is not simply these two chapters, but the entire sequence of Isa. 36.1–39.8 (// 2 Kgs 18.13–20.19) which forms a coherent and consistent unit. All four chapters belong together and form a single unit which can be appropriately called the 'Deliverance Narrative'. It possessed a literary history of its own which best accounts for the duplications which Stade noted and which formed the basis of his critical analysis. It must

8.   See n. 1 above.

certainly at one time have existed as a separate document; it has a consistent and coherent purpose; it maintains a clear and intelligible theme and presents an interpretation of the saving of Jerusalem in 701 BCE, as understood later in the light of the events of 598 and 587 BCE. It also displays a progressive heightening of concern with the supernatural element of miraculous intervention and with the significance of the promise of Yahweh to the ancestral King David.

Certainly this 'Deliverance Narrative' has been put together on the basis of earlier versions of the story of the momentous escape of Jerusalem from destruction by Sennacherib's forces. This point was quite accurately observed by B. Stade who recognized the duplication of the central theme and plot in which the superiority of Yahweh above other deities worshipped in the region (especially Bethel and Samaria) was emphasised.[9] It is also evident from the structural form of the narrative and the sequence of prophecies which are ascribed to Isaiah that the interest in the unique importance attached to the ancestral promise to King David has been introduced into it at a very late stage. Its underlying concern was to present a charge against Sennacherib that he had committed a blasphemy against the God of Jerusalem. Concern with the royal house of David was initially a minor issue, but has been made into a major one by the introduction of the prophetic addendum of Isa. 37.35 (2 Kgs 19.34) and the stories about Hezekiah's illness and recovery and the giving of a 'sign' that both Jerusalem and its king would be saved. There is certainly no necessity to defend the repetition as a deliberate literary ploy to give added emphasis. The retention of the duplication undoubtedly achieves this effect, but the point that the final form of the Deliverance narrative has been built up on the basis of earlier versions of the 'miracle' of 701 BCE is sufficient to explain their usefulness. Established literary materials have been edited and revised in the light of later events and later reflection. Most especially the disastrous happenings of the early sixth century which left Jerusalem in ruins and its king imprisoned in a foreign land was reason enough to demand some amplification of the story of Jerusalem's 'finest hour'.

The underlying theme of these three stories concerning Hezekiah is the claim that, in saving Jerusalem, Yahweh was acting 'for the sake of his servant David'. The story of the visit of the envoys from Babylon fits in with this pattern, but presents its message in an oblique and unexpected way. The

---

9. Smelik, *Converting the Past*, pp. 105-23, defends the use of repetition as 'a literary device in order to clarify the author's intention and to enhance the reader's suspense' (p. 123). This is, no doubt, the effect of the repetition in the present co-ordinated narrative, but it is more convincingly explained as having originated with loosely parallel narratives which had different emphases and which the final editor has combined for their overall impact.

need to demonstrate that the tradition of the divine promise to the dynasty of David remained valid for future generations of Israel reveals why it was significant to draw attention to the disaster of 598 BCE, and to ignore that of 587 BCE. The latter event marked an end for which there could be no compensatory act of renewal and rebirth. In the case of the events of 598 BCE, however, this was not true. By deporting Jehoiachin and his family to Babylon, and keeping him there, even in humiliating circumstances, Israel's God could nevertheless be seen to have provided heirs of the line of David who could one day flourish again. From their humiliation and weakness they could hope to restore the family's former glory.

The key towards understanding why one event, and not the other, is reported in such detail is because the deportation of Jehoiachin gave hope for the future, whereas that which marked the end for Zedekiah did not. The author's interest is wholly focused on this potential future of the ancient royal house and its message for Jerusalem. In this regard Hezekiah's foolhardy showing of his treasures to the Babylonian envoys had brought him, and his dynasty, trouble; but it had not destroyed them.

That the providential deportation of Jehoiachin should have led to the survival of an active line of the ancient royal family remained a matter of political importance when this story was composed. It was a feature filled with both religious and political potential. From this perspective what had happened in 598 BCE was interpreted in the light of what had happened earlier in Hezekiah's time. Far from showing the emptiness of the divine promise to the dynasty of David, Jehoiachin's deportation to Babylon was singled out as further evidence that this promise still retained its power to shape the future of Jerusalem.

In this story, as in the cases of the royal sickness and its mysterious sign, the intention of the author appears focused on pointing out that, in the midst of tragedy, there were signs of hope. God had prepared through the deportation of Jehoiachin a way of securing the continued effectiveness of Judah's ancient royal family. As in the case of the other two narrative episodes the message is discretely and obliquely conveyed, but it affirms belief in the positive lasting importance of the Davidic royal family. In the case of the two other accompanying stories, as well as the final combined version of the events of 701 BCE, the reader is challenged by a summons to restore faith in the claims of this royal family. The focus was clearly on Jehoiachin's heirs in Babylon which reached a peak of political significance with the involvement in a restoration movement in Judah in the late sixth century BCE involving the royal pretender Zerubbabel.

In this regard it is important to note the presence of a further story concerning Jehoiachin which relates directly to the miscellanies of Hezekiah. This is recounted in 2 Kgs 25.27-30 and reports the eventual release of

Jehoiachin from his Babylonian imprisonment and the exceptional treatment that he received after his release. I have examined this episode in detail elsewhere[10] and the numerous historical and ideological issues that it raises. It is sufficient to note that it reveals several similar exegetical features comparable to the treatment accorded to Hezekiah in these narratives and must have been composed in order to serve as a sequel to it. It appears to have drawn many of its details from extant written texts, in this case in royal psalms. Moreover its purpose is in close alignment with the Hezekiah stories: it points to the continued importance of the divine promise to the royal house of David after the disasters of the early sixth century BCE had brought the dynasty near to total eclipse.

To the modern reader the words which bring the episode of the third of the Hezekiah narratives to a conclusion:—'For he thought, "There will be peace and security in my days"'—appear to be strangely self-indulgent. The visit of the Babylonian envoys had opened a door for future distress to Israel's royal family which is presented as regrettable, but unavoidable. Yet these words lose some of their coldness when read in the context of the catastrophe of the early sixth century BCE. The disasters which took place then established the authority of Babylon as the awesome power that replaced Assyria, and their consequences could not be ignored. Against this unexpected and new political threat, when Assyria's collapse had been received with justifiable celebration (cf. the Book of Nahum), it was important to show that its replacement by the power of Babylon was not devoid of hope. A similar message was incorporated into the edited version of Jeremiah's prophecies with its assurance that, fearful though they were, the days of Babylon in the person of Nebuchadrezzar were numbered in accordance with a divine plan (Jer. 25.1-29).

In spite of near-catastrophe the Davidic family survived the disasters of 598 and 587 BCE. Even the wholesale destruction of Jerusalem in the new era had not resulted in the total eclipse of the family's importance for the nation. Moreover by the time Isaiah 39 was composed the power of Babylon had evidently already yielded to that of Persia. Accordingly belief in the mysterious and unique divine authority that was associated in antiquity with kings could still cling to King David's beleaguered surviving heirs. The disasters of the first years of the sixth century BCE, which had almost destroyed forever any hope that this family would recover its traditional prestige and power, were now past and the dynasty had survived. For a brief period at the end of that century the belief in the restoration of a royal heir in some

---

10. R.E. Clements, 'A Royal Privilege. Dining in the Presence of the Great King (2 Kings 25.27-30)', in R. Rezetko, T.H. Lim and W.B. Aucker (eds.), *Reflection and Refraction: Studies in Biblical Historiography in Honour of A. Graeme Auld* (Leiden/ Boston: E.J. Brill, 2007), pp. 49-66.

authoritative role gained fresh impetus through the person of Zerubbabel. Regrettably the sequel of events that put an end to that hope is not made clear in the pages of the Hebrew Bible. There is good reason therefore to conclude that it was in this brief interval of renewed hope linked to Zerubbabel and his heirs when the story of the Babylonian visitors to Hezekiah was composed.

Chapter 9

THE HISTORICAL CONTEXT OF THE NARRATIVES
OF JERUSALEM'S DELIVERANCE

The narratives which report the miraculous escape of Jerusalem from siege and destruction by the forces of Sennacherib in 701 BCE represent a composite literary achievement. This was long ago shown conclusively by Bernhard Stade in 1886 and, although aspects of his conclusions have called for modification, as noted above they still command strong support. Such an extensive and detailed composition regarding a single event and its aftermath is unusual and indicates the significance that was attached to what occurred then. The studies set out above regarding their origin and composition show clearly that this process of composition was extended over a considerable span of time as later events drew out further, longer term, consequences from the event. Nevertheless it is the political and theological motifs woven into the accounts that represent their most striking feature; it is these that make it possible to draw conclusions regarding the background circumstances of this extensive literary development. They concern not only the superiority of Yahweh, the God worshipped in Jerusalem, over other gods of the region but also of the unique divine support for the Davidic dynasty of kings which ruled in the city. Consideration of these highly distinctive motifs sheds light on what the background events were which motivated such extensive reflection upon a brutal military campaign which affected an entire region.

1. *The Chronology of the Literary Structure*
of the Deliverance Accounts

The evidence of the literary structure of the accounts of Jerusalem's reprieve from pillage and ruin in 701 BCE points to a degree of interweaving of motifs in their formation. Dominant features of the earliest components of the narratives, as shown by the Rabshakeh's speech and the Assyrian letter to Hezekiah, were evidently a claim that the city's salvation demonstrated the unique power of Yahweh as God. These components place no special emphasis on the manner in which the failure to destroy Jerusalem was to be accomplished. In distinction from this the concluding assertion about the intervention of the 'Angel of Yahweh' is linked to the claim that this supernatural deliverance was for the sake of the royal ancestor David. Both these claims appear to be reflections that were added at a late stage to the original stories celebrating Yahweh's power. They fit in with the royalist ideology implied by the stories about King Hezekiah.[1] Their concern throughout is to focus attention on the privileged authority of the Davidic dynasty.

The fact that there is such a variety of motifs woven into the literary composition of the narratives points to certain conclusions: the full sequence of stories as they now appear in Isa. 36.1–39.8 (= 2 Kgs 18.13–20.19) was put together from a number of shorter documentary sources and constitutes a single coherent whole. The final version takes in all the episodes and includes the report of Hezekiah's meeting with emissaries from Babylon (Isa. 39.1-8 // 2 Kgs 20.12-19). The entire sequence of narratives forms a single unit and has subsequently been incorporated in two locations: the first is the extensive collection of Isaiah's prophecies and the second is the history of 2 Kings (the Deuteronomistic History'). These subsequent literary connections were, however, secondary to its original independent status. There are some significant variations of detail between the two versions, but not such as to mask the basic comprehensive unity. Overall it seems probable, in the light of the ideological links, that the connection between the narratives and the larger collection of Isaiah's prophecies was the first of the two wider literary links that was made. However this point is of less significance than recognition that the completed sequence at one time existed as a single coherent and connected literary unit.[2]

The report of an act of dramatic divine intervention by the 'Angel of Yahweh' (Isa. 37.36 // 2 Kgs 19.35) connects with the collection of Isaiah's

---

1. The question of treating the narratives of Isa. 37–39 // 2 Kgs 18–20 as a single entity is an important one for the question of dating. Cf. A. van der Kooij, 'The Story of Hezekiah and Sennacherib (2 Kings 18–19)', in J.C. de Moor and H.F. van Rooy (eds.), *Past, Present and Future: The Deuteronomistic History and the Prophets* (OTS, 44; Leiden: E.J. Brill, 2000), p. 109. In my earlier study, the treatment of the Hezekiah Narratives as separate from the Deliverance Narrative followed the pioneering proposals of P.R. Ackroyd and others, but the assignment of the saving of Jerusalem to the presence of a Davidic ruler is of a piece with the concern with the dynasty's future expressed in Isa. 39 and 2 Kgs 20. Cf. Clements, *The Deliverance of Jerusalem*, pp. 90-100.

2. A. van der Kooij expresses a preference for the primacy of the location in 2 Kings, as also do H.G.M. Williamson and Paul Evans. However, the comments of P.R. Ackroyd are relevant in noting the close links, both verbal and theological, between the narratives of Isa. 36–39 and Isa. 5–12 and 40–55. See P.R. Ackroyd, 'Isaiah 36–39: Structure and Function', in *Studies in the Religious Tradition of the Old Testament* (London: SCM Press, 1987), pp. 105-20.

prophecies in Isaiah 28–32, but in an oblique manner. The original admonitory 'woe oracles' by the prophet warned Hezekiah against participation in the ill-fated alliance with Egypt and foretold its failure. However these have subsequently been supplemented by others which declare that Jerusalem will be assured of protection. These additions to Isaiah's prophecies foretell a sudden act of divine intervention which conflicts with the prophet's forecast of a disastrous outcome. They cannot have been declared by Isaiah at the same time as the warnings without generating total confusion. They must, like the formation of the Deliverance Narratives, have arisen when Hezekiah's surrender and reprieve from near certain doom was later presented in a favourable light as a sign of the divine support for the Davidic royal house. Possibly these additions were made at the time when the narratives were joined to the prophecies, but in any case they evidently originated in the same Jerusalem court-circle, working at some distance in time from the immediate aftermath of 701 BCE. Surprisingly none of the prophecies included in the Deliverance Narratives are included in the Isaiah collection.

A point of major significance is that the claim to a supernatural intervention by 'the Angel of Yahweh' is untypical of conventional prophetic expectations. It appears to have originated from Isaiah's insistence that human help and armies (i.e. those of Egypt which headed the coalition) would not save Hezekiah. It belongs closely to the eschatological development of prophecy which has influenced the editorial reworking of the Isaiah prophetic collection more extensively and can be classed as 'apocalyptic' or 'proto-apocalyptic'.

The concluding episode of the narrative sequence describes a visit of emissaries from Babylon and foretells great future trouble for Jerusalem and its kings at the hands of the Babylonian king. This presupposes firm knowledge of events of the early sixth century BCE and must be dated accordingly. It is surprising however that, although the siege and capture of Jerusalem in 598 BCE is referred to, the worse fate of the city in 587 BCE is not. Nevertheless it is evident that this latter event had occurred by the time the narrative sequence was completed. Overall the Deliverance Narratives were clearly aimed at rehabilitating the image of Jerusalem and the Davidic royal house in the light of both these sixth century disasters. They use Jehoiachin's unhappy fate as a sign of hope to show that a divine providence had foreseen even these disastrous events.

The most striking feature of the Deliverance Narratives is the focus on the uniquely privileged status of the Davidic royal dynasty and the belief that dramatic supernatural intervention saved Jerusalem and its king in a time of extreme crisis. In view of the awareness of what occurred in the sixth century the contrast between 701 BCE and 587 BCE was clearly a primary issue for the author/editor. The unexpected claim to angelic intervention shows familiarity with a collection of Isaiah's prophecies and reflects a sensibility to Judah's military weakness.

At no point is anything said regarding the existence of a tradition that Jerusalem was a city which would always be uniquely assured of divine protection. Its safety is assumed to depend on its royal head. At most it may be taken for granted that cities in general claimed to be under the special care of the deity, or deities, worshipped as the city's guardian. The very concept of a fortified walled city was to make it defensible in time of war. Similarly the widespread belief that kings were uniquely assured of protection by their divine guardians (cf. Ps. 91.1-13) could be taken to carry some extended benefit for their royal cities and citizens. It seems unlikely therefore that the prophet Isaiah, or his editors, was a staunch upholder of an ancient 'Zion Tradition' which nurtured the belief that the city of Jerusalem was uniquely inviolable.[3] The fate of Lachish in 701 BCE was an all too vivid reminder that Judah as a whole, was not guaranteed protection from disaster. At most this was a widely accepted theme in praise of cities and their rulers. At no point do the authors of the Deliverance Narratives refer to the existence of any such belief. Rather Jerusalem's fate is shown to depend on trust in Yahweh as God on the part of the successors of King David. A key feature is the direct link with the prophecy of Isa. 7.9.[4]

In conclusion it must be noted that, since the narratives in their finished form as a coherent sequence of stories belong together and express a coherent overall 'plot', the date of their completion must take account of this. In their commitment to belief in protection by 'the Angel of Yahweh' they are closer to a form of apocalyptic, which anticipates supernatural intervention, rather than to conventional prophecy. On this point, however, prophetic narratives are not consistent and the conventional prophetic idiom seldom specified precisely how God would act in judgment.

On the basis of these conclusions the historical location of the narratives as a composite literary sequence can only have been the period when hopes for the revival of the Davidic family's fortunes revived in the late sixth century BCE. The disasters of the first half of the century are clearly acknowledged. It seems highly likely that the need to salvage something

---

3. So B.C. Ollenburger, *Zion: The City of the Great King* (JSOTSup, 41; Sheffield: JSOT Press, 1987), pp. 107-29.

4. The dependence in the Deliverance Narratives on the 'Isaiah Memoir' of Isa. 6.1–(8.18) 9.6 is a striking feature of their composition, with the key text of Isa. 7.9 in a prominent position. It cannot be ruled out that this oracular utterance is itself an addition to the 'Memoir' and its precise meaning has been much discussed. Cf. B.S. Childs, *Isaiah* (OTL; Louisville, KY: Westminster/John Knox Press, 2001), pp. 64-66. For the variant readings in Septuagint and Qumran, cf. T. Wagner, *Gottes Herrschaft. Eine Analyse der Denkschrift (Jes. 6,1–9,6)* (VTSup, 108; Leiden/Boston: E.J. Brill, 2006), p. 48 n. and the extensive further references to this key verse.

from these catastrophic events has influenced the belief in a miraculous and implausible explanation for what happened in 701 BCE. The narratives express a message of confidence in the Davidic dynasty which experienced some sort of revival with the rise of Zerubbabel.

2. *The Deliverance Narratives as Religious Propaganda*

The literary composition of the Deliverance Narratives in their extant form must be understood in relation to other writings of the period which show concern for the future of the Davidic royal house. This interest could draw on the existence of a collection of prophecies from Isaiah; it is also particularly evident in the prophecies of Haggai and Zechariah (Zech. 1–8),[5] which similarly show familiarity with a collection of Isaiah's prophecies. It must also be compared with related passages in the books of Jeremiah, Ezekiel, and The Twelve Prophets which show a deep concern with the downfall of the Jerusalem kingship culminating in the removal and death of Zedekiah.

The picture that emerges of the historical context of the Deliverance Narratives, regarded as a self-contained literary unit, is that of the late sixth century BCE.[6] This was an age of restoration for Jerusalem, not simply in the physical sense of rebuilding its ruined temple, but, more widely, of a concern for re-establishing the intellectual foundations of Israel's faith and reclaiming the religious authority of the city. A number of pointers indicate this period as a time when a substantial number of surviving literary sources were edited and re-worked to provide the basis for a renewal of faith.

The centrepiece of this activity was the formation of a written 'Mosaic' Torah which has subsequently been incorporated as the core of the book of

---

5. Cf. M.A. Sweeney, *The Twelve Prophets*. II. *Zechariah* (Berit Olam; Collegeville, MN: Liturgical Press, 2000), esp. pp. 563-67.

6. The time of origin of the narratives is significant for understanding their historical veracity. In company with many scholars I earlier proposed a date in Josiah's reign (*The Deliverance of Jerusalem*, pp. 95-102). Cf. also M.A. Sweeney, *Isaiah 1–39 with an Introduction to Prophetic Literature* (FOTL, 16; Grand Rapids: Eerdmans, 1996), pp. 476-85. C. Hardmeier, *Prophetie im Streit vor dem Untergang Judas. Erzählkommunikative Studien zur Entstehungssituation der Jesaja- und Jeremiaerzählungen in II Reg 18–20 und Jer 37–40* (BZAW, 187; Berlin: W. de Gruyter, 1990), suggests a date sometime after 588 BCE, seeing in the royal ideology of the narratives the basis of opposition to Jeremiah and the optimistic expectations that encouraged Jehoiakim's misguided rebellion against Nebuchadrezzar. The link with the 'royal' prophecies in Jeremiah is of importance, but it seems more probable that the record of these also has been subjected to extensive editing in the light of the final collapse of the Davidic dynastic rule and the pinning of fresh hopes on the survival of Jehoiachin in Babylon. Cf. van der Kooij, 'Hezekiah and Sennacherib (2 Kings 18–19)', pp. 116-19.

Deuteronomy. Of significance to this, and to all the literary developments of this period, was the necessity of upholding the claim of Jerusalem as the centre of Israel's administrative authority. At the same time it was essential to take full cognizance of the existence of 'Jews' living in scattered communities in several lands in a condition of 'exile'.[7] The Torah was therefore required to be 'exile-friendly', since it had to accommodate to the circumstances of these scattered communities.[8]

3. *The Deliverance Narratives in the Context of Jerusalem's Restoration*

The Deliverance Narratives provide an instructive example of the aims and creative skill of scribes working in this period. (1) They make full use of earlier written sources in the form of earlier accounts of Jerusalem's escape in 701 BCE (mainly B. Stade's B1 and B2 accounts) which portray the event as a demonstration of the superiority of Yahweh. These can be readily classed as a form of religious propaganda. (2) The addition of the Hezekiah Narratives shows that, in the light of the sixth century disasters, the original stories called for fuller amplification. (3) These further additions show further dependence on a written body of Isaiah's prophecies and also on other written sources, especially royal psalms. Most evident is dependence on the central message of Isa. 7.9: 'If you do not stand firm (have faith) you will not be established (on the throne of Jerusalem)'.

In effect the completed sequence of episodic stories, as augmented and interpreted by the 'Hezekiah Narratives', forms a coherent and integrated core text which links Jerusalem's escape from destruction in 701 BCE to the presence in Jerusalem of an heir of King David. (4) The concern in the narratives with the fate of Jehoiachin is supported from other literary sources of this period. His deportation and imprisonment was evidently held in some circles to indicate the effective line of royal succession through which the promise to the ancestral David was maintained. This is shown by the following passages:

---

7. Cf. R. Albertz, *Israel in Exile: The History and Literature of the Sixth Century B.C.E.* (trans. D. Green; Leiden/Boston: E.J. Brill, 2004).

8. The concept of exile has increasingly come under scrutiny since it masks the complexity of the varied relationships of Jewish communities resident in alien lands outside Judea. In many respects the formation of a more comprehensive socio-religious concept of exile was a gradual development as these communities nurtured their own particular arrangements and lifestyles. The tension between 'torah', as the basis of a formal social order and 'eschatology' as a semi-political acceptance of the 'provisional' nature of the contemporary setting was susceptible of varied emphases. Cf. the essays included in James M. Scott (ed.), *Exile: Old Testament, Jewish and Christian Conceptions* (JSJSup, 56; Leiden/Boston: E.J. Brill, 1997).

(i) The book of Ezekiel retains a chronology for the period of Ezekiel's deportation calculated from the accession of Jehoiachin in 598 BCE (Ezek. 1.2; etc.).[9] This is maintained throughout the period of the prophet's activity and ignores the king's situation in exile. His status appears to be that of a recognized heir of the ancestral promise to King David.

(ii) The concluding historical note in 2 Kgs 25.27-30 telling of the release of Jehoiachin from confinement confirms that this event and this king's fate was regarded as a matter of great significance. The uniqueness of his royal status above that of other rulers is made into a point of principle. However, this note is inconclusive regarding the ultimate significance for Jews of the ex-king's release and reports some details which raise doubts as to their reliability. Nevertheless it asserts that, even in exile, the status of Jehoiachin was that of a ruler, superior to that of other kings (cf. especially 2 Kgs 25.29 with Ps. 72.10).

(iii) The narrative report in Jer. 26.1-24 tells of Jehoiakim's threat to the life of the prophet Jeremiah after his arrest for prophesying a threat against the city of Jerusalem. It defends Jeremiah's right to proclaim such a warning 'in the name of Yahweh' and recalls that the prophet Micah of Moresheth had earlier proclaimed a similar threat in the eighth century. It notes that King Hezekiah and the elders of Judah had not executed Micah for having proclaimed such a dire warning (Jer. 25.19); instead the king had turned to Yahweh in prayer and had successfully entreated the deity 'to change his mind'. The threat had then been withdrawn—at least for the time being, maintaining a close parallel with the message of Isa. 39.1-8. This assumption is in line with that of the Deliverance Narratives which tell how King Hezekiah had been threatened with a sentence of death, but after turning in submission to God, the threat had been withdrawn. The Jeremiah narrative then proceeds to report a comparable situation when another prophet, Uriah-ben-Shemaiah, had prophesied the destruction of Jerusalem and Judah, but Jehoiakim had not listened to him, and had instead sentenced him to death (Jer. 25.20-23).

The purpose of these reports was evidently to establish the principle that historical events were not irrevocably fixed even when they had been prophesied by a faithful prophet. Yahweh could experience a 'change of mind' when an appropriate response of belief and submission was forthcoming. In the Jeremiah narrative the citation of the words of the prophet Micah

---

9. For the significance of this chronology in Ezekiel, cf. W. Zimmerli, *The Prophet Ezekiel* (trans. R.E. Clements; Minneapolis: Fortress Press, 1979), I, pp. 112-15.

indicates access to a written collection of prophecies which are now included in the Book of the Twelve.

The inference that is drawn from this exchange between the king, the elders of Jerusalem and the prophet Jeremiah is a major one so far as the theological understanding of prophecy is concerned. A prophetic warning, when given by an accredited prophet, must be taken seriously and listened to. It is tempting to interject into the exchange some appeal for repentance, but essentially the focus is on obedience to the word of Yahweh. The implication is that there is a degree of certainty and authority in the word of a prophet, which must be obeyed. Although the issues are focused on particular prophecies and their fulfilment, or non-fulfilment, the underlying conviction is that Yahweh's will is absolute.

It is possible to read the story of this encounter between Jeremiah and Jehoiakim as implying that Jerusalem might have been saved from destruction in 587 BCE if the word of Jeremiah had been listened to and the king and people had repented. However, no such claim is made explicit and the general emphasis is upon the absolute sovereignty of Yahweh over events which has an element of inscrutability. The alleviating factor lies in the belief that major events may be foreseen by prophets, who can then express appropriate warnings. Yahweh acts in sovereign freedom, even when this may appear arbitrary and to have only an ambiguous relationship to the behaviour of individual kings. Refusal to hear the divine word is the fault that carries the greatest penalty. The necessary human response is therefore a willingness to trust in the veracity of the prophetic word, as the word of God.

The hint of arbitrariness concerning the divine will is further echoed in Hezekiah's seemingly meek acceptance of Isaiah's forewarning about the difficult future that faces the royal dynasty in Isa. 39.8. In the book of Jonah this theological viewpoint concerning the absolute sovereignty of the will of Yahweh is expressed even more emphatically; the dramatically constructed story affirms that, when there is a submissive acceptance to the judgment of Yahweh, even the people of Nineveh may be spared. In the light of later developments it is all too tempting to interject a strong appeal for 'repentance and amendment of life', but in the biblical text, little is said to this effect, since it is a submissive acceptance of the will of Yahweh that is placed at the centre.

In the history of 1 and 2 Samuel and 1 and 2 Kings the understanding of prophecy appears similarly to be deterministic and absolute. In several key passages prophets foresee future acts of divine judgment centuries before they were accomplished; certainly no attention is paid to the legal concept of individual responsibility that intervenes between the generations of families and dynasties. Children may indeed die for the sins of their parents—even when these ancestors lived centuries earlier. Such a view can only be regarded as thoroughly fatalistic. Overall the understanding of prophecy in the Hebrew Bible, when viewed as a canonical collection of writings, is far from being consistent on this question of the determinacy, or indeterminacy of historical events. A great deal of attention is paid throughout the Deuteronomistic History to applying the lessons of military defeat and failure in the interests of bolstering opposition to idolatry and non-Yahwistic forms of worship, especially worship outside the boundaries of the Jerusalem temple. However the overall general tenor of Old Testament history-writing is in the direction of resisting a historical determinism.

Besides this feature there exists, in both Old and New Testaments, an extensive pattern of post-eventum interpretation of prophecies and signs, frequently allied to the belief that such forewarnings were given in a cryptic and coded fashion. Fatalistic and long-delayed interpretations of particular prophecies go hand in hand with assumptions that suitable acts of penitence and entreaty may have delayed, but not altogether cancelled, their fulfilment. Ultimately the will of Yahweh is held to be inscrutable, but, as an act of mercy future events may be disclosed through prophets.

This understanding of prophecy may appear to be somewhat disingenuous, since it implies that many prophecies may have been given, but their import not fully recognized, until much later events brought their fulfilment. Only then did the full meaning become clear. Yet this can be no more than a partial objection since much of the concern in the New Testament, and in the extensive literary development of prophecy in Qumran and other pre-New Testament Jewish writings, lies in the anxiety to show that major events were in conformity with a divine plan. The links between foretelling and fulfilment, even when displaying contrived literary connections, are used to affirm a preconceived divine purpose (cf. the comment in Isa. 37.26-29 regarding the deliverance of Jerusalem).

From a political perspective the most significant conclusion that can be drawn regarding the historical background of the Deliverance Narratives, and from other preserved writings of the period, is that the chief concern to recall Jerusalem's escape in 701 BCE arose in order to offset the calamitous political consequences of the later disaster of 587 BCE. In support of this setback the exiled and deposed King Jehoiachin came to be regarded as the true inheritor of the Davidic promise. This appears to have been a major motive in the lack of reference in Isa. 39.6-7 to the disaster for Jerusalem and its royal house of 587 BCE. Whether this claim for believing that Jehoiachin was the rightful heir of the Davidic promise was accepted solely among the survivors who had, like him, been deported to Babylon, or whether it also enjoyed some following by a surviving community in Judah is not clear. The evidence contained in the book of Jeremiah points firmly in the direction that it was contested, and probably represents the viewpoint of no more than a limited 'royalist' circle of fellow-exiles.

This is in agreement with the biblical evidence that from the inception of the institution of kingship there had existed in ancient Israel considerable diversity of opinion about it. This received fresh impetus when it eventually collapsed in Jerusalem in 587 BCE. The power struggle over kingship was not simply an internal, inter-tribal conflict. Since kings headed a major administrative body of authority, the collapse of which would have threatened anarchy, there was recognition that only a powerful ruler could defend a mountainous territory with few natural borders. Jerusalem's destruction would inevitably have reawakened the long-term rivalry between key cities of the region, both within and outside Israel. Even more widely there existed behind these urban rivalries the still greater power struggle between Egypt and Mesopotamia. It was in consequence of this that a new situation arose with the conflicts of the eight century BCE when Assyria sought to establish control as far as the borders of Egypt and Arabia. Such a move inevitably reinvigorated longstanding local enmities heralding the shift to a prolonged period of Mesopotamian dominance and, in effect, to a new Middle-eastern era of international imperialism.

Evident from the historical traditions preserved in the Hebrew Bible is the fact that, after 587 BCE the situation for the survivors in Jerusalem and Judah was precarious and weak. Support for the exiled former king Jehoiachin, and the emergence of the exaggerated accounts of the events of 701 BCE in the Deliverance Narratives were the outworking of a major concern to restore Jerusalem's influence.

In the late sixth-century Zerubbabel's unexpected appearance in Jerusalem claiming a historic royal authority formed part of the effort to restore the city's eminence by exploiting the reputation of the Davidic monarchy. The final outcome of this bid to restore the dynasty's and Jerusalem's status is unknown. Zerubbabel disappears from the scene in unknown circumstances, but eventually the Jerusalem temple, the restoration of which he had supported, returned to full activity and a renewed cultic life flourished. The underlying motif that has promoted the complicated and extensive structure of the book of Isaiah, and with it also the story of the rise and fall of the First Kingdom of Israel, is that of Jerusalem's status. It is a divinely chosen centre, the 'City of David', the focal point for a great 'Pilgrimage of All Nations'. It is both an administrative centre of great authority, a goal for religious pilgrimages, but it is also a symbol of hope for the ultimate unity and peace of all nations (so Isa. 2.1-4).

The consequences of this sixth century development continued into the following century and beyond, and marked the beginning of the recovery of the authority and eminence of Jerusalem. Both in Judah, and among the scattered heirs of the former kingdom, a regard for the city and its religious authority became a form of idealized citizenship. In place of the old kingship the role of the cultus in the restored temple acquired added significance as a priestly ministry on behalf of all Israel—'both those who were near and those who were far' (cf. Dan. 9.7). A striking assertion of this reclaimed authority for Jerusalem is expressed in a late passage in Isaiah:

> For out of Zion shall go forth torah
> And the word of Yahweh from Jerusalem (Isa. 2.3).

The remarkable feature of this linking of the authority of torah with the eminence of the city of Jerusalem lies in its lack of dependence on the institution of kingship. For centuries this had been the institution, through control of the administration of defence, law and priesthood, which had conferred authority on the city and upheld its control over the surrounding region. It is the city where the sacred 'hill of Zion' was held to have been 'chosen' by Yahweh as the location where his 'Name' was to be invoked (cf. Deut. 12.11, 21; etc.).

Extensive biblical development of this early 'Zionist' pro-Jerusalem ideology is to be seen in the numerous expansions and additions to the collection of the prophecies of Isaiah. The later additions to the book of the prophet become, in effect, a celebration of Jerusalem and its place in the divine plan for Jews scattered among the nations. In this respect the two parts of the book of Isaiah display distinct ideologies; nevertheless these are closely related to each other so that the cultic-urban ideology of the second part (chs. 40–66) is dependent on the royalist ideology of the first part (chs. 1–39).

This ideological shift promoted the growth of a concept of 'exile' as a prominent feature of the ethos and apologia of an increasing number of scattered migrant communities. Until the Hellenistic era after 332 BCE the absence of any strong Jewish political voice was compensated for by a form of idealized citizenship. The literary expression of this in Isaiah 40–66 represents a significant development of the older 'book' of Isaiah's prophecies in which Yahweh's commitment to 'the House of David' was the dominant theme. By the addition, first of Isaiah 40–55 and then of further prophecies relating to Jerusalem in 56–66 and 1–4 the transition from 'royal messianic' to 'Zionist' ideologies took shape in forming the enlarged book. The historic divine promise to David was recast in a highly distinctive fashion as an assurance of protection for all Israel (Isa. 55.3-6).

This had become necessary after the failure of Zerubbabel to win the expected crown that was forecast for him in Hag. 2.23. With the disappearance of this prince of royal blood from Jerusalem's history a new understanding was called for concerning the meaning of the divine promise to David for the destiny of Israel. It might have been expected that this historic theme would simply be dropped when there ceased to be an immediate prospect for the restoration of a king in Jerusalem. However, this is clearly not what happened.

The assurance in Isa. 55.3-6 that this historic covenant would be upheld is categorical in its positive aspect, but is far from being transparently clear as to what it implies. Elsewhere I have suggested that, in line with the assurance in Psalm 72 that kings of the earth would pay homage to David, it was taken to offer assurance of respect and protection for the 'citizens of Jerusalem' living among the nations. This situation is firmly demonstrated in the royal addendum to the history of 2 Kings regarding the respect shown to Jehoiachin in Babylon. Overall it would appear that it was felt to be imperative in the period of Judah's recovery and renewal in the fifth century BCE to recall the greatness of King David in reclaiming authority for the city of Jerusalem and its temple.[10]

The variety of prophetic and narrative traditions regarding the Davidic kingship which are preserved in the Hebrew Bible reflects the divided loyalties that emerged over the restoration of a monarchy after its collapse in 587 BCE.[11] After the destruction of the temple, kingship as an institution came under a dark cloud. The story of the First Kingdom in the 'Deuteronomistic History' (Joshua–2 Kings) is equivocal about the institution and has evidently combined within its extensive compass both traditions that were strongly pro-monarchic and pro-Davidic and also others that were distinctly critical.[12] It celebrates kings as representing the 'voice of God to the people', but, at the same time, blames their laxity towards alien cult traditions as the primary reason for the nation's downfall. The Deuteronomic 'law of the king' in Deut. 17.14-20) similarly shares this reserve about the institution of kingship. Not only does it prescribe restrictions for the actions and lifestyle of kings, but carefully avoids presenting such a primary political office as mandatory. The importance devoted to the coming of a 'Branch of David' in Isa. 11.1-5 is similarly left in uncertainty on account of the absence of a clear historical date for the inclusion of this key prophecy. Nor is it evident that it represented the view of more than a small minority. In the sixth century BCE

10.   Cf. my essay, 'A Royal Privilege: Dining in the Presence of the Great King (2 Kings 25.27-30)', in R. Rezetko, T.H. Lim and W. Brian Aucker (eds.), *Reflection and Refraction: Studies in Biblical Historiography in Honour of A. Graeme Auld* (VTSup, 113; Leiden/Boston: E.J. Brill, 2007), pp. 49-66.

11.   The issue is an important one, especially in the light of the 'liberal' nineteenth-century tendency to affirm the importance of the ethical judgments of the biblical prophets, but to minimize, or even dismiss altogether, the notion of prophetic foretelling of events. For further reflections of the difficulties, cf. the discussion in R.W.L. Moberly, *Prophecy and Discernment* (Cambridge: Cambridge University Press, 2006), pp. 1-40.

12.   The problem of the diversity of attitudes shown towards the last kings of Judah in the prophecies of Jeremiah is discussed by J.B. Job, *Jeremiah's Kings: A Study of the Monarchy in Jeremiah* (SOTS Monographs; Aldershot/Burlington: Ashgate, 2006).

the question of restoring a monarchy in Jerusalem appears to have been a short-lived issue since, with Zerubbabel's disappearance, the possibility of any immediate return of a Davidic prince to the throne came to an end.[13]

Nevertheless, in the wake of this failure the issue that came to the fore as the most significant for the future development of Judaism was the recovery of the authority and leadership of Jerusalem, both in its religious (priestly) dimension and its more overtly political role under a governor approved by the Persian suzerain. In a sense this situation was an attempt to rewrite the story of Hamlet without the king of Denmark since it was the reputation of the royal dynasty of David which had first placed the city on the map of world history. In an oblique fashion the Deliverance Narratives were a contribution to this task.

4. *The Theological Significance of the Deliverance Narratives*

In the second volume of his *Old Testament Theology*,[14] Gerhard von Rad devotes a major part of his treatment of the message of the eighth century prophet Isaiah to an examination of this question, focused on the theme of faith. His conclusions are centred on the claim that the fundamental message of the prophet was based on belief in the divine election of the royal house of David to rule over Israel which was linked inseparably to the election of Mount Zion as the seat of the divine presence. This theme was enshrined in the 'Zion Tradition', proclaimed in several prominent psalms, which upheld belief that a divine umbrella of supernatural protection hovered over the city of Jerusalem. The message of the Deliverance Narratives, with their claim that something wholly extraordinary occurred in 701 BCE, and that of the prophet Isaiah, with his insistence that Egypt's forces would not save Hezekiah, is made into a demonstration of the absolute power of Yahweh, God of Jerusalem. Hezekiah's faith in Yahweh's commitment to the house of David is declared to have saved him and his city in their hour of greatest need. His predecessor, Ahaz, had failed to demonstrate such faith by his appeal to Assyria which had proved to be so costly for Judah and Israel. Hezekiah's initial response to Isaiah's summons to faith had similarly been negative (and Lachish had duly suffered as a result), but, after his encounter with a near-fatal sickness, he trusted in Yahweh's word and events proved the wisdom of doing so.

13.   Cf. the essays included in John Day (ed.), *King and Messiah in Israel and the Ancient Near East* (JSOTSup, 270; Sheffield: Sheffield Academic Press, 1998). The essay by H.G.M. Williamson, 'Messianic Texts in Isaiah 1–39', pp. 238-70, is particularly relevant to the present discussion. See also his studies *Variations on a Theme: King, Messiah and Servant in the Book of Isaiah* (Carlisle: Paternoster Press, 1998).

14.   G. von Rad, *Old Testament Theology*. II. *The Theology of Israel's Prophetic Traditions* (trans. D.M.G. Stalker; Edinburgh: Oliver & Boyd, 1965), pp. 155-69.

Such an abbreviated summary of this key section of von Rad's theological treatment of Isaiah can only focus on one issue, but it nevertheless draws attention to the theme that pervades the Deliverance Narratives. This serves to explain the tension between Isaiah's prophecies warning Hezekiah against his misguided trust in Egypt and the successful outcome of events as described in the narratives. In spite of the appearance of a gross discrepancy which has encouraged the fruitless search for some unreported event that occurred after Hezekiah's surrender there is a recognizable point of connection. This focuses on Isaiah's claim that Hezekiah could not secure his throne by trusting in human armies (Egypt), but must trust in Yahweh's power alone.

Both the narratives and the prophecies reflect the centrality of the summons to faith in Yahweh, although, ultimately the narratives have resorted to the claim of a wholly supernatural intervention to achieve Jerusalem's deliverance. The question whether Isaiah gave this assurance on the basis of a long-standing 'Zion Tradition' of the kind von Rad outlines, or whether this belief was not itself a consequence of the biblical version of the events of 701 BCE, has continued to be a contested historical issue. Quite clearly the mutual interaction of this singular event and the cluster of traditions relating to cities, kingship and the absolute power of deities have become intermingled in both poetic and narrative developments. As a consequence of being spared the fate of Lachish in 701 BCE Jerusalem was elevated into an ideal, supernaturally endowed, and ultimately eschatological, city.[15] The historical and logistical factors which led to this outcome have certainly been exaggerated in the narratives, but the broader point remains of importance that, as a result of its occurrence Jerusalem obtained a considerable advantage in its long-standing rivalry among its neighbours.[16] This is the issue that was to have the greatest consequence for the future and was ultimately to create a legacy which has endured into modern times. Zion was celebrated as a city like no other because Yahweh had delivered it in its hour of greatest peril.

There can be little doubt that, behind this narrative tradition there was an influential royal dynastic ideology which affirmed that a unique act of divine election had singled out a particular royal family to rule over Israel. The

15. For the importance of the rise of Jerusalem and the development in prophecy of an extensive religious mythology built around the notion of Jerusalem as the centre of the world, cf. J. Vermeylen, *Jérusalem, centre du monde. Développements et contestations d'une tradition biblique* (Lectio divina, 217; Paris: Editions du Cerf, 2007).

16. Vermeylen, *Jérusalem, centre du monde*, pp. 145-226. Cf. J. Middlemas, *The Problems of 'Templeless' Judah* (Oxford Theological Monographs; Oxford: Oxford University Press, 2005), and my essay, 'The Deuteronomic Law of Centralisation and the Catastrophe of 587 B.C.', in John Barton and David J. Reimer (eds.), *After the Exile: Essays in Honour of Rex Mason* (Macon, GA: Mercer University Press, 1996), pp. 5-26.

building of a temple in Jerusalem was a further visible expression of this bond that linked city, temple and the royal dynasty together as objects of special divine favour. The power and wisdom of kingship was believed to be conferred by deities and, through such rulers, to be a blessing to the communities which they governed. From a political perspective the passage from tribal chieftainship to kingship of a city-state has been widely researched by social anthropologists and no doubt has many facets. Nevertheless, this fundamental political development can be seen to have given rise to a range of religious assurances, expressed through priests and prophets. Such a principle of dynastic succession remained for centuries an intrinsic feature of this ideology of 'sacral' or 'divine' kingship. What is significant in respect of the Deliverance Narratives is that they show how this royal tradition was transferred to a city, and, at the same time, gave rise to a remarkable ideology concerning the 'presence' of a deity. The effect of this transfer was of highest significance in the 'spiritualizing' of the idea of a divine being which contributed to the distinctiveness of Judaism as a religion of scattered communities and, in a similar direction, to a monotheistic faith.

A central feature of this tradition rests in its claim that Yahweh, the deity worshipped in the temple of Jerusalem, acted uniquely to protect the city in its hour of greatest danger. When, later, a similar deliverance did not occur in the face of another major threat more searching questions required to be asked. Much research has focused on attempts to trace the roots of the tradition behind the time of the prophet Isaiah. Arguments have frequently built heavily on the claim that the tradition not only antedated the prophet, but even antedated the Israelite conquest of the city of Jerusalem. Certainly a wide variety of ancient elements, some of which had mythological connections, formed part of this belief. Celebrating the role of cities as places of refuge and military defence quite properly reflected their primary purpose and origin.

Several elements of the symbolism and formalised language of divine nearness and protection, which appear in the Psalter in connection with Zion, can be traced much further back in the ancient Near East in relation to other cities. This applies to the symbolism concerning sacred rivers and high mountains, which far exceed the geographical realities of Jerusalem. It appears likely that it was also the case with the portrayal of mighty kings who laugh their opponents to scorn and who win overwhelming victories over mighty armies outside the gates of their cities. Such themes are popular word-pictures that were prominent motifs in various ancient mythologies. They belong to the essential character of ancient cities as places of protection, trade and the administration of justice.

The so-called 'Zion tradition' of ancient Israel, was undoubtedly heir to this far wider cluster of traditions. Yet it acquired a unique character as a result of its distinctive history and its relationship to the book of Isaiah. Not least the belief that something altogether unprecedented and unexpected had happened in 701 BCE provided a key motif for the veneration of Isaiah's prophecies. From this the theme was developed in the Psalter and eventually passed over into Christian liturgical tradition.

The stories of what happened to Jerusalem in 701 BCE contain features which brought together these traditional religious themes. These stories served as a catalyst for a number of themes and expectations concerning divine providence. They established a particular Israelite-Jewish 'Zion Tradition', the results of which can still be found in biblical psalmody.

The idea that a fully-rounded belief in Jerusalem's inviolability from military threat was already well established before Isaiah and that the prophet simply endorsed this in relation to a number of contemporary threats is mistaken. Several prophecies ascribed to him warn of the fearful danger posed by Assyria to King Ahaz of Judah, and this was repeated subsequently when King Hezekiah embarked on policies that incurred a similar threat. Isaiah's repeated warnings would make little sense if either the city of Jerusalem or its king were believed to be guaranteed full protection by God. The prophet would then have been accused of encouraging a policy that invited disaster. Quite possibly, at a later time, the popularity of such beliefs did foster reckless and irresponsible policies.

The Zion tradition, as it emerged after 701 BCE, appears as a cluster of beliefs that drew on a variety of sources and used the city's escape from destruction as a catalyst to fuse them together. The rich variety of such themes illustrates both dangerous political expectations, strong royalist motifs, but also, ideas of divine nearness and support in adversity. It is these more spiritual expressions of trust in the presence of God on Mount Zion which have remained the most enduring legacy of this distinctive theme. They came to convey a sense of spiritual support which reached beyond geographical or historical limitations.

The royal ideology of dynastic kingship was undoubtedly a central factor in the process of eliciting from Jerusalem's survival in 701 BCE a wider message about the city and its destined role among the nations. Reflections on the event drew on elements of the controversial history surrounding the Davidic royal family by claiming that Jerusalem had been demonstrably preferred and protected by Yahweh, in contrast to the tragic fates of Bethel and Samaria. This was a feature that sought to give a partisan political interpretation to the tradition. However, a significant contribution was also made by ideas of 'Holy War' with expectations of divine assistance to confer victory when that would otherwise have been impossible. There can be no doubt long-cherished ideas about divine help in winning battles played a role at a period when the small kingdom of Judah was fearfully aware of its weakness and inadequacy to counter Assyrian supremacy. David's defeat of the Philistine Goliath served as a paradigm of such victories and the broad network of alliances that formed a background to Isaiah's prophesying was a consequence of this inadequacy.

A prominent feature of this 'Deliverance Narrative' tradition celebrating the saving of Jerusalem from destruction in 701 BCE is the claim that this was a victory for which divine help was uniquely responsible, without the intervention of human forces. The prophet Isaiah's words, which have good claims to being authentic, denigrated to the point of contempt King Hezekiah's trust in the power of Egypt to protect his kingdom. Such trust was ridiculed as a misguided reliance on human ability to resist the overwhelming power of God—an attitude which was regarded as self-evidently absurd. A certain element of irony exists therefore in the eagerness with which several modern scholars have sought to find evidence that it was, in the end, Egyptian intervention which led Sennacherib to abandon his planned assault on Jerusalem. Isaiah's message had so categorically insisted that to put trust in Egypt to protect Judah would be folly. It would therefore do little for the reputation of biblical prophecy if, in the last resort, it turned out to have been Egyptian help which saved Hezekiah.

In the light of the many reconstructions of the actual events of 701 BCE it is noteworthy that the biblical narratives which recount the story set out to endorse the truth of Isaiah's prophesying without qualification by insisting that it was 'the angel of Yahweh' who intervened to bring salvation. Yahweh, God of Jerusalem, had defended the city, not human agency. This contention lies at the very heart of the pro-Davidic, pro-Jerusalem, narrative constructions that recorded what had taken place.

The rise of this 'Zion Tradition' has continued to exercise an influential part in the development and verbal symbolism of the Jewish-Christian concept of God. It marks an important step in freeing the idea of God from the confines of geographical limitations, paradoxically by identifying the presence of God very directly to a specific sanctuary and location. However, in a broader spectrum it transcends unduly physical and localised concepts of a divine being. In company with the prohibition on idolatry it carries a rejection of the localised symbolism of a divine presence, and forms an indispensable aspect of an emphasis on the hiddenness of God. By doing so it has in a unique fashion spawned a whole range of unique vocabulary and imagery which continues into the present. Language that, in its literal sense, relates directly to the ancient city of Jerusalem has taken on a unique spiritual meaning. Imagery and symbolism used in the Hebrew Psalter has been carried over into Christian liturgy and hymnody, shaping ideas of providence and divine protection. This geographical terminology has developed into a convenient metaphorical language affirming spiritual values similar to the continued use of anthropomorphic imagery to describe divine attributes.

When taken in a literal sense, with all its historical and geographical connections, such language is strange, and can easily border on the absurd to those unfamiliar with its origins. Nevertheless it has generated a range of metaphors that require an understanding of the history of the Hebrew Psalter and of its adoption by the early Christian communities for it to be intelligible. Already, it must be argued, this semantic development had progressed to a considerable extent in Jewish communities living in the diaspora before the Christian era.

However, it is not simply the extension of local and geographical terminology that is at issue, but a deeper and more complex understanding of the nature of God. Has God a 'presence'? In a straightforward response to such a question it is evident that, in antiquity, the majority of worshippers would have answered in the affirmative and pointed to a huge range of divine images, or symbolic ciphers or signs which abounded in homes, sanctuaries and open countryside in the ancient world. Explanations of why and how an image was able to express, or provide access to, a silent and unseen deity would certainly have varied greatly, or even been repudiated as unanswerable and meaningless. Such has been the complex power of art and imagery in the symbolism of religion.

Nevertheless, so far as the Hebrew Bible is concerned the existence in Jerusalem of a temple to the God Yahweh provided a point of connection for ideas of the presence of deity. It was this temple which nurtured the stereotyped language of Hebrew psalmody and from there it has passed over into later Jewish and Christian worship. In the various stages through which this complex development in religious language took place two steps were undoubtedly of greatest significance. The first was the historical tradition that a remarkable act of divine intervention saved the city of Jerusalem from destruction in 701 BCE. It is not the simple historical record of Hezekiah's surrender which was so triumphantly recorded in Sennacherib's Chronicle that has dominated popular memory, but the inflated and supernaturally endowed version of the Hebrew Bible. The second major event was the destruction of the temple in 587 BCE, echoed later in the similar destruction of its even greater successor by the armies of Rome in 70 AD. The complex symbolism of religious language, when faced with the inevitable vulnerability of all material architecture, gave rise to a verbal iconography regarding the Being and Presence of God which has endured to the present day. Samuel Terrien has described this as 'The Elusive Presence'.[17]

Only the biblical context of the symbolism of temples and temple-building provides the necessary interpretive key for understanding how and why this language has survived and what it conveys about the nature of deity. The links with the book of Isaiah are of major significance for the origin and development of this distinctive theme.

17. S. Terrien, *The Elusive Presence: Toward a New Biblical Theology* (New York: Harper & Row, 1979).

Chapter 10

THE LITERARY CONTEXT OF THE STORY
OF JERUSALEM'S DELIVERANCE

1. *The Story of Jerusalem's Deliverance as a Literary Source*

A major conclusion of these studies regarding the narrative sequence which tells what happened when Jerusalem was spared from destruction in 701 BCE is the contention that it at one time formed an independent literary unit. This applies to the entire sequence of episodes in Isaiah 36–39 (// 2 Kgs 18.13–20.19). Although it is now preserved in slightly varied versions in two distinct locations, it was originally self-contained and expressed its own unique message. Indications are that, at one period a considerable number of such literary compositions existed and have been drawn upon to form the longer books which make up the Hebrew Bible, with its foundation in the Pentateuch and the Former Prophets. This extensive literary activity must have been undertaken in the Persian era after the first efforts to re-establish a temple community in Jerusalem in 520–516 BCE.

Its internal structure shows that the core text of this particular 'Deliverance Narrative' is based on two earlier, loosely parallel, accounts of how Jerusalem was spared in 701 BCE. It has been carefully edited and supplemented by further stories which shed light on the fate of King Hezekiah and Jerusalem. The resulting sequence of episodes makes up into a coherent documentary source that forms a connected story about 701 BCE; it is self-contained, editorially structured and has a clear beginning and conclusion. It conveys a coherent message celebrating the power of Yahweh, the God worshipped in Jerusalem, to deliver the city from the military force of the mighty Assyrian oppressor Sennacherib. Its general character and purpose as an expression of anti-imperialist (anti-Assyrian/Babylonian) propaganda is evident. It celebrates the power of Yahweh, the God of Jerusalem as superior to that of Sennacherib and also to that of the other gods worshipped in the region. Because of this historic religious association the narrative shows Jerusalem to be superior to other cities of the region, whose gods failed them when confronted with the might of Mesopotamia (Assyria and Babylon). It also shows Egypt to be a weak and failing partner in resisting Mesopotamian might. To this extent the narrative has a message focused on a particular historical event, and also a larger political warning about the regional 'balance of power'.

As a piece of religious propaganda this narrative compilation is typical of the kind of celebratory praise that affirms the superiority of one god over others. Moreover it affirms this superiority in a specific historical context and develops its claims in order to take account of subsequent events of immense political significance. To some extent the extravagance of the claims about how Jerusalem was saved from defeat and destruction is rendered intelligible by the severity of the humiliating disasters which followed in the sixth century at the hands of the king of Babylon. A special focus is on the contrast between the fate of other cities of Judah and the preservation of Jerusalem (Isa. 36.1 // 2 Kgs 18.13-16). From being a story of the merciful deliverance of one particular city threatened with destruction it is made into a propaganda document highlighting the regional importance of this city and the royal dynasty which had first made it a major factor of Israel's political life. It affirms that the destiny of Jerusalem was linked to a promise made by Yahweh to King David. An element of theodicy is undoubtedly present but is subordinated to more specific political claims.

Overall the sequence is self-explanatory and its message is unmistakeable. It does, nevertheless, contain elements that are surprising. Foremost is the claim that the saving of the city occurred as the result of an intervention by the 'Angel of Yahweh' to save the city in its moment of greatest peril. The timing of this intervention heightens the startling impact of the action since by the time it occurred all the fortified cities of Judah had been lost. The most significant action only took place when the situation of Jerusalem and its kings appeared hopeless. The king is portrayed as on the brink of despair and with no alternative except to strip the sacred temple of its treasures and to submit to the Assyrian king's demands (Isa. 37.1). The report of the timing and manner of Yahweh's intervention has evidently been based on Isaiah's insistence that human (Egyptian) help on which Hezekiah had pinned his trust, would be unable to save him and his city.

The contrast between divine and human power is a major theme of the narrative, rather mocking the attempts of modern scholarship to look for a human factor to explain the story of angelic intervention. The tension generated by the king's initial submission and subsequent vindication is further explained in the form of a parable of the king's sickness and recovery. This reflects his initial lack of trust in Yahweh, when he faced imminent death, followed by his recovery of trust in the God of his royal ancestor. This is then further maintained in spite of forewarnings about future disasters that will overtake the royal house (Isa. 39.1-8). The coherence and consistency of the storyline is excellent throughout and is only disturbed when set alongside other information contained in the larger literary contexts in which it is preserved. K.A.D. Smelik argues that the repetition of events, which forms the basis of B. Stade's source division, can be accounted for as a stylistic device to give added emphasis.[1] However, this claim somewhat overpresses its force. To a large extent Stade's observations appear to be valid, but draw attention to the point that earlier accounts have been skilfully edited into a longer report to which fresh features have been added. When this observation is combined with the availability of extra-biblical evidence, this has encouraged a tendency to disregard the consistency of the narrative story-line that is present. This is not the first instance where a search for earlier 'sources' of a story has undermined the capacity to understand it as a well-crafted whole in its extant form. Such re-editing of older text units appears commonplace in the literary development of biblical prophecy.

A further surprising feature is that the reason given for the remarkable angelic intervention is the existence of a promise made by Yahweh to King David in the distant past (Isa. 37.35). Although the precise content of this promise is not spelled out, the inference is that it contained assurance of divine protection for kings of this royal lineage (cf. Ps. 91; etc.). The completed sequence of stories looks ahead explicitly to the disaster that overtook the royal house of David in 598 BCE, but their general tenor also assumes familiarity with the bigger disaster of 587 BCE. Clearly it was the despair created by these setbacks for Jerusalem and its royal house that helped to shape the dramatic nature of the narrative sequence as a whole. It is a piece of propaganda aimed at restoring the prestige and authority of Jerusalem, but it does so by focusing attention on the ancient line of kings who ruled there. It does this at a time when hope for their restoration to power remained a contemporary issue, i.e. probably around 540–520 BCE.

At no point in the narratives, or in the prophecies that are cited in them, is any reference made to the existence of a unique 'Zion Tradition' affirming the city's guarantee of protection. The city's fate is clearly shown to depend on the presence of Yahweh's temple there and the divine promise to the dynasty of David; the saving of Jerusalem in 701 BCE is directly linked to this special relationship. It appears certain that, had a tradition regarding Zion's unique inviolability from hostile armies been widely current, it would have featured in the story line. At most it is taken for granted that this is what walled cities were for. There is a particular concern for the reputation of Jerusalem, but this prestige is taken to be dependent on the deity Yahweh and the family of kings who had reigned in the city for more than four centuries.

---

1. K.A.D. Smelik, *Converting the Past: Studies in Ancient Israelite and Moabite Historiography* (OTS, 28; Leiden: E.J. Brill, 1992), pp. 105-109.

The purpose and historical point of origin of this literary composition cannot be in doubt, but questions nevertheless emerge about the reason for its incorporation into larger documents which do not fully share its viewpoint. This is certainly true so far as the Former Prophets ('Deuteronomistic History') is concerned which is very critical of the role of the royal dynasty of David, although it recognizes its historical importance. In the case of the book of Isaiah the situation is more complex since, although the first part (chs. 5–35) shows high regard for the Davidic dynasty this is substantially changed in the second part (chs. 40–66).

Why retain a document celebrating the uniqueness of the Davidic dynasty, when the future of that dynasty had lost credibility and authority? Part of the answer to this lies in the fact that the narrative no longer appears as an independent and self-contained work. Nor is the fate of the royal house the sole institution that is at issue, since the unique claim of the city of Jerusalem is also prominent, as also is the superiority of the god worshipped there over other deities venerated in the region. The incorporation of the narrative into these larger contexts substantially affects the message that it contains. Overall the reason for incorporating this narrative sequence into longer books can only be that it gives great prominence to the historic importance of the promise of Yahweh to the royal house of David. This had begun as a major political issue centuries earlier, but it remained a controversial issue in the post-exilic age, eventually continuing into the New Testament era and down to modern times. Both the longer contexts in which the narrative is preserved are at great pains to uphold the claims of Jerusalem to be Israel's first city and religious centre. They both also display a strong concern to carry over the primary basis for this claim from the royal dynasty which brought the city international fame to the city itself.

2. *The Deliverance Narrative in a Post-587 BCE Setting*

Both the book of the prophet Isaiah and the Deuteronomistic History (i.e. Joshua–2 Kings) are major documents which acquired their extant shape in the Persian Period and both are long composite productions that incorporate large extracts from older documents. They represent a form of literary pastiche, held together by a chronology and formed around several major themes. In the case of the History these include official records which are named, popular tales of heroic figures, such as the prophets Elijah and Elisha and contemporary records of Judah's twilight years. The hands of more than one author/editor are strongly evident. The finished work is given a thematic structure with a strong didactic purpose condemning idolatry and deviation from the exclusive worship of Yahweh alone as God. As a consequence these can conveniently be classed as 'Deuteronomistic' ideals of religious allegiance.

In both Isaiah and 2 Kings the narrative sequence dealing with 701 BCE forms only a small part of a much longer literary composition. In both of them the broader themes of Jerusalem's eminence, the greatness of the royal dynasty of King David, and the incomparable power of Yahweh, the God worshipped in Jerusalem play a big role. These institutional interests serve to identify Israel as the people of Yahweh, and they range over wider issues than simply those of Jerusalem and its kings. Nevertheless in both of them the saving of Jerusalem in 701 BCE plays a significant part although they differ greatly in the emphasis placed upon this event. In both works the major crisis-point for the stories they have to tell concerns Israel's final downfall in the sixth century BCE, when the Jerusalem temple was destroyed and the Davidic dynasty removed from the throne. In consequence the telling of what happened in 701 BCE acts as a counter balance to accounts of the greater threats and crises that lay ahead. This is made explicit in both contexts by the episode of the visit of the Babylonian emissaries.

Since the entire Hebrew Bible is a corpus of texts which have been drawn from a wide range of ancient, shorter texts, some of them of considerable antiquity, the concern of modern scholarship to identify the age of these sources and their probable historical locations is wholly laudable, but fraught with obvious limitations. It is unnecessary at this point to note the many diverse proposals regarding these presumed 'sources' of both the Former and Latter Prophets. The 'Deliverance Narrative', is simply one such source and its repetition in both the first and second parts of the division known as 'the Prophets' is a matter of surprise. All the more is this so when it is evident that its message about an angelic intervention in support of an ancient royalist promise fits rather differently in the two locations.

For the book of Isaiah such a dramatic sudden overthrow of great imperial forces is repeated as a thematic motif which reveals the ultimate goal of all human history. In contrast the story recounted in the Former Prophets is more narrowly focused on the rise of the people Israel to greatness and their subsequent downfall through relapse into idolatry and religious apostasy. Jerusalem's near-disaster in 701 BCE is not, however, linked to this prevalent motif of idolatry since at no point does Hezekiah compromise his claim on Yahweh's protection by resorting to other gods. Instead he trusts in the power of Egypt to protect him and his city. The inclusion of the story in 2 Kings therefore appears to have been motivated primarily in order to focus on the fate of the Davidic dynasty and the special significance of the city of Jerusalem. It asserts the uniqueness of the city, by linking it to an event and to the royal house which had first brought it to eminence in Israel.

A strong sense of the rivalry between the cities of Samaria and Jerusalem is a prominent feature. The city which remained loyal to the house of David (i.e. Jerusalem) was saved from the clutches of Sennacherib; the cities which defected from that loyalty (i.e. Bethel and Samaria) were not saved. The lesson for the reader is obvious. The important point for the present-day reader to grasp is that this rivalry between Jerusalem and Samaria was a long-running and bitterly contested aspect of life in post-exilic Judah. In this regard the present emphasis of the story is less about what happened at the close of the eighth century BCE and more about what was continuing to happen in the fifth century BCE. This is in line with the dominance of the contemporary 'Deuteronomistic' claim that the city was the place where Yahweh had chosen 'to set his name' (Deut. 12).

Examination of these wider literary contexts helps explain why the story of 701 BCE continued to fulfil a uniquely significant role in the movement for the restoration of religious life in Judah and Jerusalem under Persian authority. As a consequence the story has played a unique role in the development both of biblical historiography and the formation of a canonical corpus of written prophecy. In spite of some variants in the respective texts the versions in Isaiah 36–39 and 2 Kings 18–20 are sufficiently close to show that they are editions of the same basic narrative sequence. Which of the two is the older has been variously estimated, but, since B. Stade showed that both are developments of earlier accounts, this question of literary priority is not of great importance. Far more significant is recognition that, in both of them substantial editorial efforts have been made to present a coherent and intelligible message about Jerusalem, the God worshipped in the temple there and the line of kings who ruled there.

The story of 701 BCE, as a historical event, is not difficult to explain or justify. Towards the close of a major punitive campaign in the Levant by Sennacherib, Ruler of Assyria, Jerusalem was spared the fate that overtook Lachish and other cities of Judah, and much of the surrounding region. The reason, as 2 Kgs 18.13–16 confirms, was that, after Lachish was besieged and destroyed, further resistance became impossible. Hezekiah surrendered, but was allowed to keep his throne on payment of a heavy indemnity (2 Kgs 18.16). What may, or may not have happened to induce such comparatively lenient terms from a cruel oppressor has never passed beyond the realm of speculation. The biblical narrator, mindful of later disasters to Jerusalem and its royal house, has constructed a story about an angelic visitation, drawing on clues from Isaiah's prophecies, other stories preserved in Israelite tradition, and a general desire to magnify the superiority of Jerusalem over Samaria and of Jerusalem's God over the oppressive rulers of Mesopotamia. The story of a fortunate escape amid a ruthless campaign of destruction and barbarism has been elevated into one of miraculous divine intervention.

In its comprehensive final form, the story of Jerusalem's deliverance is one that serves a significant purpose in defining who Yahweh, the God of Israel is. It shows why the city occupies a unique place in the divine government of Israel; it explores conventional propaganda motifs about kingship, and it exalts Jerusalem over Samaria. It does all this in reporting a specific historical occurrence and links this to a promise made by Yahweh to the royal house of David. To this extent it both harks back to old rivalries and strongly reflects contemporary ones. Since The story carries firm evidence regarding its time of origin in the late sixth, or early fifth, centuries BCE. By this time the link between Jerusalem and the royal House of David had been severely compromised and Jerusalem's claim to eminence was at a very low point. It had evidently lost out in the eyes of the Persian administration in favour of Samaria. For half a century at least the city had been in decline, if not in complete ruin, and the prestige and authority of its historic rivals had flourished.

The so-called 'Zion Tradition', which has emerged among scholars as a traditional motif associated with Jerusalem, appears to have arisen as the result of this significant shifting of focus from the royal dynasty of David to the city of Jerusalem. The difficulty was that the survivors of the dynasty no longer carried the authority which had once been theirs. The rise of the 'Zion Tradition' marked a fundamental shift from a conventional political theology relating to a royal dynasty of kings to the concept of a uniquely chosen 'city of God'.

Of the two versions of the Deliverance Narrative, the 'Isaianic' version is noticeably the longer through the incorporation of the psalm celebrating Hezekiah's recovery from sickness (Isa. 38.10-20). Considerable effort has been expended on a comparison between the two versions and the results have not been decisive in according priority between them. Whereas a majority of critics have accorded priority to the version in 2 Kings 18–20, K.A.D. Smelik has emphasised that the consistency and coherence of the finished account, shows clearly its original independence as a literary unit. A similar conclusion is implicit in the formative study by P.R. Ackroyd which has been fruitful in focusing attention on this unique piece of narrative prophecy. The incorporation of the document in these longer literary settings is secondary, both in literary history and also in the religious significance drawn from the story. By the time these larger literary compositions were completed the hope of restoring the Davidic dynasty to power through Zerubbabel must certainly have foundered. The immediate purpose of the story—to support the claims of a Davidic prince—had therefore suffered a major setback. However its more lasting impact was in support of the claims of Jerusalem over those of Samaria. It is in this context that its most enduring impact was felt and its inclusion in the longer contexts of the books of Isaiah and the Former Prophets fully reflects this.

3. *The Story of Jerusalem's Deliverance in the Context of the Book of Isaiah*

From a literary perspective the question of how Isaiah 36–39 relates to the book of Isaiah rapidly divides into several subordinate issues. As modern critical studies have decisively shown, the book of Isaiah, like all the prophetic books, is not one book, nor even two or three. It is a composition that has been constructed and shaped from several different documentary sources and finally given an overall shape at a relatively late period in the 'post-exilic' era. Even this epithet is misleading in the case of the book of Isaiah since, in this work the belief in an Israel that is 'postexilic' is focused on the future (so especially Isa. 60.1-22). A fundamental assumption that pervades it is that 'Israel's exile' is an ongoing feature of life which demands a message of hope about its end.

It is in this context that upholding the claims regarding the special religious significance of the city of Jerusalem in the present stood out as an issue that called for the strongest backing of tradition. The story of how Jerusalem was saved from the grip of Sennacherib in 701 BCE was one that deserved to be told and retold with the strongest acclaim. It was a waypoint of Israelite history—a story of divine protection, preservation and trust that pertained to a city. It generated the idea of a form of 'spiritual citizenship' for all those in whose hearts the 'love of Zion' had taken hold (cf. Ps. 122). Perhaps even more immediately relevant for communities living as aliens in a foreign environment was the sense of divine protection that is implicit in the story (so especially Ps. 124).

Two particular issues come to the fore in establishing a perspective regarding the part played by the story of 701 BCE in the formation of the larger book of Isaiah. The first lies in the widely noted feature that, both from a literary and theological perspective, Isaiah 36–39 fulfils a pivotal role in the overall structure of the book. The claim that Jerusalem was ultimately saved by the 'Angel of Yahweh' from destruction by the imperialist power of Assyria forms a fitting conclusion to the warnings of impending disaster that began in Isaiah 5 with the threat to King Ahaz at the time of the Syro-Ephraimite crisis. Moreover it confirms, even if in a dramatically supernatural manner, the theme of the sovereignty of Yahweh which reverberates through Isaiah's 'Memoir' of Isa. 6.1–(8.16) 9.6. The incomparable power of Yahweh is amply demonstrated by the story of the angelic intervention which saved Jerusalem from Sennacherib. Furthermore Isaiah 39, with its warning of perils still to come, forms an excellent bridge to the prophecies of Isaiah 40–55. Since the connection between the 'First Isaiah' of chs. 1–39 and the 'Second Isaiah' of chs. 40–66 is the most significant connection of the entire book, Isaiah 39 provides the major 'pivot point' for this. However this bridging function applies to the whole unit of Isaiah 36–39 and not just the final episode. A further relevant point is that Isaiah 35 appears to have been composed as the re-assuring conclusion to the major literary collection of Isaiah 5–35. Its focus is on the end of 'exile' through a return to Jerusalem.

A number of considerations provide clues about the sequence in which the first part of the book of Isaiah has been shaped and the reasons why connections were made between its separate components. So far as the Deliverance Narrative of Isaiah 36–39 is concerned the following factors are of most importance:

(1) The arguments advocated by Hermann Barth regarding an 'anti-Assyrian' edition of a collection of Isaiah's prophecies during the reign of Isaiah have received widespread subsequent support, notably by M.A. Sweeney.[2] However, it is evident that whatever shape may have been given to such a collection during Josiah's reign, this primary collection has subsequently undergone extensive subsequent revision and expansion in the light of Jerusalem's humiliation at the hand of the King of Babylon. It is, in general, hard to believe that any collection of Isaianic prophecies from the eighth century could have been preserved without extensive revision after the disasters of the sixth century.

(2) The theological perspective of the Deliverance narrative, with its claim for a dramatic intervention by the 'Angel of Yahweh' displays links with several prophecies attributed to Isaiah in Isa. 28.1–32.8. Those that are relevant to Sennacherib's campaign of 705–701 BCE have been carefully edited and expanded to take account of Isaiah's claim that Yahweh's action would demonstrate that divine, not human power would determine the outcome of the threat to Judah. It would be dramatic, direct and overwhelming. Furthermore the prophecies relevant to this Assyrian campaign have been expanded (notably in Isa. 30.27-28, 29-33; 31.8-9) to present a proto-apocalyptic message giving an absolute assurance of divine protection. In this way general assurances of divine protection have been elaborated into a story about divine intervention to save Jerusalem in its hour of direst need. Prophecies have been elaborated into an exemplary story of supernatural divine action.

The authors of the Deliverance Narrative evidently shared essentially the same political world-view expressed in Isaiah's contrast between divine and human help. Admittedly there are qualifications, but, in general the assertion of the superiority of Yahweh to human help, and those who trust in it, is shared by the Deliverance Narrative. It is developed also in a number of

---

2. M.A. Sweeney, *Isaiah 1–39 with an Introduction to Prophetic Literature* (FOTL, 16; Grand Rapids: Eerdmans, 1996), pp. 353-58.

prophecies ascribed to Isaiah. The simplest conclusion can only be that the authors of the narrative were linked with the editors/authors of the prophecies attributed to Isaiah in Isaiah 28–32.

(3) A further feature which supports this conclusion is present in the pro-Davidic royalist stance of the Deliverance Narrative which is shared by the similarly royalist stance of Isaiah 28–32 (notably in Isa. 32.1-8). The most noteworthy aspect of this is the absence of any such pro-Davidic, royalist position in the prophecies which follow in Isa. 32.9–35.10 (Isa. 33.17 is the only exception to this). The shift from the notion of the divine election of a royal dynasty—a familiar concept in the ancient Near East—to one of Jerusalem as a chosen city to which the survivors of Israel will return is made strikingly prominent in Isa. 35.1-10. The conclusion drawn by O.H. Steck that this chapter at one time formed the conclusion of a major collection of 'First Isaiah' prophecies can then be substantiated.[3] Such a shift would be wholly in agreement with the change of political expectation that followed the collapse of Zerubbabel's brief moment of power.

The overall message of Isaiah 5–35 can then be seen as one which sought to uphold the authority of the city of Jerusalem in the situation that emerged in the fifth century BCE under the wider orbit of Persian administrative control. It reveals the religious and political background to the activities of Ezra and Nehemiah.

In conclusion to this reflection on the relationship between the Deliverance narrative and the prophecies of Isaiah 5–35 two points come clearly into the forefront. The first is the light that the narrative sheds on the central contention of the 'Deuteronomistic' political theology that Jerusalem had been chosen by Yahweh as the place where the divine name was located and was to be invoked. In the Deuteronomic law-book the location is not even named, although this becomes clear in the narrative history of the Former Prophets. Since Jerusalem had come into eminence as a major city of the kingdom of Israel as a result of King David's capture of it and the building of a temple there under Solomon, its status was wholly dependent on this royal connection. It was 'the city of David' and the Deliverance Narrative exploits this royal link in order to account for the city's being spared the fate of Lachish.

Yet the political implications of this royal connection were fraught with dangers, as Jerusalem's enemies could point out (cf. Ezra 4.11-16). If Jerusalem was to recover its position as the leading city of the region there was need to establish a different, non-royal, non-Davidic, basis for the city's claim. This is attempted in the Deuteronomic ruling regarding the divine

---

3. O.H. Steck, *Bereitete Heimkehr: Jesaja 35 als redaktionelle Brücke zwischen dem Ersten und Zweiten Jesaja* (SBS, 121; Stuttgart: Katholisches Bibelwerk, 1985).

choice of a place for the offering of worship and prayer. It continued as a primary issue during and after the move for the restoration of the temple area in the late sixth century BCE. Could Jerusalem recover its position as the leading city of the region? Such a question carried with it immense religious implications in the face of the rival ambitions of Bethel and Samaria. This rivalry proved to be a long-lasting point of contention, carrying within its compass far-reaching issues of priestly authority and doctrinal conformity. The most acute of these later consequences are to be seen in the Samaritan controversy.[4]

4. *Later Developments of the Story of 701 BCE*

The completed account of how Jerusalem was saved from the armies of Sennacherib in 701 BCE at one time existed as a single coherent literary unit. Its incorporation into the emerging book of Isaiah cannot have taken place until sometime after 500 BCE. Whether its inclusion in the narrative history of the Former Prophets (the 'Deuteronomistic History') was prior to this can only remain a matter of conjecture. The evidence for assigning a chronological priority is not decisive. The whole range of literary issues regarding the origin, compilation and constituent elements, which now form this long historical work have themselves become the subject of extensive debate which cannot be entered into at this juncture. In any case, these questions have only a secondary bearing on the origin and structure of the Deliverance Narrative itself.

Of direct relevance is the claim by some scholars to discern within the finished Deliverance account elements which may originally have belonged to the 'Deuteronomistic History' and which have been taken up in the story of Jerusalem's escape. Most at issue here is the claim by Paul Evans that a core version of the story of how Jerusalem was saved from Sennacherib at one time formed a sequel to 2 Kgs 18.13-16 reporting Hezekiah's surrender.[5] Similarly the claim that the account of the visit of the emissaries from Babylon now contained in 2 Kgs 20.1-8 forms a 'bridge' unit anticipating the disasters of the sixth century BCE is a point of note. A similar argument has been widely canvassed in respect of the importance of this latter story as a 'bridge' between the first (Assyrian) and second (Babylonian) parts of the book of Isaiah.

---

4. R.J. Coggins, *Samaritans and Jews: The Origins of Samaritanism Reconsidered* (Oxford: Blackwell, 1975).

5. P.S. Evans, *The Invasion of Sennacherib in the Book of Kings: A Source-Critical and Rhetorical Study of 2 Kings 18–19* (VTSup, 125; Leiden/Boston: E.J. Brill, 2009), pp. 39-85.

In all of these instances, however, the question of whether some parts of the account of a miraculous divine intervention to save Jerusalem in 701 BCE were original to the Deuteronomistic History are highly speculative and questionable. The arguments put forward by Smelik are fully convincing. Of far greater significance than any search for 'Deuteronomistic' elements in the Deliverance Narrative is recognition that, in spite of the duplications and unevenness that appear within it, its present form is carefully structured, consistent in its message and plot, and holds together as a single coherent literary unit. That it should have existed at one time in two different versions—the 'Isaianic' and the 'Deuteronomistic'—in no way detracts from this. Of greater importance is recognition that the overall theme and message of the completed narrative is more thematically central to the overall structure of the present Book of Isaiah than it is to the Deuteronomistic History. In the case of Isaiah it provides an important key towards understanding how the very negative and admonitory prophecies of the prophet directed towards both Ahaz and Hezekiah came to be viewed retrospectively as a favourable message regarding the divine support for, and promising future of, the Davidic royal dynasty after the disaster of 587 BCE. In the case of the Deuteronomistic History, however, its presence is noticeably enigmatic. In this work in its final form there is a sharply marked and repeated criticism of kingship generally including the Davidic kings.

However the whole issue of the presentation and ideological intentions of the so-called Deuteronomistic Historian in regard to the institution of kingship represents a major issue in itself and many important questions remain unresolved. They cannot be dealt with here and it is sufficient to note in this connection that, even allowing for the emphasis on faith and trust in Yahweh which pervades the Deliverance Narrative, the assertion that Jerusalem was miraculously saved by 'the Angel of Yahweh' in 701 BCE 'for the sake of Yahweh's servant David' appears surprising in a narrative in which most kings are condemned out of hand and even the best of the Davidic line do not escape sharp criticism. Such a comment can only be understood in regard to King Hezekiah and the events of 701 BCE after the siege and destruction of Lachish.

The question that arises therefore cannot be whether the Deliverance Narrative contains a number of significant elements which once formed part of the Deuteronomistic History, but rather why was this completed narrative introduced into it at all? It is not immediately clear that the story of the twilight years of the royal house of Judah required the introduction of this narrative, since it places the figure of David and his royal dynasty in a highly favourable light. Without its inclusion the general picture of decline from Hezekiah to Zedekiah is perfectly intelligible and, with responsibility for this decline laid at the door of the royal palace of Jerusalem and its misguided trust in the power of Egypt to protect Judah, the story is coherent. It is the miracle of 701 BCE that stands out as a strange anomaly. Why had Yahweh acted so differently in 587 BCE from 701 BCE? The story of Hezekiah's misguided welcome to emissaries from Babylon (2 Kgs 20.1-8) only partially explains such a change of attitude.

No clear and convincing explanation for the apparent strangeness of this discrepancy is forthcoming, but three points require to be noted.

(1) The first is the most obvious and concerns the fact that what happened in 701 BCE is recalled as a favourable event for Jerusalem and its royal head, even though this came at the cost of a humiliating act of royal surrender. It could then be understood as the end-point of the 'years of woe' and devastation of the land as foretold by Isaiah (cf. Isa. 6.9-13). The fate of the many other cities of Judah that fell victim to the forces of Sennacherib (2 Kgs 18.13) is then tacitly overlooked.

(2) 701 BCE was in any case an event that could not be ignored and was evidently remembered in some circles as a form of historical 'proof' that the destiny of the Davidic royal house was providentially guided and upheld. Any chronicle of Judah's decline could not then ignore such an event, nor leave out of the reckoning the complacent and congratulatory interpretation of it as an act of divine favouritism. If this favourable interpretation of what had happened in 701 BCE had become the occasion of a dangerously complacent political policy, then, by placing it in a wider context of national disasters, this could be countered. The inclusion of a version of the Deliverance Narrative in the extended 'Deuteronomistic History' served as a warning that its message required considerable caution and amendment in the light of other events.

(3) A third consideration must also be given consideration. This concerns the strangely enigmatic episode set as the conclusion of the entire history in 2 Kgs in 25.27-30. The story of the release of Jehoiachin from his Babylonian imprisonment and the honour accorded to him as an exiled ruler in Babylon is surprising and appears confusing in its implications. It has, at times, been taken to imply that, after all the failures and disasters of the early sixth century BCE, the survivors of the Davidic royal house were nevertheless destined to play a role in Judah's, and Jerusalem's future. However, if this was the implication it is certainly not spelt out with any clarity. Nor does this episode contain any indication that it was intended to support the expectations of a return of Zerubbabel to the Jerusalem throne in the late sixth century BCE.

The most plausible explanation for the inclusion of this episode, which raises doubts concerning its historical veracity, is that it is intended as a sequel to the prophetic forewarning of Jehoiachin's fate in 2 Kgs 20.1-8. The historic promise of Yahweh to David that his sons should receive honour and respect among other kings of the earth (as Ps. 72.10-11) was fulfilled for Jehoiachin, even though he was a prisoner in Babylon. In this way Yahweh's honour was upheld, but no return to actual kingship in Jerusalem took place. The story of Jehoiachin's release serves as the necessary sequel to the warning of his ignominious deportation and removal from the throne. The striking feature of this linking of the two episodes is that it affirms that Yahweh's promise was fulfilled, but does not hold out any prospect of a return of a descendant of David to the throne in Jerusalem. The two events are thereby understood in relation to each other and Jehoiachin's fate is made into a paradigm of the meaning of the Davidic promise. Instead of a return to the throne in Jerusalem—an event for which some may have hoped—it shows that the ancient promise of Yahweh to David was fulfilled in the unexpected setting of a Babylon royal palace. So many other former citizens of Jerusalem would spend their lives living 'among the nations'. Yet they could trust that, like Jehoiachin, Yahweh's promise to David would be fulfilled for them in that they would be the subjects of providential care and respect.

Jehoiachin was a son of David living among the nations, and he received honour accordingly. Yet he remained in exile, as a majority of Judah's former citizens were destined to do. The point that is made is that the promise of Yahweh to King David would be fulfilled in an unexpected way.

Further developments of the central theme of the Deliverance Narrative appear in the later chapters of the Isaiah book (Isa. 40–66) and in the extensive development of Isaianic prophecies in the books of Haggai and Zechariah. The favourable interpretation of Jerusalem's escape in 701 BCE is made into a paradigm of divine providence. Further developments of its basic themes are contained in the Chronicler's reworking of the story of the rise and fall of the First Kingdom of Israel and the whole event is seen very differently in Samaritan texts.

These developments of the basic literary unit of the Deliverance Narrative move outside the scope of the present study which is primarily focused on its importance for the formation of the Book of Isaiah. As a result of its importance to this book it plays a significant role in the emergence of an apocalyptic future hope. Of first importance must be recognition that, irrespective of evaluations regarding its time of origin, its central themes are integral to the making of the Book of Isaiah. The favourable interpretation of the events of 701 BCE is employed to demonstrate the power of Yahweh, God of Jerusalem, over the nations. This motif then becomes the thread that binds together the distinct parts of the Book of Isaiah.

The preference among scholars for regarding the incorporation of the Deliverance Narrative in 2 Kings as earlier than its insertion in the Isaiah book has tended to hide recognition of this point. Whereas it is indispensable to understanding the structure of the Book of Isaiah, this cannot be said of the so-called Deuteronomistic History with its plethora of literary uncertainties. Once the original independent character of the narrative as a well-planned literary whole is recognized then, along with its post-587 BCE origin, a better understanding of its importance is forthcoming. The excessive attention to a search for a historical explanation of its most controversial episode—the slaughter by the 'Angel of Yahweh'—has encouraged a disregard for its unique literary features.

A further point is also relevant in respect of its time of origin and its place in the corpus of Old Testament prophecy. The major shift of focus in research into the formation of the prophetic books has drawn greater attention to the extreme difficulty of reconstructing any convincing chronology of the editorial formation of the prophetic writings, including the great 'Deuteronomistic History'. Quite obviously a rich library of documents in one form or another existed in the early sixth and fifth centuries BCE. This rich inheritance from an earlier age, and most especially from the time when the last vestiges of the First Kingdom of Israel collapsed, was available and was drawn upon to create a new series of 'books'. From an inherited treasure store of ancient texts a new work began, intent on creating a new literature for a new age in which the readers were no longer a conveniently identifiable nation but scattered groups in many lands. Such a work must have started soon after the restoration of the temple in 516 BCE. The identity, authorship, literary form and *locus* of preservation of the material on which this new literature could draw are no longer known and can only be estimated with the greatest caution. Nevertheless, out of the labours of this new generation of editors/authors/scribes a new kind of authoritative literature emerged. This was 'The Law and the Prophets' from which the extant Hebrew canon was formed. It was the birthplace of the concept of a Bible as a literary phenomenon and these unknown editors were, in the fullest sense, the 'authors' of the Hebrew Bible which has been preserved into the present.

PART III

THE BOOK OF ISAIAH IN A PERSIAN CONTEXT

Chapter 11

ISAIAH 14.22-27:
A CENTRAL PASSAGE RECONSIDERED

The publication in 1960 of the second volume of G. von Rad's *Theologie des Alten Testaments*[1] dealing with the prophetic traditions of Israel raised several new questions relating to the interpretation of the message of the prophet Isaiah. In particular his analysis of the influence of the 'Zion tradition' upon the prophet regarded this as firmly evident in the passage Isa. 14.24-27. G. von Rad then further compares Isa. 10.27b-34; 14.28-32; 29.1-8 and 31.1-8. This was then followed up by B.S. Childs in a study of the message of Isaiah in relation to the siege of Jerusalem by Sennacherib in 701 BCE.[2] Childs undertook a close form-critical analysis of the unit, finding in it a manifestation of the 'summary-appraisal' form in which a measure of didactic wisdom influence upon the prophet was to be discerned. In the light of these researches the passage has come to be regarded by a number of scholars as a major witness to the preaching of Isaiah in regard to the threat against Jerusalem posed by the Assyrians. Whether the prophecy is to be dated to 715 BCE, as Isa. 14.28 might suggest, or more immediately to the crisis of 705–701 BCE then makes little difference to its place in determining the prophet's attitude to the Assyrian threat. Isaiah was affirming to his king and nation that God would defend his city of Jerusalem and overthrow its Assyrian attackers, because he was the special divine Guardian of Zion.

In his commentary on Isaiah 13–39 O. Kaiser[3] has challenged the assumption of the authenticity of the passage on a number of grounds, and has pointed back to arguments to this effect from B. Stade in the nineteenth

---

1. G. von Rad, *Theologie des Alten Testaments*. II. *Die Theologie der prophetischen Überlieferungen Israels* (Munich: Chr. Kaiser, 1960). Eng. translation, *Old Testament Theology*, II (trans. D.M.G. Stalker; Edinburgh: Oliver & Boyd, 1965), pp. 155ff.

2. B.S. Childs, *Isaiah and the Assyrian Crisis* (SBT, 2/3; London: SCM Press, 1967), pp. 38ff.

3. O. Kaiser, *Der Prophet Jesaja. Kapitel 13–39* (ATD, 18; Göttingen: Vandenhoeck & Ruprecht, 1973); Eng. translation, *Isaiah 13–39* (trans. R.A. Wilson; London: SCM Press, 1974), pp. 45ff.

century. Far from recognizing any influence upon the prophet of the ancient 'Zion tradition', Kaiser has drawn attention to its proto-apocalyptic character and the relationship of the passage to other similar sayings which are to be found scattered throughout Isaiah 1–39.

More recently still the American scholar J.D.W. Watts[4] has sought to redefine the unit that we are concerned with as Isa. 14.22-27, thereby whatever we determine about the nature and origin of the passage we must recognize its central importance for an assessment of other passages, closely similar in content, which are to be found in the book in chs. 1–39. Furthermore we cannot ignore the relationship of the pronouncement regarding the overthrow of 'the Assyrian' made in v. 25 to the narrative account set in 2 Kgs 18.17–19.37 (= Isa. 36.2–37.38). Since I have earlier offered a study attempting to reconstruct what took place in 701 BCE in regard to the Assyrian threat to Jerusalem, a reconsideration of Isa. 14.22-27 would seem to be a necessary step in evaluating some very diverse approaches to the interpretation of Isaiah 1–39.[5] The questions have, in any case, been accorded added interest in the light of Hermann Barth's study[6] of the 'anti-Assyrian' prophecies incorporated into the Isaianic prophetic corpus at a relatively early stage of its literary growth.

As an initial starting-point for the study of Isa. 14.22-27 we may draw attention to two features which have served to encourage rather premature and over-hasty conclusions in regard to its time and purpose of origin. The first is the marked fact that G. von Rad, by listing a relatively small number of comparable passages in which he thought to identify the influence of the Zion tradition upon the prophet Isaiah, has encouraged a tendency to treat these passages in isolation from a larger number of other similar passages which are preserved in the book. These also may be thought to have a 'proto-apocalyptic' character. By proceeding in this fashion G. von Rad has pointed to something in the nature of a block of 'Zion prophecies' in the book of Isaiah which have then been allowed to stand too much apart from passages in the book with which they ought necessarily to be compared. Furthermore, we may claim that differences between what is affirmed in these passages, which are often quite marked, are then neglected. A quite false sense of coherence and consistency is thereby created which may be misleading.

---

4. J.D.W. Watts, *Isaiah 1–33* (WBC, 24; Waco, TX: Word Books, 1985), pp. 212-16.

5. R.E. Clements, *Isaiah and the Deliverance of Jerusalem: A Study of the Interpretation of Prophecy in the Old Testament* (JSOTSup, 13; Sheffield: JSOT Press, 1980).

6. H. Barth, *Die Jesaja-Worte in der Josiazeit. Israel und Assur als Thema einer produktiven Neuinterpretation der Jesajaüberlieferung* (WMANT, 48; Neukirchen–Vluyn: Neukirchener Verlag, 1977), especially pp. 103-17.

If we are to discern in these verses evidence of the influence upon the prophet Isaiah of the 'Zion tradition' evidenced in Psalms 46, 48 and 76, then this too raises further questions. Not only is this the case in respect of the date of these psalms, but clearly also in regard to the fact that, if some common similarity of content is to be found in both the psalms and the Isaianic prophecies, then quite obviously this could be accounted for in a variety of ways. Possible as it appears to be that these psalms antedate Isaiah's prophesying in the eighth century BCE, the overall extent to which they express a content of mythological ideas which can be closely linked to the 'anti-Assyrian' prophecies in the book of Isaiah remains open to further investigation. All assumptions regarding the manner in which the prophet Isaiah was influenced by the Jerusalem background must then be considered separately.

1. *The Structure and Origin of Isaiah 14.24-27*

As a first point of our investigation we may note a feature which is strikingly obvious. The two verses Isa. 14.22-23 provide a summarising conclusion to the series of prophecies which precede it dealing with Babylon. They announce that God will rise up against Babylon and destroy it, leaving the city a perpetual ruin. This event is clearly assumed to be still in the future and, since there are no reasons for thinking that anywhere other than the real Babylon is intended, this would point to a time prior to the capture of Babylon by Cyrus in 538 BCE. We can press beyond this, however, since a time prior to the rise of Cyrus in establishing a major threat against Babylon, which we may put at ca. 546 BCE seems most probable, The prophecies against Babylon in Isa. 13.1–14.23 make no reference to the human agents who will bring about Babylon's downfall. This would certainly lead us to conclude that the prophecy of Isa. 14.22-23 is of earlier origin than chs. 40–55 of the book of Isaiah in which Cyrus and the kingdom of the Medes are named.

When we turn to the immediately following verses in Isa. 14.24-25 it is striking that these refer explicitly to 'the Assyrian' as the enemy of God's people who is to be overthrown. This prophecy, like the one that precedes it, is also making a pronouncement about a yet future event which, it is declared, will take place upon the soil of Yahweh's land ('my land', v. 25). I can see no reason for thinking that some power other than the real Assyria is intended, whose control over Judah finally came to a complete end with the overthrow of Nineveh in 612 BCE. The prophecy would therefore appear to have originated prior to this time and to have seen in the overthrow of Assyria an end to its imperial rule over Judah which had begun more than a century earlier.

A third point is significant, and can surely not be unrelated to what we have already drawn attention to. This is that vv. 26-27, which follow these pronouncements of judgment upon Babylon and Assyria, extend the references further. The defeat of the enemy upon what God refers to as 'my land' is extended to cover 'the whole land', just as the powers which threaten God's people are extended to cover 'all the nations' (v. 26). In view of the fact that, with the excision of vv. 25b and 26b, both G. von Rad and H. Barth regard Isa. 14.24-27 as a single unit, this feature needs to be examined carefully. The deliberate way in which the fate that is declared to be awaiting Assyria has been extended to apply to 'all nations' shows unmistakably that vv. 26-27 are secondary to vv. 24-25. Moreover it would also appear to be the case that vv. 22-23 had by this time been linked with vv. 24-25 so that the threats against both Babylon and Assyria were now being extended in a universal direction. This is the justification for considering the six verses of Isa. 14.22-27 together. They comprise three quite separate threats addressed respectively to Babylon, Assyria and 'all nations'.

We can discern that within this section therefore are the marks of three major phases in the history of the tradition of Isaiah's prophecies: an anti-Assyrian redaction, an extension of this to include Babylon, and a subsequent apocalyptic redaction in which a universal frame of reference is introduced. This latest addition radically changes the understanding of the passage by giving to it a final eschatological character. Out of a pronouncement concerning a defeat of Assyria that was understood to stand within the series of historical events a more ultimate event that would ensure the vindication of Israel at the 'end time' has been developed. It is noteworthy that H. Donner[7] noted that vv. 26-27 reflect, in their pronouncement of a judgment upon 'all nations', the apocalyptic character of the post-exilic era, but was unwilling to draw the full implications of this in respect of its late time of origin.

If the conclusion is valid that a clear distinction exists between the declaration of Yahweh's plan to defeat 'the Assyrian' (vv. 24-25) and that which asserts that his purpose is to overthrow 'all nations' who fight against Jerusalem-Zion (vv. 26-27), then we must surely accept the conclusion that the same distinction applies in respect of other comparable passages in the book of Isaiah. This especially concerns Isa. 8.9-10, 17.12-14 and 29.5-8. The first of these passages is a warning uttered against 'all you far countries' who plot against Judah (Isa. 8.9). The second passage threatens a divine rebuff to be delivered against 'the nations' who are not more precisely defined. The third passage then pronounces a sudden and dramatic defeat which is to be inflicted by Yahweh of hosts 'with whirlwind and tempest' (i.e. non-human forces) against 'the multitude of all the nations that fight

---

7. H. Donner, *Israel unter den Völkern* (VTSup, 11; Leiden: E.J. Brill, 1964), p. 146.

against Ariel' (Isa. 29.6-7). These pronouncements must all be regarded as consciously universalizing affirmations of Yahweh's plan to defend and exalt Jerusalem at the expense of the many nations which threaten the city. They can therefore best be understood as post-exilic apocalyptic pronouncements concerning the final eschatological vindication of Jerusalem and the remnant of Judah who are destined to find protection in Zion (Isa. 14.32; 31.9 etc.). The idea that such passages can simply be understood as indicative of the influence upon the prophet Isaiah of the ancient *Völkerkampf* motif celebrated in the Jerusalem cult must then be discarded. It does indeed appear probable that we are faced here in this motif with an ancient tradition celebrated in the Jerusalem cultus, which is also to be traced in the psalms (cf. Pss 46.5, 9; 48.3), but this must be considered carefully in relation to the history of the redaction of Isaiah's prophecies. At what point the cult-mythological motif has found entry into the tradition of Isaiah's prophesying must be left at this stage as a separate question.

There is a second feature which also has a direct bearing upon the understanding of the nature and origin of the unit Isa. 14.22-27. Quite clearly v. 25b makes allusion back to the royal coronation prophecy of Isa. 9.3 concerning the removal of the yoke of foreign domination through the power of God working through the Davidic king. The presence of this citation here has almost certainly come by way of the comparable usage to be found in Isa. 10.27. The primary occurrence is that of Isa. 9.3 affirming the Davidic kingship to be a defence against foreign domination and both Isa. 10.27 and 14.25b draw upon this and give to it a specific application. There is no reason why we should regard Isa. 14.25b as of later origin than the short unit in which it is now set. On the contrary, it must be argued that it occupies a determinative position since it is Yahweh's respect for the Davidic kingship which is taken to provide the assurance that he will overthrow nations that oppress Jerusalem and Yahweh's land as a whole. We should therefore oppose the widespread assumption—that Isa. 14.25b can be regarded as a later gloss. It is in any case markedly evident, not only in the case of Isa. 10.27 but also in a host of other passages, that a considerable number of prophetic metaphors, images and affirmations that belonged to the written collection of Isaiah's prophecies have been elaborated upon and expanded as that collection was enlarged.[8] It also appears to be a highly probable conclusion, so far as the history of the redaction of this part of the book of Isaiah is concerned, that 14.24f. was once linked with the contents of ch. 10, especially 10.5-14.[9]

---

8. Cf., for example, the development of the 'briers and thorns' imagery from Isa. 5.6 in 7.23-25; 10.17; 27.4. An abundance of other examples are to be found.

9. J. Vermeylen, *Du prophète Isaïe à l'apocalyptique*, I (Paris: J. Gabalda, 1971), p. 253.

We may then arrive at the conclusion that Isa. 14.24-25 affirms that the overthrow of 'the Assyrian' will take place upon Yahweh's land and that assurance for this hope was found in the collection of Isaiah's prophecies, especially that concerning the Davidic kingship (Isa. 8.23; 9.6). This royal coronation oracle has provided a focal point for such a future hope since it links Yahweh's support for the Davidic dynasty with a belief in the rebuttal of all attempts at foreign domination over Yahweh's people who are to be ruled by such a king. Furthermore this pronouncement regarding the defeat of Assyria on Yahweh's land was at one time linked editorially with other comparable prophecies preserved in Isa. 10.5-15. These have a closely similar import, but have now also undergone subsequent expansion. The intrusion of the material concerning Babylon in Isa. 13.1–14.23, followed by the still later intrusion of the promises of Israel's return and restoration in 11.1 and 12.6, have resulted in the separation of 14.24-25 from other comparable sayings which threatened Assyria.

The question remains whether the pronouncement concerning Assyria's coming downfall set out in Isa. 14.24-25, could have originated with the prophet himself. This must surely be ruled out on both formal and material grounds. In form the appeal in 14.25b to the Davidic royal promise of 9.3 must be regarded as a mark of secondary compilation. There is no obvious indication to suggest that this clause was not an original element in the saying of vv. 24-25. On the contrary it provides a motive for establishing the assurance that Yahweh does intend to remove the yoke of all foreign oppressors from his territory. It is typical of the extensive employment of such midrashic type citations of prophetic metaphors and phrases to be found throughout Isaiah 1–39. It further points us in the direction of recognizing that the appeal to the Davidic royal ideology reflected in this short prophetic saying belongs to the broader background of Yahweh's intention to defeat 'the Assyrian'. This is precisely in line with the motivation expressed in the narrative regarding the events of 701 BCE (2 Kgs 19.34 = Isa. 37.35). The use of the citation, both here and in 10.37, also lends support to the recognition that the coronation prophecy of Isa. 8.23–9.6 held a very formative position in the collection of Isaiah's prophecies. It is possible to defend its Isaianic origin as marking the end of the reign of Ahaz and the accession of Hezekiah.[10] What is evident is that Isa. 14.24-25 has been composed with the

---

10. In my commentary of 1980 (*Isaiah 1–39* [NCBC; Grand Rapids: Eerdmans, 1980], pp. 103ff.) I held to the conclusion that the birth of the 'Saviour-king' of Isa. 8.27–9.6 was a reference to the replacement of King Ahaz by Hezekiah. Other commentators would see in this royal birth a reference the kingship of King Josiah. No firm indication is possible and the primary purpose would appear to be to affirm that the future of the Davidic dynasty was assured. In this way the absence of a specific royal name was itself significant. By a process of *relecture* it was shown that it was the future of the dynasty that was important.

aid of a citation from Isa. 9.3. To this we must add an objection on the grounds of content.

Certainly it must be admitted that a measure of circularity attends the discussion of the Isaianic authenticity of this saying and its possible connection with the prophet's attitude to the events of 701 BCE. The case that, either during the build-up to the threatened siege or possibly a little earlier, Isaiah declared that Yahweh would defend Jerusalem and humiliate the Assyrian forces, depends for its cogency on such passages as this and the few closely related affirmations to be found in Isaiah 1–39. I see no reason for deviating from the position that I adopted in my earlier study of *Isaiah and the Deliverance of Jerusalem*[11] that the prophet vigorously opposed Hezekiah's rash act of rebellion and foretold a fearful outcome to it. The eventual aftermath was apparently less catastrophic than Isaiah had foretold it would be, but this in no way softened the prophet's sharp castigation of Jerusalem and its leaders for what had taken place (Isa. 22.14). All that we can safely conclude is that the saying of Isa. 14.24-25 is apparently intended to be understood in relation to the events of 701 BCE, although even this point needs some more careful examination. Overall therefore we must conclude that the saying concerning the dramatic defeat of 'the Assyrian' expressed in Isa. 14.24-25 did not originate with the prophet Isaiah, but has been composed secondarily and linked with the prophet by means of the citation of the promise of the removal of the 'yoke of the oppressor' from Isa. 9.3. It appears likely that it has been deliberately intended to modify and clarify the position adopted by the prophet in relation to the events of 701 BCE, although it is precisely this issue that now requires investigation.

2. The Relationship of Isaiah 14.24-25 to the Narrative of 2 Kings 18.13–19.37 (= Isaiah 36.1–37.38)

Once it is accepted that the prophecy of Isa. 14.24f. was intended to refer to the real Assyria and that the extension of the promised protection to cover 'all the nations' (Isa. 14.26) has been made later, them its purpose must be understood in one of two ways. Either it refers to a still future defeat of 'the Assyrian' on the soil of Judah, which had not taken place at the time that the prophecy was composed, or alternatively it could have been intended to refer to the deliverance of Jerusalem and Hezekiah in 701 BCE from the threatened consequences of Sennacherib's siege. In this latter case the prophecy must have been composed after the event had taken place and with a view to making clear a certain point in regard to Isaiah's message at the time which was thought to be in danger of being misunderstood.

---

11. Cf. Clements, *Isaiah and the Deliverance of Jerusalem*, pp. 58ff.

It is the former possibility for understanding the origin and purpose of the anti-Assyrian saying of Isa. 14.24-25 that is advocated by H. Barth.[12] The prophecy genuinely looks forward to the time when Assyrian power over Judah will be broken and thus it effectively amounts to a promise of the cessation of Judah's vassal status. It belongs therefore to the 'anti-Assyrian Redaction' (AR) of Isaiah's prophecies and must have originated at some time during the reign of King Josiah (639–609 BCE). The fact that there was no such dramatic overthrow of Assyrian forces in the land of Judah, but only a gradual withdrawal, would not then materially affect its particular intention. A certain degree of poetic hyperbole has been introduced, which would be wholly within the accepted character of prophetic utterance (or scribal composition).

Such an interpretation is clearly intelligible, and we can well understand how it would have related directly to the political ambitions of Josiah's court followers and their eventual fulfilment in the reform of 622 BCE. What is less than convincing about such an interpretation of the origin of the anti-Assyrian saying of Isa. 14.24f. is the complete separation that it implies between such an expectation of the future overthrow, by Yahweh himself, of Assyrian forces on the soil of Judah and the narrative tradition which asserts that such took place in connection with the events of 701 BCE. By far the most plausible explanation must surely be that the prophetic announcement that the Assyrian forces would be divinely overthrown on the land of Yahweh and the narrative tradition which affirmed that this had indeed taken place when Sennacherib confronted Hezekiah are connected with each other. Otherwise we must suppose that the belief that such a defeat would take place in dramatic fashion has been allowed to reflect backwards onto the formation of a tradition which eventually led to the conviction that it had taken place in 701 BCE.

If this were thought to be the case then it would suggest that a form of re-application of the prophecy has taken place, referring it back to an event of almost a century earlier than its expected time of fulfilment. Such a position appears to me to be a most implausible explanation of the situation. By far the most straightforward understanding is that the prophecy of Isa. 14.24-25 is nothing other than a more forthright and emphatic pronouncement of Yahweh's plan to thwart the attack of Sennacherib which is expressed in the prophecies of Isa. 37.22-35. These are more modest in what they assert about the manner of defeat to be inflicted on the Assyrian, but are fundamentally similar in intent. What we must now consider are what possible aims and intentions could have given rise to the belief that Yahweh had declared through Isaiah that he would deliver a crushing blow to Sennacherib's forces when they threatened Jerusalem.

12.　Barth, *Die Jesaja-Worte*, p. 240.

In this regard I must express my indebtedness to the major study by F.J. Gonçalves[13]of the narrative traditions of 2 Kgs 18.17–19.37. Since the work of B. Stade it has been clear that the account which has been designated as the B narrative is composed from two separate traditions which we can designate B1 and B2. These narratives contain signs of a progressive heightening of the dramatic elements of divine intervention to protect Jerusalem, and this is especially the case if, as I have argued earlier, the action of 'the angel of Yahweh' in 2 Kgs 19.35 (= Isa. 37.36) is the latest element of this heightening to have been made.[14] It is wholly in line with the warning of Isa. 31.8 that the defeat of the Assyrian forces will be brought about by a supernatural agency ('a sword, not of man').

What I find to be significant in the study by Gonçalves is the contention that the B2 narrative of Jerusalem's deliverance in 701 BCE is a composition that has attained its final form after the destruction of the city in 587 BCE.[15] As has been made increasingly evident by recent study there is a marked element of contrasting of the differing fates of Jerusalem in 701 BCE and 587 BCE in the way in which the redaction of Isaiah's prophecies in Isaiah 1–32 has been made.[16] Awareness of what happened to the Davidic royal house in 598 BCE permeates the story of the coming of the emissaries from Babylon to Jerusalem in 2 Kgs 20.12-19 (= Isa. 39).[17] There is much to be said in support of the claim of Gonçalves that the B2 account of how Jerusalem was divinely protected in 701 BCE has been composed in its extant form after the catastrophe of 587 BCE. The narrative is designed to show that, under the obedient response of a faithful king, God does act to protect and uphold his people.

If this is the case in respect of the B2 narrative, then it must surely also be true of the saying we are primarily concerned with in Isa. 14.24-25. This too has been composed after 587 BCE and its purpose is thereby revealed as a concern to provide a qualified re-affirmation of the importance of the Davidic dynasty and the city of Jerusalem in the divine plan. By contrasting the fate of the city and its king in 587 BCE with what took place in 701 BCE it was thought to be possible to retain a positive role for both the Davidic kingship and the temple on Mount Zion in the divine plan for Israel. By such

---

13. F.J. Gonçalves, *L'expédition de Sennacherib en Palestine dans la littérature hébräique ancienne* (EBib, NS, 7; Paris, 1986), pp. 441ff.

14. Clements, *Isaiah and the Deliverance of Jerusalem*, pp. 60ff.

15. Gonçalves, *L'expédition de Sennacherib*, pp. 480ff.

16. Cf. R.E. Clements, 'The Prophecies of Isaiah and the Fall of Jerusalem in 587 BC', *VT* 30 (1980), pp. 421-36.

17. Cf. R.E. Clements, 'The Isaiah Narrative of 2 Kings 20: 12-19 and the Date of the Deuteronomic History', in A. Rofé and Y. Zakovitch (eds.), *Essays on the Bible and the Ancient World: Isaac Leo Seligmann Volume*, III (Jerusalem: E. Rubinstein's, 1983), pp. 209-20.

means the desirability of restoring both institutions was affirmed. The city of Jerusalem could, it was believed, be supernaturally protected by the very angel of Yahweh (cf. Isa. 14.32) when the proper spiritual conditions were fulfilled. The fulfilling of these conditions through the agency bf a devout and obedient king of the Davidic royal house is the primary purpose of the inclusion of the story concerning Hezekiah's sickness (2 Kgs 20.1-11 = Isa. 38*). We may venture to draw the conclusion therefore that the 'anti-Assyrian' saying of Isa. 14.24-25 owes its origin, along with the comparable saying of Isa. 31.8 and the B2 narrative now combined in 2 Kgs 18.17–19.37, to the desire to re-establish a rationale for restoring the Davidic kingship and for rebuilding the Jerusalem temple in the wake of what happened to both institutions in 587 BCE. There is also an inseparable element of theodicy implicit in such an undertaking which cannot be ignored. Both Davidic kingship and Jerusalem temple were valuable instruments of divine protection, but only when these institutions were recognized and upheld in a context of faith and obedience.

If such a viewpoint concerning the origin of the anti-Assyrian saying of Isa. 14.24-25 is a valid one, then this also offers to us a way of understanding how the inclusion of the anti-Babylon prophecies of Isa. 13.1–14.23 has been brought about. A central key is provided by a pre-occupation with the fate of the Davidic kingship and the Jerusalem temple, especially the former. The Assyrian intrusions into Israel and Judah in the second half of the eighth century had threatened both, especially with Sennacherib's siege of Jerusalem in 701 BCE. Both Jerusalem and the Davidic kingship had survived without major harm at that time, but had not been so fortunate at the hands of the Babylonians first in 598, and then more drastically in 587 BCE. In this way a concern with Babylon was attached to the collection of Isaiah's prophecies and the shadow of 587 BCE has been allowed to fall over the edited form of them. Inevitably in the process questions concerning the 'how long' (cf. Isa. 6.11) of Babylonian rule over Judah arose. So it becomes intelligible that a prophecy concerning Babylon's eventual downfall (Isa. 14.22-23) should have been linked with one relating to Assyria. By the time this addition was made the story of Assyria's fall was already a fact of past history, although that of Babylon at first was still only a matter for faith in the future. In time, however, Babylon too had fallen, permitting the yet fuller and more universal extension of the same trust in Yahweh's protection to be expressed in Isa. 14.26-27. Overall therefore three very meaningful stages in the development and extension of Isaiah's prophetic message have been made in Isa. 14.22-27, all of them ultimately taking their point of origin in the coronation oracle of Isa. 8.23–9.6.

Chapter 12

ISAIAH 53 AND THE RESTORATION OF ISRAEL

It is useful to begin a study of the controversial 'Suffering Servant' passages in Isaiah 40–55 by summarizing briefly some fundamental, if necessarily provisional, conclusions regarding their literary and historical setting. Doing so in the wake of the publication of T.N.D. Mettinger's short essay bidding farewell to them is to accept that he has succeeded in removing the most unlikely lines of interpretation, but has still left unresolved some other, potentially fundamental, questions regarding their significance.[1] His primary aim has been to take out of the discussion the radical attempt of Bernhard Duhm to interpret these passages in historical and literary isolation from their present context in Isaiah 40–55.[2] Already J. Lindblom had argued for a closely related position by seeking to interpret the Songs in direct relation to their context.[3] Overall there is no doubt that the main lines of scholarship since the 1930s have been in the direction of seeking an interpretation which does not depend on the kind of radical literary dislocation of the Songs that Duhm proposed.[4]

1. Some Basic Perceptions and Assumptions

We may begin by setting out the following basic perceptions:
1. There is no sufficient evidence to demonstrate that any of the four Servant passages needs to be ascribed to an author, or authors, different from, and chronologically separate from, the rest of Isaiah 40–55.

1. T.N.D. Mettinger, *A Farewell to the Servant Songs: A Critical Examination of an Exegetical Axiom* (Scripta minora; Lund: C.W.K. Gleerup, 1983).
2. Bernhard Duhm, *Das Buch Jesaja* (Göttinger Handkommentar zum Alten Testament, III.1; Göttingen: Vandenhoeck & Ruprecht, 1st edn, 1892 [4th edn, 1922 = 5th edn, reprinted 1968]).
3. J. Lindblom, *The Servant Songs in Deutero-Isaiah* (LUÅ, NS, 1.47.5; Lund: C.W.K. Gleerup, 1951); *Prophecy in Ancient Israel* (Oxford: Blackwell, 1962), pp. 268ff.
4. See H.H. Rowley, 'The Servant of the Lord in the Light of Three Decades of Criticism', in *The Servant of the Lord and Other Essays on the Old Testament* (Oxford: Blackwell, 2nd edn, 1965), pp. 4-7.

2. In light of this statement the degree to which these four passages are themselves to be regarded as standing significantly apart from, and therefore not directly related to, the rest of Isaiah 40–55 is questionable. In most respects their character, form, and subject matter show them to be integral to the material in these sixteen chapters. We can note in passing that recent studies have drawn attention to the links between these sixteen chapters and the earlier (chs. 1–39) and later (56–66) parts of the book of the prophet Isaiah.[5] The extent to which this changed perspective has relevance for understanding the mission and work of Yahweh's Servant is not our immediate concern.

3. There are undoubtedly difficulties of translation, chiefly within the fourth passage (Isa. 52.13–53.12). Nevertheless the major problems of interpretation are not resolved by resort to a revised, and more radical, translation of the text, even though there are clearly significant difficulties for the translator.[6]

4. The primary problem for the interpretation of the figure of the Servant lies in the highly individual portrayal of the Servant's suffering set out in the final Song (Isa. 52.13–53.12) and the significance of this suffering for those who are identified by the use of the first-person 'we' in the fourth Song.

5. Elsewhere in Deutero-Isaiah Yahweh's Servant is identified as the collective figure of Jacob-Israel (Isa. 41.8-9, Jacob/Israel; 44.1, 2 [Jacob–Jeshurun], 21, etc.). In the MT of Isa. 49.6 the Servant is addressed as 'Israel', and this would support the corporate interpretation of the figure from directly within the second of the Servant passages.

This last fact, combined with a recognition of the close links between the Songs and their immediate context (Lindblom; Mettinger), would appear to be decisive for a collective understanding of the figure. Yet the textual reliability of Isa. 49.6 does not appear to be above question, and extensive debate has hinged precisely on the issue of whether the context must be

5. W.A.M. Beuken, *Jesaja*, IIIA/B (Nijkerk: Callenbach, 1989); H.G.M. Williamson, *The Book Called Isaiah: Deutero-Isaiah's Role in Composition and Redaction* (Oxford: Clarendon Press, 1994); O.H. Steck, *Studien zu Tritojesaja* (BZAW, 203; Berlin/New York: W. de Gruyter, 1991).

6. See D. Winton Thomas, 'A Consideration of Isaiah LIII in the Light of Recent Textual and Philological Study', *ETL* 44 (1968), pp. 79-86; M.J. Dahood, 'Phoenician Elements in Isaiah 52.13–53.12', in H. Goedicke (ed.), *Near Eastern Studies in Honor of William Foxwell Albright* (Baltimore: The Johns Hopkins University Press, 1971), pp. 63-73; R.N. Whybray, *Thanksgiving for a Liberated Prophet* (JSOTSup, 4; Sheffield: JSOT Press, 1978).

regarded as determinative for the complex portrait given in the fourth Song. In this the highly specific descriptions of suffering have led even such otherwise convinced advocates of a collective view as H.H. Rowley to recognize some fluctuation between collective and individual viewpoints.[7] We are compelled to reckon either with a remarkable compression of images of violence and injustice inflicted onto one single person, leading to his death, or to some exceptional poetic, or psychological, representation of a community's experience.

The literary background to all four passages concerning the identity of the Servant would undoubtedly support the claim that we are faced here with a person who fulfils some form of representational collective role. Yet this leads to problems for the interpreter in understanding what kind of historical background has given rise to so impressive a picture of an individual's fate. Moreover, it leaves open many details regarding what precisely has happened to the Servant and how his fate is understood to benefit the onlookers, who are themselves not more fully identified. To a considerable extent the mystery of the Servant's identity is closely intertwined with the questions of the identity of those for whom his sufferings bring deliverance and of how his death can deliver the onlookers from guilt and disease (Isa. 53.4-5). What is implicit in the affirmation that his sufferings are counted as an 'offering for sin' (Heb. *'āšām*; Isa. 53.10)?

The claim that the sufferings endured by an individual are effective in bringing healing and forgiveness to a larger group is what lends the portrait of the Servant much of its uniqueness. The very notion of sacrificial offering is brought directly into the human sphere and incorporated into an understanding of how human experiences, which have no overt cultic intention, may fulfil a ritual purpose.

The task of interpretation therefore uncovers a need to understand how the individual role of the unidentified Servant can link the distinctively personal experiences which are ascribed to him with the corporate identity of the Servant-Israel. There is evidently some degree of differentiation between the Servant and the community he serves, even though they share much of an inherited Servant imagery. The solution would appear to lie in a recognition that one leading figure in a community may serve as its representative, so that he, or she, may at times be wholly identified with it, while at other times standing out in opposition to it.

2. Individual and Collective Interpretations

By looking at certain representational roles in other areas of Hebrew literature we may hope to find some explanation for the fluctuation between

---

7. Rowley, 'The Servant of the Lord', pp. 51-60.

the experience of the individual and the community which appears in the Songs. In this fluctuation the fate of one individual in some way both embodies, yet redeems, the fate of the larger group. We might have been tempted to conclude that all we are encountering is a very extended and forceful use of a literary figure of speech in which the group is personified. This would then make the text a close parallel to the description of the fate of Babylon which the prophet describes in terms of the humiliation and abuse inflicted on a well-brought-up young woman (Isa. 47.1-15). Yet few scholars have found such a literary explanation convincing, since, in the fourth Servant Song, the individual experience appears too exceptional, and the details of the suffering too precise, for a straightforward poetic device to have led to its creation. Some deeper ideological or institutional understanding of an individual's representative role appears to underlie the portrait of the suffering of the Servant in this passage.

Three major fields of ancient Israel's traditions have suggested themselves. We shall then look, in turn, at the roles of kingship, prophecy, and the Deuteronomic portrait of Moses, all of which appear to have some useful parallels and features by which the portrait of the suffering Servant may be understood. Before doing so, however, it is as well that we should remove from the discussion what appears largely to have been a false trail in the path of exegesis. This relates to the attempt, most closely associated with the name of H. Wheeler Robinson,[8] to accept that Israelite thinking displayed a characteristic so fundamentally different from our own that the individuality of a person was merged into that of the group to which he or she belonged.[9] This could be described as a concept of 'corporate personality' and was held to be a manifestation of 'primitive thinking'. It based itself upon the suggestions of L. Levy-Bruhl and a related school of anthropologists and rested on a theory about the nature of self-awareness and self-identity in the thought world of antiquity.[10]

From both the anthropological and theological perspectives, a claim that people of antiquity embraced a fundamentally different mode of thinking from our own cannot be sustained.[11] To a degree the very concept of community representation is at issue here, since awareness of a fun-

---

8. See H. Wheeler Robinson, *Corporate Personality in Ancient Israel* (Edinburgh: T. & T. Clark, rev. edn with a new introduction by C.S. Rodd, 1981), pp. 37-41; originally published as 'The Hebrew Conception of Corporate Personality', in P. Volz, F. Stummer and J. Hempel (eds.), *Werden und Wesen des Alten Testaments* (BZAW, 36; Berlin: A. Töpelmann, 1936), pp. 49-62.

9. Robinson, *Corporate Personality in Ancient Israel*, pp. 32-34.

10. See J.W. Rogerson, *Anthropology and the Old Testament* (Oxford: Blackwell, 1978), pp. 46-65.

11. Rogerson, *Anthropology and the Old Testament*, pp. 55-56.

damental distinction between the individual and the group was important for an understanding of how the group could be set under the authority and power of a representative leader. Although the theory of 'corporate personality', as applied to the Hebrew Bible, had the merit of drawing attention to the way in which social groups could share a common interest and feel a sense of a shared destiny, it erred by seeking to explain this characteristic by a different psychology. It assumed that primitive communities suffered from blurred and poorly defined perceptions, rather than recognizing that different communities experienced differing pressures which controlled the interaction between the group and the individual. As a way of drawing attention to the varied social forces at work in a community the idea had a certain value, but as a claim that a different kind of mentality was the cause it resorted to implausible theorizing.

3. *The Royal Servant*

We may turn then to consider the institution of kingship as a background to the Servant Songs. In general, the book of the prophet Isaiah, to a greater degree than any other book in the canon, is deeply affected by questions relating to the Davidic kingship.[12] I. Engnell, in an original adumbration of the theory that royal features, largely connected with the ritual function of the king, had been woven into the portrait of the Servant of Yahweh, drew heavily upon aspects of the Mesopotamian royal cultus.[13] This heavy dependence upon supposed ancient Near Eastern parallels cast a shadow of uncertainty over such an interpretation. Yet O. Kaiser has been able to explore a more distinctively Israelite development of the notion that kingly traits colour the portrayal of the Servant and his experience.[14]

One strong reason for thinking of such a royal background to the portrait of the Servant lies in the fact that, of all the institutional personages of ancient Israelite society, the divinely chosen and appointed king appears to have exercised most strongly a representative function on

---

12. See A. Laato, *Who Is Immanuel? The Rise and Foundering of Israel's Messianic Expectations* (Åbo: Åbo Academy Press, 1988); P.D. Wegner, *An Examination of Kingship and Messianic Expectation in Isaiah 1–35* (Lewiston, NY: Edwin Mellen Press, 1992).

13. I Engnell, 'The *'Ebed* Yahweh Songs and the Suffering Messiah in Deutero-Isaiah', *BJRL* 31 (1948), pp. 54-93.

14. O. Kaiser, *Der königliche Knecht: Eine traditionsgeschichtlich-exegetische Studie über die Ebed-Jahwe-Lieder bei Deuterojesaja* (FRLANT, 70; Göttingen: Vandenhoeck & Ruprecht, 1959).

behalf of the nation.[15] Insofar as early Israel gave voice to an ideology of the state, it did so in terms of claims of royal divine election. Nor is there any doubt that the issue of the divinely elect status of the Davidic dynasty was a central issue which served to shape the early prophetic pronouncements of the prophet Isaiah.[16]

In a closely connected manner it is evident that the disasters of the last days of the kingdom of Judah, which initiated the period of the Babylonian exile, fell particularly heavily upon the representatives of the Davidic royal line. The tragic fates which befell in succession Josiah, Jehoahaz, Jehoiakim, Jehoiachin, and his uncle Zedekiah occupy a prominent place in prophecy and contributed to the confusion and horror at Judah's downfall.

One strong reason for thinking of such a royal background to the portrait of the Servant lies in the fact that, of all the institutional personages of ancient Israelite society, the divinely chosen and appointed king appears to have exercised most strongly a representative function on behalf of the nation. Insofar as early Israel gave voice to an ideology of the state, it did so in terms of claims of royal divine election. Nor is there any doubt that the issue of the divinely elect status of the Davidic dynasty was a central issue which served to shape the early prophetic pronouncements of the prophet Isaiah.

In a closely connected manner it is evident that the disasters of the last days of the kingdom of Judah, which initiated the period of the Babylonian exile, fell particularly heavily upon the representatives of the Davidic royal line. The tragic fates which befell in succession Josiah, Jehoahaz, Jehoiakim, Jehoiachin, and his uncle Zedekiah occupy a prominent place in prophecy and contributed to the confusion and horror at Judah's downfall. That there took place a period of anxious reflection is highlighted by the extraordinarily high expectations which, in the face of all the facts of experience, still clung to these last representatives of a discredited and failing institution. This tension between the traditional expectations surrounding Judah's prestigious royal family and the experienced realities of history are to be seen both in prophecy and in the guarded, and seemingly contradictory, implications of the Deuteronomic reporting of the end of the monarchy (2 Kgs 25.27-30).

It is wholly plausible that the fate of such kingly figures should have provoked deep spiritual reflection in the mind of a prophetic herald seeking to make sense of the events which overtook the last representatives of

15. S. Mowinckel, *He That Cometh: The Messiah Concept in the Old Testament and Later Judaism* (trans. G.W. Anderson; Oxford: B.H. Blackwell, 1956).

16. See R. Kilian, *Die Verheissung Immanuels, Jes 7,14* (Stuttgarter Bibelstudien, 35; Stuttgart: Katholisches Bibelwerk, 1968).

Judah's long-surviving royal dynasty. In particular the experience of Jehoiachin, in his prolonged Babylonian imprisonment, must have given cause for thinking afresh about the divine significance of such a fate. From within the Deutero-Isaianic corpus of material the enigmatic pronouncement of Isa. 55.3-5 concerning the future of the Davidic dynastic promise is itself more than a little ambiguous concerning the significance of this piece of political theology for the renewal of Israel.

So the fate of Judah's last kings, when linked to the hope of restoring one of the surviving royal heirs to a major position in a renewed Israel, could well have exercised a formative role in shaping the figure of the suffering Servant. Royal personages had suffered grievously at the hands of their Babylonian enemies, and yet the dynasty had not been totally eclipsed. It could indeed be regarded as both stricken and abused, yet replete with hope that it would 'prolong its days' and 'see his offspring' (Isa. 53.10). If this is the case, then the conventional ideology in which the king embodied the hopes and divine blessing which were promised to the nation more generally can be readily understood. For many the idea of a restored independent nation without a king must have appeared to be an impossibility.

4. *The Servant as Prophet*

The second line of interpretation that has provided a strong basis for the fluctuation between the individual and the collective features of the Songs is to be found in the role of prophecy, and of particular prophets, within the life of Israel as a community. Already the Deuteronomic presentation of prophecy set out in 2 Kgs 17.23 views the prophet as a rejected figure who has spoken the truth from God, but who has been refused a responsive hearing. Already we are well on the road toward recognition of the prophet as a martyr figure who suffers for the truth. Moreover, in the written collection of the canonical prophets each is firmly presented as one who addresses the nation of Israel in its entirety. He stands between God and the nation so that even the lines of political demarcation between Judah and Israel become more than a little blurred.

The use of the autobiographical first-person form in the second and third Songs, and to a more limited extent in the fourth also, strongly points toward accepting that the experiences of individual prophets, and most emphatically of that prophet whom we have come to know as Deutero-Isaiah, have heavily influenced the Servant's portrait in the fourth Song.[17]

17. Mowinckel, *He That Cometh*, pp. 248-53; Whybray, *Thanksgiving for a Liberated Prophet*, pp. 79-92.

By this time it certainly appears that a sufficiently strong pattern had become established among prophetic circles which viewed the true prophet as a rejected and oppressed figure. This pattern has markedly shaped the presentation of the narrative of Isa. 6.1-13 which has, in turn, exercised a far-reaching influence across the remainder of the book. The prophet speaks God's truth, but is refused a hearing and becomes mocked and despised by those whom he addresses. Yet he knows in advance that he will be rejected, mocked, and set aside by the audience, and they, in turn, are hardened in their rebellion against God. They become blind and deaf (see Isa. 42.18-20; 43.8), whereas the prophet becomes isolated and outcast (see Isa. 8.11-15) until such time as the judgment falls.

This interpretive pattern has certainly coloured the presentation in Jeremiah, in which the impossibility that the prophet could fulfil any role as intercessor and deliverer in the manner of Moses or Samuel is emphatically stressed (Jer. 15.1). We know almost nothing of the details of experiences which befell the author of Isaiah 40–55, but the preserved record of such a prophet as Jeremiah indicates that suffering and rejection could become a necessary accompaniment of a prophet's work, leading ultimately to the eventual renewal of the community. A major impulse toward the preservation of a written, and ultimately canonical, collection of prophecies foretelling judgment on Israel lay in the experience of rejection and isolation which befell the major prophets who had foretold Israel's and Judah's downfall. These experiences gave rise to the idea of the true prophet as a martyr figure.

Yet the prophet remained an individual, and it still remains difficult to understand how the variety of misfortunes and ignominies heaped upon the suffering Servant, according to the fourth Servant Song, could have befallen one single person. We should be led to think of the experiences of several prophets being brought together and vested into one typified 'ideal' prophet. But such a line of interpretation does not help much in clarifying how the prophet could suffer at the hands of his people, be rejected by them, and yet, at the same time, recognize that his sufferings avail to bring them deliverance. The language employed in the fourth Song draws heavily upon cultic rites which go beyond what might typically have been regarded as the role of a prophet (so especially v. 10). Even the language of intercession, and the necessary role accorded to the prophet in the Songs, appears insufficient to account for the declaration that the surrendered life of the Servant may serve as a 'sin offering' (Heb. *'āšām*).

5. *Moses and the Servant*

There does, however, remain a central figure of Israelite tradition whose portrait in the biblical literature combines a significant number of kingly and prophetic features. This fact at least suggests that the undoubtedly unique figure of the suffering Servant was not without biblical parallel. The exilic age, after the debacles of 598 and 587 BCE, led to a profound magnification of the role of Moses in the formation of Israel as a nation (so the Deuteronomic literature generally, but most especially Deut. 1–11; 29–34). The influence of G. von Rad has reawakened interest in the influence of the historical figure of Moses upon the portrait of the Servant of the LORD in Isa. 40–55.[18]

That some connection existed was adumbrated, but later abandoned, by Ernst Sellin.[19] The suggestion proposed here is not that a direct intention existed to use the historical traditions about Moses as the prototype for the suffering Servant, but rather that essentially the same theological concerns which helped to shape the Deuteronomic portrayal of Moses have shaped those of the suffering Servant. More precision is devoted to showing Moses as a righteous individual who stood over against his people, yet who nevertheless suffered with them and on their account. Thereby this portrait could undoubtedly lead to the idea that the death of the righteous one was made necessary by the unrighteousness of the many. At the same time this signal experience of injustice could achieve renewal and sanctification, which made such a death a 'sin-offering'. The argument hinges firmly on recognizing that such an offering became necessary as a means toward restoring the holiness of the community, rather than serving as legal substitution of one victim for another.[20]

From a historical and literary perspective it is all too easy to overlook the extent to which the record and presentation of the person and work of Moses occurred relatively late in the development of Israelite historiography. All the indications appear to be that the earliest drafts of the so-called Deuteronomic History began in typical ancient Near Eastern fashion as a hagiographic type of royal chronicle. Then, in a major recasting, the hagiographic royal annals which celebrated the rise and authority of the royal house of David were transformed into a chronicle of the Mosaic origins of the nation of Israel and its steady fall from grace as progressive generations flouted the laws which Moses had given. The hero-kings

18. G. von Rad, *Old Testament Theology*. II. *The Theology of Israel's Prophetic Traditions* (trans. D.M.G. Stalker; Edinburgh: Oliver & Boyd, 1965), pp. 261-62.

19. Rowley, 'The Servant of the Lord', pp. 10-11.

20. Objections to such an idea are set out by Whybray, *Thanksgiving for a Liberated Prophet*, pp. 29ff.

became villains and a new mysterious and all-commanding superhero was introduced as the lead figure of the entire story. This figure was Moses.[21]

Both the introduction to the Deuteronomic law and its epilogue place the most exceptional degree of emphasis upon the role of Moses, recasting and enlarging upon two aspects of the earlier tradition which had previously appeared incidental. This is all the more surprising in view of the almost total absence of Moses from the central Deuteronomic law code in chs. 12–26. It is significant that the sole reference to him in this code comes only implicitly in the regulations governing prophecy (Deut. 18.15-22).

In the introduction to the code the foremost feature of the role ascribed to Moses is that of the greatest and most efficacious of the intercessors who had intervened with God on Israel's behalf. He had thereby rescued the nation from certain judgment and oblivion by putting his own life on the line and surrendering even his own hope of survival in order that Israel might be spared.[22] A second, and even more surprising, feature is the emphasis placed in Deuteronomy upon Moses as the victim who, on account of Israel's rebelliousness, was denied the privilege of participation in the nation's entry into the promised land. He had to die, having seen the land, but without having set foot upon a single part of it.

This portrait of Moses as intercessor and victim has certainly arisen in the light of the events that befell Judah in the first half of the sixth century BCE. The fate of the nation's leader is a fate with which others can identify and in which they may see some of their own misfortunes mirrored. Clearly the motif of Israel's rebelliousness has passed through various interpretive stages, but, in its Deuteronomic expression, is used to highlight the innate untrustworthiness of Israel's claims to loyalty.[23] The nation appears as irretrievably immersed in faithless self-doubt and complacent self-deception. Only Moses stands apart, to the extent that God offers to build a new nation from this one figure alone! Yet this cannot be, since Moses has committed himself wholly to the Israel that exists, with all its wayward tendencies.

The most surprising, and theologically unexpected, feature of this heroic and grand action on the part of Moses lies in the tradition which insists that, in spite of his courageous faith Moses must die outside the

---

21. Cf. G.W. Coats, 'Legendary Motifs in the Moses Death Reports', *CBQ* 39 (1977), pp. 34-44.

22. E. Aurelius, *Der Fürbitter Israels: Eine Studie zum Mosebild im Alten Testament* (ConBOT, 27; Stockholm: Almqvist & Wiksell, 1988), pp. 41ff.

23. G.W. Coats, *The Murmuring Motif in the Wilderness Traditions of the Old Testament: Rebellion in the Wilderness* (Nashville: Abingdon Press, 1968).

promised land in the same manner that the generation which had listened to the demoralizing warnings of the spies had had to perish. The one concession granted to Moses is that he should at least view the land from afar (Deut. 32.52).

So in the Deuteronomic portrait of Moses it is not only the guilty who must perish in the fires of judgment, but many of the innocent. It undoubtedly appeared to many that 'the way of the LORD is unfair' (Ezek. 18.25). The very arbitrariness and unreality of Ezekiel's doctrine of the individual's freedom to repent (Ezek. 18.23) draws attention to this sense of grievance. Misfortune not only befell the wicked, but struck out aimlessly and mercilessly in many directions.

All the greater interest attaches therefore to the unexpected epilogue to the Song of Moses, which generally emphasizes the justness of the doctrine of retribution. God addresses Moses with a harsh and unexpected judgment:

> You shall die there on the mountain that you ascend and shall be gathered to your kin, as your brother Aaron died on Mount Horeb and was gathered to his kin; because both of you broke faith with me among the Israelites at the waters of Meribath-kadesh in the wilderness of Zin, by failing to maintain my holiness among the Israelites (Deut. 32.50-51).

The reason given is surprising, since it draws upon the conceptual field of holiness and the cult, which is quite distinct from the juridical ideas of retributive justice.[24] In spite of his successful intercessory role, Moses fell victim to the nation's sin in that he too had failed to maintain the divine holiness among the people. Sin in such a field of thinking was not simply an individual's failure, but a community experience which had consequences that could not be averted. The innocent were drawn into suffering along with the guilty. Kaminsky rightly draws attention to the fact that it is a more wilful and glaring sin, carrying similar consequences, which is highlighted as the offence of the unfortunate Achan in Joshua 7. The rules concerning warfare appear only at the edge of the action which brought destruction upon Achan and his entire family. His behaviour had disrupted and nullified the holiness which served as a protective envelope upholding Israel. When the envelope was intact, Israel could expect to receive remarkable divine blessings and victories. However, when the rules of holiness were broken, the divine power was believed to be withdrawn, and dire consequences ensued.

In the light of this perspective we can understand why it was important that the sufferings of the Servant of Yahweh in Isaiah 53 should act as an

---

24. J.S. Kaminsky, *Corporate Responsibility in the Hebrew Bible* (JSOTSup, 196; (Sheffield: Sheffield Academic Press, 1995).

'āšām—a sin-offering. That the context is drawn primarily from cultic ideas and imagery is already indicated by the assertion that the Servant delivers the community (indicated by 'us', 'we', and 'our' in Isa. 53.3-5) from 'diseases' and 'infirmities' (v. 4) besides 'transgressions' and 'iniquities' (v. 5).

The entire experience of defeat and exile had sentenced Israel to 'die among the nations in an unclean land' (see Amos 7.17). Only by recovering its status as a 'holy nation' (Exod. 19.5f.) could there be a renewal of life and a recovery of a life-giving relationship with Yahweh as God. Yet the very agency and means by which holiness had, in past years, been assured to Israel, namely, the temple of Yahweh in Jerusalem, had been destroyed and rendered ineffective. Without the temple there could be no sin-offering to guarantee the continuance of a holy relationship to Yahweh. The ravages of guilt and disease, understood as the threats and misfortunes from which divine holiness brought deliverance, could no longer be held at bay. Yet now Deutero-Isaiah introduces his boldest of assertions, that God will accept the sufferings of the Servant-Israel, perhaps largely focused on the specific sufferings of the unnamed prophet himself, as the *'āšām* by which the restored nation will be purified.

Two passages from the book of Ezekiel enable us to grasp this background of cultic ideas which have served to shape the language. The first is in Ezek. 11.16, where the prophet insists that, during the period in which Israel was threatened with the uncleanness of the lands and countries into which they had been driven, God himself would be 'a sanctuary for a little while'. The language is vague and indeterminate. It amounts to an assertion that God would make a unique, though temporary, provision for those Judeans who had been driven into foreign lands, into a realm of danger and uncleanness. There they were no longer under the umbrella of holiness that the temple had secured for them when they had been in Jerusalem. God had withdrawn the presence of the divine glory from the temple and left it to its destroyers, but for those driven far off into strange lands, a temporary sanctifying presence of God would be granted.

The second passage occurs as Ezekiel looks ahead to the time when these scattered former members of Israel will return out of the unclean lands into which they had been taken to live in their own land. There God would 'sprinkle clean water' upon them in order to remove all the uncleannesses with which they had been tainted during their years of exile (Ezek. 36.25). Although the cultic imagery differs from that of Isaiah 53, the underlying ideas are essentially the same as in Isa. 53.10: God will make special provision to restore the survivors of Israel to the status of a holy nation. The land would again become holy as traditional assertions had claimed before the disasters of 587 BCE.

Seen in such light the flow of imagery and ideas in Isaiah 53 is wholly coherent and consistent, so that the uniqueness of the idea that a human life could serve as a sin-offering belongs within the context of Israel's need again to become a holy people. Since there could be no authorized sin-offering by which the people could be protected from sin and disease while the Jerusalem temple lay in ruins with its altars desecrated, Yahweh would make special provision. The sufferings of Servant-Israel would be the offering by which the relationship of all the scattered nation with Yahweh would be renewed. Israel would once again be returned to the sphere of blessing and divine protection, which its own sins had nullified in the past. Just as a sin-offering was needed so that Aaron could be consecrated to the office of high priest, so the sufferings of Israel among the nations would count as an offering that the ruined temple in Jerusalem could no longer provide.

Much of the difficulty concerning the idea of vicariousness has arisen on account of a rigid preoccupation with juridical notions and the attempt to understand the language of Isaiah 53 against a background of legal practice. Against such the language appears both alien and strained. Yet once the language is understood in its proper cultic setting it makes excellent sense. Plunged into the uncleanness of living among the nations, Israel could do little to escape the threat posed by disease and guilt.

Yet without the temple cultus to make atonement to remove the effects of such guilt, Israel appeared helpless and faced an impossible dilemma. Guilt-ridden and threatened by disease, it had no avenue through which to secure atonement, since unauthorized offerings would simply have added to the nation's disobedience. Here in this remarkable prophetic insight, Isaiah 53 asserts God's unique resolution. Until the regular sin offerings can be restored, the Servant-Israel's own suffering among the nations will be the sin-offering by which that nation's guilt will be cleansed and its diseases carried away.

The incident in Acts 8.26-40 in which the Ethiopian eunuch alludes to Isa. 53.7-8 quite correctly understands the Isaianic context with its concern for uncleanness and the threat of alienation. The Ethiopian was doubly excluded from the cultic community of ancient Israel on account of his physical defect (Deut. 23.1) and his Ethiopian origin (see Isa. 45.14). Yet the context adumbrated the promise of a new path to holiness and wholeness which the eunuch deeply coveted. Philip then shows that this renewal had now become possible and real through the death of Jesus and proceeded immediately to lead the eunuch to Christian baptism. The eunuch's uncleanness and alienation were removed. It seems impossible that, both in the original Isaianic setting and in that of Acts 8.26-40, before the beginning of the Christian mission to the Gentiles, the importance of a larger cultic background was not intentionally being drawn upon. God had provided a new form of sin-offering through the sufferings of a righteous Servant, by which uncleanness could be removed.

As to the identity of the Servant in Isaiah 53 the fundamental issues that were noted at the outset of this survey still remain. These concern the seeming fluctuation between the collective identification of the Servant of the LORD, through his association with such titles as Israel and Jeshurun, and detailed description of the fate of an individual prophet-teacher. On this issue it certainly appears necessary to accept and accommodate such fluctuations and tensions without destroying, or denying, the reality of both aspects. An individual may embody and represent the destiny of a nation, as we see in the Deuteronomic emphasis upon the representative role of Moses, the obedient leader who nevertheless suffers along with his people. The overall balance of the four Servant Songs, however, points strongly in the direction of some form of typified collective identification of the Servant. They are as those Israelites who had endured suffering in exile. Their fate was the fate of individuals, yet also in a real sense they embodied the fate of the former nation, since the central thrust of Isaiah 40–55 appears designed to uphold the claims of those taken into exile to be the true and faithful Israel.

The second issue, concerning the sense in which the sufferings of the Servant are understood to be vicarious and to bring deliverance to the community he represents, can be answered more adequately. Once the proper cultic background to the language is understood, then the supposed difficulties of the concept of vicariousness recede. In what sense can a human being remove the sins of a community? Just as the Deuteronomic history treats the death of Moses as an action which had become necessary because of Israel's sins in the wilderness, so the Servant suffers both for, and with, the community he represents. Moses too had done no less. The shared background of ideas in Isa. 53.10 and Deut. 32.50-51 consists of notions of holiness and wholeness by which a community is protected. Those, like Achan, who threaten that holiness must suffer for what they have done.[25] Yet Moses, too, even though he had challenged the disobedience which Israel chose to pursue, became a victim of the broken holiness which resulted. Since there had to be a sin-offering to effect restoration once the holiness of the people was infringed, Isaiah 53 insists that the Servant's misfortunes will provide that essential offering.

---

25. Kaminsky, *Corporate Responsibility in the Hebrew Bible*, pp. 67-95.

6. *Conclusion*

That the imagery of a suffering Servant whose misfortunes lead to re-demption and eventual triumph has a complex origin should not occasion surprise. In a number of respects the notion lacks precise definition, and it represents a confluence of imagery and ideas embracing both prophetic and cultic traits. Nevertheless comparison with the near contemporary development of the redrawn portrait of Moses as intercessor and national leader (Deut. 9.6-29; 32.48-52) and with the insistence in Ezekiel that Israel must be washed from the uncleanness of its existence in exile provides a rewarding fresh understanding. God provides the very sin-offering by which Israel can be healed, cleansed, and forgiven.[26]

26. For more information, see O. Eissfeldt, 'The Promises of Grace to David in Isaiah 55.1-5', in B.W. Anderson and W. Harrelson (eds.), *Israel's Prophetic Heritage: Essays in Honor of James Muilenburg* (London: SCM Press, 1962), pp. 196-207; P.D. Hanson, *Isaiah 40–66* (Interpretation Commentaries; Louisville: Westminster/ John Knox Press, 1995); C. Houtman, 'De dood van Mozes, de knecht des Heren: Notities over en naar aanleidung van Deuteronomium 34.1-8', in *De Knecht: Studies rondom Deutero-Jesaja, door collega's en oud-leerlingen aangeboden aan Prof. J.L. Koole* (Kampen: Kok, 1978); D.T. Olson, *Deuteronomy and the Death of Moses: A Theological Reading* (Overtures to Biblical Theology; Minneapolis: Fortress Press, 1994); and J.W. Rogerson, 'The Hebrew Conception of Corporate Personality: A Re-examination', *JTS* NS 21 (1970), pp. 1-16.

Chapter 13

A LIGHT TO THE NATIONS:
A CENTRAL THEME OF THE BOOK OF ISAIAH

The book of Isaiah is a very complex structure, so much so that, even in the present, it is open to contend that modern scholarship has encountered very considerable difficulty in elucidating its message. Indeed, it remains possible to question whether there is an overall series of propositions that can properly be called 'the message of the book', or whether we must not rather settle for a simple acceptance of a whole variety of 'messages' that belong to the various prophets who have contributed to its separate parts. For more than a century, the contention that the book must be regarded as composed of at least three separate prophet 'books', or collections, has dominated scholarship. As a result it has become commonplace to treat the various sections separately in histories of Israelite prophecy—the so-called First, Second and Third Isaiah—and to look for different authors to contribute introductions and commentaries to each of them. There is then little expectation that the unity of the book will prove an issue that requires careful examination and detailed treatment. All too often, it is taken apart before the question of whether it belongs together as a unity is ever considered.

1. *Isaiah as Prophet and the Prophetic Book*

All these assumptions and procedures now stand in radical need of revision and rethinking, and far more attention needs to be paid to the canonical form and structure of the book, not simply as a literary salutation to the canonical, or final form of the text, but as a theological and literary concern to understand its essential character and purpose.[1] After all, we know very little of

---

1. Cf. my essay, 'The Unity of the Book of Isaiah', *Interpretation* 36 (1982), pp. 117-29; J. Vermeylen, 'L'unité du livre d'Isaïe', in *The Book of Isaiah* (BETL, 81; Leuven: J.P. Peeters, 1989), pp. 11-53; C.R. Seitz, 'Isaiah 1–66: Making Sense of the Whole', in C.R. Seitz (ed.), *Reading and Preaching the Book of Isaiah* (Philadelphia: Fortress Press, 1988), pp. 105-26; E.W. Conrad, *Reading Isaiah* (Overtures to Biblical Theology; Minneapolis: Fortress Press, 1991).

how prophetic books were expected to appear to assume that the book of
Isaiah is somehow extraordinarily odd, or should really be regarded as three
separate books. During the past decade a considerable change of outlook has
taken place, a revision of methods of critical analysis and a generally altered
angle of perception in the study of the prophetic literature. Inevitably, this
has had considerable impact on the study of the book of Isaiah.[2] We may
claim with confidence that the hypothesis of a basic three-part division of the
book, as advocated by Bernhard Duhm in his commentary of 1892,[3] is obsolete and must now be considered as simply a provisional, and recognizably
inadequate, attempt to understand its origin and to interpret its significance.[4]
In seeking to trace the processes which led to the formation of the book, and
which can explain its present structure, such a hypothesis concedes too little
to its compositional complexity and ignores too much of the undoubted
internal connectedness of its various component parts.

The recent studies by C.R. Seitz,[5] Marvin Sweeney[6] and H.G.M. Williamson[7] have shown that those parts of chs. 40–66 which were at one time
thought to be unrelated to the earlier section of the book must certainly be
interpreted in relation to it. So far as chs. 40–55 are concerned the case is
modest but sufficiently clear to be decisive. Similar changes of outlook have
taken place in regard to chs. 56–66, which were left in Duhm's analysis as a
rather forlorn miscellany.[8] They have subsequently been rather hesitantly
ascribed either to the mysterious Deutero-Isaiah or, more probably, to his
less poetically inspired disciples. As the result of the studies by a number of
scholars, most especially O.H. Steck[9] and W.A.M. Beuken,[10] the close
relationship to the earlier parts of the book of these seemingly errant and
orphaned eleven chapters is becoming much clearer.[11]

---

2. A full and extensive survey of these changes is to be seen in the volume by
M.A. Sweeney, *Isaiah 1–39 with an Introduction to the Prophetic Literature* (FOTL, 16;
Grand Rapids: Eerdmans, 1996).

3. B. Duhm, *Das Buch Jesaja* (HAT; Tübingen: J.C.B. Mohr, 1892, 5th edn, 1968).

4. Cf. the critique by C.R. Seitz, *Zion's Final Destiny: The Development of the Book
of Isaiah* (Minneapolis: Fortress Press, 1991), pp. 37-46.

5. Cf. especially the works cited above in nn. 1 and 4.

6. M.A. Sweeney, *Isaiah 1–4 and the Post-Exilic Understanding of the Isaianic
Tradition* (BZAW, 171; Berlin: W. de Gruyter, 1988) and the work cited in n. 2 above.

7. H.G.M. Williamson, *The Book Called Isaiah: Deutero-Isaiah's Role in Composition and Redaction* (Oxford: Clarendon Press, 1994).

8. Duhm, *Jesaja*, pp. 7-10, 14-15, 418-19.

9. O.H. Steck, 'Tritojesaja im Jesajabuch', in J. Vermeylen (ed.), *The Book of Isaiah*
(Leuven: Leuven University Press, 1989), pp. 11-53.

10. W.A.M. Beuken, *Jesaja deel IIIA, deel IIIB* (Nijkerk: Callenbach, 1989).

11. Cf. the valuable critique and review in G.I. Emmerson, *Isaiah 56–66* (OTG;
Sheffield: Sheffield Academic Press, 1992).

Nor can we leave aside the importance of the studies by Rolf Rendtorff[12] in recognizing the close internal connections between the various parts of the great Isaiah collection. In a rather surprising fashion, therefore, it appears that these chapters, which at one time appeared of least importance to the book as a whole, and of only marginal interest theologically, have, nevertheless, provided some of the most important clues to understanding the whys and wherefores of its structure and formation. The reason for this is that they display with varying degrees of clarity a concern to hark back to, and to develop, themes and imagery which have appeared earlier. To a startling degree, they serve as a kind of historical and theological commentary on the earliest parts of the book which must certainly date back to the eighth century BCE.

It is a major point of significance in the two volumes of commentary on Isaiah which John Watts has published[13] that they undertake to provide a treatment of the whole book and seek to elucidate from its contents the message of the 'vision of Isaiah, the son of Amoz'.[14] Clearly, this cannot simply be a statement about authorship, relating only to those sayings and prophetic images which were declared by Isaiah of Jerusalem when the major threat to Israel from Assyria first materialized. It becomes readily apparent that there is much material in the book which must incontrovertibly be dated to a time long after the original prophet's death if it is to be adequately understood.[15]

Nevertheless, the book is a unity of some sort. There is reason why it is headed by the name of the prophet Isaiah, and it becomes evident on close examination that it seeks to maintain a kerygmatic consistency. It proclaims a reasonably coherent, connected and integrated message concerning God's purpose for Israel. It sees this purpose as directly related to Jerusalem—Zion, to the central role of the royal dynasty of David, and to the leadership that Israel is to assume among the nations. These themes recur in different ways and with different emphases, showing that they needed continual revision and development in the light of events. God's word is presented as two-edged, on one side voiced through the mouth of a prophet and on the other confirmed, modified and realized through historical events. Its vitality

12. R. Rendtorff, 'The Composition of the Book of Isaiah', in *Canon and Theology. Overtures to an Old Testament Theology* (trans. M. Kohl; Edinburgh: T. & T. Clark, 1994); Rendtorff, 'Isaiah 56.1 as Key to the Formation of the Book of Isaiah', in *Canon and Theology*, pp. 181-89.

13. J.D.W. Watts, *Isaiah 1–33; Isaiah 34–66* (WBC, 24, 25; Waco, TX: Word Books, 1985, 1987) regards the literary form of the Isaianic vision as complete by approximately 435 BCE (*Isaiah 1–33*, p. xxiv).

14. Watts, *Isaiah 1–33*, pp. xxiv-xxix.

15. Watts, *Isaiah 1–33*, pp. xxiv-xxix.

was necessary because the perspective of the reader was ever-changing. Its message was open-ended because it pointed to a future which came under the category of not yet!

Two concepts in particular dominate the Isaianic perception of Israel as its separate prophecies came to terms with the destruction, disappointments and internal conflicts which characterized a period of several centuries since the year in which king Uzziah died (Isa. 6.1). One was hope based on belief in the unique importance of the royal dynasty of David to impose peace on all nations. The other related belief was that the city of Jerusalem occupied a primary place in the divine purpose to bring this rule of peace to the warring nations of humankind (Isa. 2.2-4). Both the city and its Davidic king experienced a remarkable escape from catastrophe in 701 BCE and this event provided the focal point for both these hopes. Yet disaster and further upheaval befell Judah and Jerusalem during the years which followed the events of 701 BCE and the death of the main participants in that confrontation brought new threats and dangers. Those years witnessed the dismemberment of the Northern Kingdom, which was eventually followed a century later by the destruction of Judah and its chief city.

Prophecy was a means of rescuing events from the category of being meaningless to becoming meaningful. Against such a background, it can be seen why the images of 'remnant'[16] and 'servant'[17] are taken up and developed in the book of Isaiah to serve as fundamental themes which recur several times, and which proved capable of being developed and applied in different ways as it became necessary to comprehend both disaster and deliverance within the divine scheme of things. They show how Judah, the Davidic dynasty, and the city of Jerusalem could function and maintain hope for the nation of Israel more broadly within the context of the disasters and humiliations suffered during this period. Through judgment, pain, suffering and national break-up neither the purpose, nor existence, of God were denied, but they were inevitably subjected to new limitations and qualifications.

In turn these qualifications brought to birth new insights and possibilities which did not nullify the vision of Israel's final triumph but set it in a larger, and more rounded, perspective. It should not occasion surprise for us, therefore, that the book of Isaiah provides us with two of the most durable and meaningful concepts by which a variety of scattered communities maintained their belief in their religious identity. These are precisely the images

---

16. Cf. R.E. Clements, 'A Remnant Chosen by Grace (Romans 11.5)', in D.A. Hagner and M.J. Harris (eds.), *Pauline Studies: Essays in Honour of F.F. Bruce on his 70th Birthday* (Exeter: Paternoster Press, 1980), pp. 280-300.

17. Cf. W.A.M. Beuken, 'The Main Theme of Trito-Isaiah: The Servants of YHWH', *JSOT* 47 (1990), pp. 67-87.

of 'remnant' and 'servant' which were to become central to the Christian New Testament's reinterpretation of Israel as an *ekklesia*—a Church.

Without such qualifying metaphors the destructive triumphalism of election without suffering or service takes over, making the notion of spiritual power into an arrogant delusion. More than once in its history the Christian Church has proved as blind and deaf to the challenge of God's calling, as the prophet Isaiah saw to be true of his contemporaries! In this light, the book of Isaiah can be claimed to represent a 'Bible in miniature', since its central themes have subsequently provided two key Christian guidelines for reading the Bible as a canonical whole.

Surprisingly, the theme of Israel's land and of the various territorial units into which Israel was broken up during the pain-ridden centuries in which the book of Isaiah came into existence figure only marginally in its contents, contrasting sharply with the near-contemporary development of the Deutero-nomic literature. All too often in the prophecies of the book of Isaiah the geographical horizons and descriptions which appear are difficult to focus with any sharpness. At times it becomes impossible to ascertain even where the prophet is himself located, leaving open, for instance, the question of whether a common geographical setting is to be presupposed for the whole of 40–55 where 'Zion' is explicitly addressed, but where a virtual imprison-ment in Babylon is openly referred to. Instead, we find that geographically vague, but theologically highly charged and meaningful, designations are employed extensively. They have left us with imagery which has made it possible to transpose the Isaianic poetry into wholly new Christian environ-ments. Accordingly such terms as 'Zion', 'the coastlands', 'the ends of the earth', and even 'the nations' figure prominently. Israel's relationship to YHWH God is seen as established through worship and total spiritual loyalty, making the language of servanthood and remnant into primary terms through which the bond between God and the nation is given expression.

2. *Prophecy as Metaphor*

One of the major gains of the recent recovery of the awareness that the book of Isaiah has been fashioned to create an intricately woven tapestry of care-fully arranged themes and images is that it re-emphasizes the need to under-stand it as a whole. However blurred some of its pictorial images are, it has been intended to present a theological and literary unity. This is not because it all has the same author, but because it all bears witness to the same God and to a belief that a whole sequence of events reveals a divine plan and purpose. Seen in such a light, the path is open to trace the development of certain basic themes within the book through their various stages of development.

In historical perspective we are well aware that from earliest times such a method of study has been employed by scribes and scholars, pursued simply by associating different occurrences of the same, or closely related, words, frequently with little real consideration whether any connection was ever intended or can properly be construed. There are, however, a significant number of key words, images and themes to be traced in the book of Isaiah which recur in such a fashion as to indicate that they were themselves intended to serve as signposts and markers within a complex process of prophetic imagery and compositional development. It is this fact that has made them key features in the book's structure and which makes them central to what can be called the book's message.

High on a list of such themes, the idea of Israel as a 'remnant' must be placed. This undoubtedly originated with the name Shear-jashub given to the oldest and first-mentioned of the prophet's children. Similarly, the metaphor of the 'briers and thorns' which ruin the vineyard of YHWH of Hosts (Isa. 5.6) provides a cover term for the various enemies and threats which emerged within Judah's history,[18] as does the portrayal of the 'blindness and deafness' of Israel which the prophet regarded as afflicting the majority of the people.[19]

The number of such themes can readily be added to, and attention has already been drawn to the fact that the metaphor of 'The Servant of YHWH' provides a further example of just such a central image which proved capable of being developed and applied in a variety of ways. For more than a century, attention to the actual literary contexts in which the theme appears has been a regrettable casualty of the scholarly frustration of trying to elucidate who 'the Servant of YHWH' might have been and what actually happened to him. By separating a mere four so-called Servant Songs from the rest of Isaiah 40–55, and no less frustratingly from the rest of the book of Isaiah, it is not surprising that scholars have found themselves unable to provide a solution. Throughout the book the theme is used frequently but applied in a number of diverse ways in relation to changing events. In very similar fashion, the way in which the concept of the 'remnant' is used does not have one single, all-encompassing, application. It carries both judgmental as well as saving overtones.

Besides these terms, however, attention should also be given to the manner in which other powerful metaphors are used and re-used in the

---

18. Cf. Isa. 7.3-25; 27.4.

19. Cf. R. Rendtorff, 'Isaiah 6 in the Framework of the Composition of the Book', in *Canon and Theology*, pp. 170-80; R.E. Clements, 'Patterns in the Prophetic Canon: Healing the Blind and the Lame', in G.M. Tucker, D.L. Petersen, and R.R. Wilson (eds.), *Canon, Theology and Old Testament Interpretation: Essays in Honor of Brevard S. Childs* (Philadelphia: Fortress Press, 1988), pp. 189-200.

prophecies, enabling them to carry much of the meaning which must, in the very nature of prophetic language, remain enigmatic. Truths and imagery by which the meaning of an event is to be apprehended must often be mysterious, and even ambiguous, in exposing to a human audience the feelings and intentions of God. So imagery of the tree with its cycles of growth and decay provides a major cluster of metaphors to show how God deals with Israel and the nations. Similarly metaphors drawn from the familial relationships of parenthood, and especially motherhood, are employed in order to engage the attention of the reader in a direct and inescapable manner. They are transparent in the directness with which they convey a sense of the emotional burden latent in fundamental human relationships and, by implication, point to the high level of passion which must be construed as shaping the divine purpose. The reader is not left searching for a non-existent dictionary of theological concepts because the prophet's imagery lies freely exposed in the everyday world of persons and things. His metaphors become part of an argument which insists that if human beings feel like this then how much more must God experience such pain and passion.

3. A Light to the Nations

It is against this background of recognizing the extent to which several of the basic metaphors that are to be found in Isaiah reappear in distinctive literary and historical contexts that it is valuable to reconsider one of the most popular of them. This concerns the imagery of light as a metaphor of salvation and its use in a number of key texts within the collection. All told the noun 'light' (Heb. *'or*) occurs no less than twenty-two times in Isaiah, but we should probably add to these the four occurrences (Isa. 24.15; 31.9; 47.14; 50.11) of the closely related noun for 'brightness, fire' (Heb. *'ur*). It appears that at least some of these occurrences make a deliberate play on the similarity of sound with the noun for 'light', perhaps because fire was the simplest and most immediate way of bringing light out of darkness. In any event it must be noted that in Isa. 10.17 the fact that the metaphor of 'light', implying salvation, could also convey a sense of 'fire', bringing judgment, becomes a significant feature of the Isaianic imagery. Once again, ambiguity is deliberately employed, as in the metaphor of the 'remnant', in order to show that both judgment and salvation can be comprehended within a single series of events. The actions which bring salvation to some, imply judgment for others:

> The light of Israel will become a fire,
>   And his Holy One a flame;
> And it will burn and devour
>   His thorns and briers in one day (Isa. 10.17).

A similar contrast is to be found in Isa. 50.10-11 where those who fear God, but who walk in darkness, are assured of security and salvation. The irony of the ambiguity is skillfully expressed in vv. 10-11:

> Who among you fears YHWH
>   And obeys the voice of his servant.
> Who walks in darkness
>   And has no light,
> Yet trusts in the name of YHWH
>   And relies upon his God?
> But all of you are kindlers of fire,
>   Lighters of firebrands.
> Walk in the flame of your fire,
>   And among the brands that you have kindled!
> This is what you shall have from my hand:
>   You shall lie down in torment.

Our primary intention in following the most prominent of the occurrences of the imagery of 'light' through the book of Isaiah is to note two points which appear to be of primary exegetical significance. The first of these is that it certainly appears to be the case that the imagery of light, which is so familiar a feature of life as to make it a readily available, and almost obvious, metaphor of salvation, provides an important counterpart to the imagery of blindness which occupies a central place in the Isaianic theology. The second point is that the association of light with fire makes it a convenient metaphor for elucidating what it means that Israel is to become 'a light to the nations'.

The first point, that light will serve to remove Israel's blindness, becomes particularly evident in the introduction of the theme as a metaphor of salvation in Isa. 9.2 (9.1 in the Hebrew):

> The people who walked in darkness
>   have seen a great light;
> those who lived in a land of deep darkness
>   —on them light has shone (Isa. 9.2 [Heb. 9.1]).

From a structural point of view, the royal messianic oracle of 9.2-7 (Heb. 9.1-6) forms a conclusion to the unit, built around the three sign-names given to the prophet's children in 7.1–8.4, which began with the account of the prophet's call in 6.1-13. In this the fundamental theme of the 'blindness and deafness' of Israel is introduced and given a powerful reinforcement in 8.22 where no less than three nouns describe the intensity of the darkness that will afflict Israel. It transpires that this is not a physical darkness but rather the spiritual darkness which accompanies Israel's blindness. It is, then, of great importance to the Isaianic understanding of how salvation will come and how new light will arise for Israel. It will take the form of a new deliverer-king.

The actual, royal, messianic oracle of 9.2-7 is probably among the most contested passages of the entire corpus of prophecy, and I have discussed it extensively elsewhere.[20] It is sufficient to reiterate the conclusion that it is an accession oracle for a new king, not directly foretelling the birth of a specific royal heir but rather of announcing the glory that will accompany the arrival of a new heir of the Davidic house to the throne of Israel. Within the structure of the book, it is evidently intended to point to the accession of Hezekiah in succession to Ahaz, with whose policies the prophet Isaiah had strongly disagreed.

Within the larger setting of the book, the significance for the use of the imagery of light as a metaphor of salvation is its direct link to the royal, messianic claims of the Davidic dynasty. There seems little doubt that the reference in 10.17 to the light of Israel' which will become a flame to devour 'thorns and briers' intends an allusion back to 9.2 (Heb. 9.1), just as the 'thorns and briers' refer back to 5.6. The passage, however, must probably be regarded as among the very latest to have been incorporated in Isaiah 1–12 along with other material in 10.16-27 which throughout shows every indication of being a kind of commentary on various key metaphors taken from 6.1–9.6.[21]

The Deutero-Isaianic development of the metaphor of light is taken up in 42.6-7 where the conjunction of the imagery of light, darkness and blindness, strongly suggests that the earlier occurrence of these metaphors in Isaiah 6–9 is being openly alluded to:

> I am YHWH, I have called you in righteousness,
>   I have taken you by the hand and kept you;
> I have given you as a covenant to the people, a light to the nations,
>   to open the eyes that are blind,
> to bring out the prisoners from the dungeon, from the prison
>   those who sit in darkness (Isa. 42.6-7).

The close connection between the metaphor of light as a sign of salvation and the ending of the darkness' of Israel's spiritual blindness is then further elaborated in 42.16:

20. R.E. Clements, 'The Immanuel Prophecy of Isa. 7.10-17 and its Messianic Interpretation', in E. Blum, C. Macholz, and E.E. Stegemann (eds.), *Die hebräische Bibel and ihre zweifache Nachgeschichte: Festschrift für R. Rendtorff zum 65. Geburtstag* (Neukirchen–Vluyn: Neukirchener Verlag, 1990), pp. 225-40. Cf. also the extensive study of the importance of this prophetic oracle within the context of Isa. 1–35 by P.D. Wegner, *An Examination of Kingship and Messianic Expectation in Isaiah 1–35* (New York: Edwin Mellen Press, 1992).

21. O. Kaiser, *Isaiah 1–12: A Commentary* (OTL; trans. J. Bowden; Philadelphia: Westminster Press, 2nd edn, 1983), pp. 221-28; J. Vermeylen, *Du prophète Isaïe à l'apocaplyptique* (EBib, 1; Paris: J. Gabalda, 1977), p. 442.

> I will lead the blind
>> By a road they do not know,
> By paths they have not known
>> I will guide them,
> I will turn the darkness before them into light,
>> The rough places into level ground,
> These things I will do,
>> And I will not forsake them (Isa. 42.16).

The further extensive development of the theme of Israel's blindness and deafness in 42.18-20 points yet again to the dependence on the earlier material of chs. 6–9 for an understanding of the links that serve to relate words to ideas.

It should not escape attention that 42.1-4 provides the first of the so-called Servant Songs and that vv. 5-9 are taken, either as an original part of such a servant passage, or more plausibly as an intended commentary upon it. Moreover, it also deserves attention that the phrase 'a light to the nations' has proved to be one of the most memorable, if also one of the more controversial, features of the prophetic development in chs. 40–55 of the book. What exactly is meant by such a phrase? Does it mean, as most have taken it, that the gentile nations also will share in Israel's salvation, or merely that they will see the light as a sign that the time for Israel's deliverance has come?[22] The former meaning would certainly appear to be confirmed by the elaboration of the theme of 'a light to the nations' in 49.6:

> He says,
> 'It is too light a thing that you should be my servant
>> to raise up the tribes of Jacob
>> and to restore the survivors of Israel;
> I will give you as a light to the nations,
>> that my salvation may reach to
>> the end of the earth' (Isa. 49.6).

The most striking development of the metaphor of light, with its direct links to earlier occurrences in 9.2 (Heb. 9.1), 42.6 and 49.6, is then to be seen in Isa. 60.1-3. It would appear that this passage quite plainly assumes that the reader is familiar with the earlier assurances that light will dawn for Israel, marking a new era of deliverance. It should be noted, however, that the use of the same metaphor in 58.8 and 10 already anticipates the usage that is found in ch. 60. The prophecy is addressed to Jerusalem and the allusion back to the royal-messianic motifs of 9.2 is strongly evident:

---

22. Cf. the review of the various possibilities in D.W. van Winkle, 'The Relationship of the Nations to Yahweh and to Israel in Isaiah xl–lv', *VT* 35 (1985), pp. 446-58; G.I. Davies, 'The Destiny of the Nations in the Book of Isaiah', in Vermeylen (ed.), *The Book of Isaiah*, pp. 93-120.

Arise shine; for your light has come,
  And the glory of YHWH has dawned on you.
For darkness shall cover the earth,
  And thick darkness the peoples;
But YHWH will arise upon you,
  And his glory will appear over you.
Nations shall come to your light,
  And kings to the brightness of your dawn (Isa. 60.1-3).

The closeness of the reference back to the darkness covering the earth taken from 8.22 is noteworthy and the importance of the imagery of light is then given a further poetic exposition in 60.19-20. What such light implies is then interpreted in practical terms in 60.21-22.

4. Conclusion

The argument of this study has endeavoured to relate closely the three key passages in which the metaphor of light as a sign of salvation occurs in Isa. 9.2 (Heb. 9.1), 42.6 and 60.1-3. Other occurrences in the book are certainly relevant and related, but it is these key passages which are most directly concerned. It has been a consequence of the conventional division of the book of Isaiah into three separate collections of prophecies, each possessing its own context and character, that the close connections between all three passages have been largely ignored, or overlooked. The result has been that the ambiguities and uncertainties regarding what it means, in an Isaianic context, for the servant-Israel to be 'a light to the nations' is far from clear. It is also worthy of note that the close links with the royal-Zion motifs are also more fully brought out when all three passages are seen in conjunction with each other.

Seen in this broader context of the book of Isaiah as a formal and structural unity, certainly, the nations are expected to participate in Israel's salvation, not simply as onlookers and spectators, but directly as those who will enjoy its benefits. Ancient motifs, in their origin closely tied to the mythological motif of the temple mount as a divine dwelling-place and of the royal dynasty of David as bringers of truth and righteousness, are then vividly expressed in Isa. 2.2-4. Mount Zion is the location from which truth, righteousness and justice will be dispensed among all nations. Those who come there will come willingly to seek knowledge of the ways of God (Isa. 2.3). Jerusalem is to be a city of light, as the late passage 30.19-26 further affirms. It then becomes a wholly fitting rubric in 2.5, no doubt inserted by an enthusiastic scribe, to invite Israel to walk in the light of the knowledge of God, which is its treasure:

O house of Jacob, come, let us walk in the light of YHWH! (Isa. 2.5).

Chapter 14

ZION AS SYMBOL AND POLITICAL REALITY:
A CENTRAL ISAIANIC QUEST

The fact that the book of Isaiah is presented as a literary unity, but that its component parts can be clearly identified as deriving from a period spanning at least two centuries and probably considerably more, raises fundamental issues concerning the nature of biblical prophecy in general. It is possible to maintain a wide variety of opinions as to what exactly this composite authorship implies. On one side those scholars who have believed that the tradition concerning authorship is sacrosanct and that, in spite of apparently conflicting evidence, an essential unity of authorship must be upheld, have been forced to argue that prophetic prediction might possibly explain even the presence of seemingly impossible details being disclosed long in advance of the events which rendered them meaningful.[1] It is possible on the other hand to defend the book's unity as primarily a literary fact, implying little at all regarding authorship, but which must nevertheless be respected since any attempt to unravel it, or to trace its emergence, becomes fraught with uncertainties.[2] Between such positions, less stringent approaches have noted that, like other prophetic texts, the book of Isaiah shows many characteristic features of being an anthology of material, drawn from different times but carefully edited into a whole. This necessarily raises major methodological problems regarding our ability to identify levels of tradition both within the smaller sections, and even more seriously within the larger framework of the whole.[3]

1. J.N. Oswalt, *The Book of Isaiah, Chapters 1–39* (NICOT; Grand Rapids: Eerdmans, 1986); A. Motyer, *The Prophecy of Isaiah* (Leicester: IVP, 1993), pp. 25-29.
2. Cf. the approach advocated by E.W. Conrad, *Reading Isaiah* (Overtures to Biblical Theology; Minneapolis: Fortress Press, 1991), pp. 3-33.
3. Cf. C.R. Seitz, 'The Divine Council: Temporal Transition and New Prophecy in the Book of Isaiah', *JBL* 109 (1990), pp. 229-47, esp. 245-46.

1. *Intertextuality and the Structure of Isaiah*

The present essay is an attempt to offer a contribution towards a better understanding of the relationship between Isaiah 1–39 and 40–66 by noting two neglected passages which have a bearing on the issue. Within any approach to the question of this relationship it is methodologically possible to discern a measure of division of intent between the work of editors and the work of prophetic authors who have simply introduced fresh prophecies appropriate to new situations which nevertheless bear a relationship to what had already been preserved. The aim of the less prominent editors would have been to assist the reader in recognizing important points of transition. This was accomplished by marking them with superscriptions or closures, and it is the presence of a significant number of such editorial aids that is a distinctive feature of the book of Isaiah. In many cases it must be assumed that major editorial restructuring became necessary in order to take account of events that had transpired after the original prophecies had been recorded. These events called for a substantial re-orientation of earlier sayings without necessitating their abandonment altogether. It would have been necessary, in many instances to show that the foretold time of divine judgment was now ended and was soon to be replaced by renewal and restoration. A distinctive literary consequence of this is that, whereas the most pronounced message of the earliest prophets was one of threat and coming divine judgment, in their final form all the major prophetic books are broadly messages of hope for Israel's future.[4] This feature is especially relevant to understanding the division between Isaiah 1–39 and 40–66. The very nature of the book, and with it the understanding of the nature of prophecy, becomes very differently perceived once this connection between the two parts is broken.

A further aspect of the book of Isaiah lies in the presence within it of passages in which specific metaphors have been re-used and re-applied, frequently in sharply contrasted ways.[5] Thereby patterns of contrast and *inclusio* have been set up which help towards demonstrating the connection between distinct parts. The literary unity then becomes both theologically and artistically recognizable. The phenomenon of intertextual linkage within the book not only reveals important features about the manner of its origin, but is also relevant to the understanding of its overall message. It is true that in some cases repetition and *inclusio* appear as little more than artistic

---

4. Cf. R.E. Clements, 'Patterns in the Prophetic Canon', in G.W. Coats and B.O. Long (eds.), *Canon and Authority: Essays in Old Testament Religion and Theology* (Philadelphia: Westminster Press, 1977), pp. 42-55.

5. Cf. my 'Patterns in the Prophetic Canon: Healing the Blind and the Lame', in G.M. Tucker, D.L. Petersen and R.R. Wilson (eds.), *Canon, Theology and Old Testament Interpretation: Essays in Honor of Brevard S. Childs* (Philadelphia: Westminster Press, 1988), pp. 189-200.

devices to hold together diverse sayings which have little in common other than their use of the same metaphor or theme. More generally, however, the use of such devices appears intended to reflect some deeper ideological level of unity.

There is an evident need, from the perspective of a methodological enquiry, to identify the larger structural patterns within a prophetic book, as well as the intertextual significance of recurrent themes and metaphors in the various parts of it. Continuity and discontinuity, unity and difference, are all present as recognizable features, making the identification of the different growth levels a complex proceeding. Since this intricate literary production is itself a reflection of the way that prophecy was interpreted and used as a means of encouraging, and holding together, a community suffering times of extreme stress and danger, a wider theological interest attaches to it. Prophecy served as a marker for community identity[6] and the various literary techniques and devices used in it bear testimony to the manner of its origin. The edited collections of prophecies were expected to shape the lives of the community to whom they were addressed. The extent to which recent research has shown how intricate, and often seemingly arbitrary, examples of literary word-play, are used alongside more familiar rhetorical and poetic devices of oral preaching shows that prophecy developed as a scribal, as well as a rhetorical, pursuit. Examination of the phenomenon of intertextuality has thereby given rise to a significant shift in the interpretation of prophecy by showing the extent to which its development was furthered by literary techniques and written preservation. The scribe could become a prophet by exploring his literary skills and artistry. From a broader biblical perspective it is arguable that it is this literary stage in the rise of prophecy which has given to it its most enduring influence. The particular situation of the preacher was extended and reshaped by written preservation into a more universal message of the scribe who could address not one age, but many ages. Through the creation of a book Isaiah of Jerusalem could address all humanity.

A major concern of the application of an intertextual methodology to the study of the book of Isaiah must therefore be, not simply to note the interconnections within it as a literary anthology, but to seek beneath its surface for its larger structure. It is behind these that we can hope to discover those factors which gave it momentum and which provide sufficient cohesive constraint to make the notion of unity a meaningful one. To a considerable extent the search for such factors could only really begin, once the mistaken belief in the unity of authorship of all sixty-six chapters was finally abandoned. That unity was explicable in terms of a single author became a

---

6.   Cf. P.D. Hanson, *The People Called: The Growth of Community in the Bible* (San Francisco: Harper & Row, 1986), pp. 253-90.

dangerous device for failing to note the real basis of the book's unity. At the same time, the attempt to counter this by assuming that we are essentially dealing with two, or more probably three, separate and unconnected books of prophecy, with a corresponding trinity of authors, has also proved misleading.

It is then an exciting and stimulating advance of recent methodology to have begun the task of tracing carefully the basic motives and themes which give to the book its essential unity. In this research it is an immense pleasure to pay tribute to the rewarding and pioneering insights of a scholar whose commentaries have contributed richly towards the fulfilment of such a goal.

2. Isaiah—One Book or Two?

We may set as a matter of first importance the question which undoubtedly stands as the most central of those which the book presents. This is whether we are seeking to interpret two books which have been joined together at some unknown point of time, or whether we are not seriously and essentially seeking to interpret one single book which has been built up and augmented in a manner unique to the nature of prophecy. It is this question which bears directly on the nature, and underlying assumptions, of the connection between chs. 1–39 and chs. 40–66. Already a substantial range of exegetical studies has drawn attention to the many intertextual connections which exist between the two parts.[7] These links and interconnections undoubtedly exist. The need is therefore to explain them in relation to the way in which prophecy was understood to provide an ongoing medium for revealing the will of God.

A point of immediate significance, which provides a central point of focus for the present study, concerns the nature and purpose of the connections between the original Isaiah call-narrative of Isa. 6.1-13 and the opening address to Zion-Jerusalem in Isa. 40.1-11.[8] That the latter has been

---

7. Cf. R.E. Clements, 'Beyond Tradition-History: Deutero-Isaianic Development of First Isaiah's Themes', *JSOT* 31 (1985), pp. 95-113 (repr. in R.E. Clements, *Old Testament Prophecy: From Oracles to Canon* [Louisville, KY: Westminster/John Knox Press, 1996], pp. 78-92, and also in P.R. Davies [ed.], *The Prophets: A Sheffield Reader* [Sheffield: Sheffield Academic Press, 1996], pp. 128-46); now also esp. Seitz, 'The Divine Council'; Seitz, 'How is the Prophet Isaiah Present in the Latter Half of the Book? The Logic of Chapters 40–66 within the Book of Isaiah', *JBL* 115 (1990), pp. 219-40; H.G.M. Williamson, *The Book Called Isaiah: Deutero-Isaiah's Role in Composition and Redaction* (Oxford: Clarendon Press, 1994), and the extensive secondary literature cited by these scholars.

8. Cf. especially R Rendtorff, 'Jesaja 6 im Rahmen der Komposition des Jesajabuches', in J. Vermeylen (ed.), *The Book of Isaiah* (BETL, 81; Leuven: Leuven University Press, 1989), pp. 73-82 = 'Isaiah 6 in the Framework of the Composition of the

influenced by the former and makes clear and demonstrable allusions back to a number of its central assertions appears sufficiently evident as to be accepted as a datum. It then becomes important to explore the implications of this more fully.

It remains something of a legacy of the claim that we are primarily dealing with two distinct and identifiable prophetic individuals that the link between the two passages should be understood in terms of a prophetic call and the sense of a new call, or commission, by which a further message from God is to be added to that of Isaiah by a new prophet. Accordingly, as Isaiah 6 presents the story of the call of Isaiah of Jerusalem, so Isa. 40.1-8 (11) has been viewed as the call-narrative of Deutero-Isaiah.[9] In this way something of the *persona* and sense of divine commissioning appropriate to the originating figure of Isaiah is taken up and renewed through the new prophet.

Clearly there is a measure of validity for such an approach since different individuals undoubtedly stand behind the text. However it is striking that if the unit is taken as comprising 40.1-11 so that vv. 9-11 are an integral part of it, the address is explicitly to Zion—Jerusalem, rather than an individual prophetic figure. The city itself has become personified as the message-bearer of the good news. This links up with the form of the opening address to an unknown comforter in vv. 1-2 who is bidden to 'speak reassuringly' to Jerusalem. Seitz would see this as a prophetic employment of the form of a speech from within the heavenly council of Yahweh.[10]

The case is strong, however, for regarding Jerusalem-Zion as the intended addressee throughout the passage, with a natural progression from a rhetorical appeal to an unspecified comforter for Jerusalem to one in which the city itself becomes the message-bearer whose changed fortunes constitute the good news of the new message. Since the content of the message is one of comfort and re-assurance for Jerusalem the different modes of address are simply different ways of drawing attention to this. It would seem that the idea of an extended form of call-narrative as the explanation of the unexpected form of Isa. 40.1-11 is largely occasioned by the conscious harking back to the call narrative of Isa. 6.1-13. In other respects it is not particularly significant since the new passage is emphatically concerned to demonstrate that what is now revealed is not wholly distinct, but is the essential continuation of the earlier message. It presents a call to declare the 'new things' which are to replace the 'former things' which have now been fulfilled.

Book', in R. Rendtorff, *Canon and Theology* (Overtures to Biblical Theology; Minneapolis: Fortress Press, 1993), pp. 170-80; Seitz, 'The Divine Council', pp. 238-43.

9. Cf. Seitz, 'The Divine Council', pp. 231-32; Williamson, *The Book Called Isaiah*, pp. 151-54.

10. Seitz, 'The Divine Council', pp. 229-33.

In reality the connection between chs. 1–39 and 40–66 can be fully understood in terms of the centrality of the theme of Zion-Jerusalem as the centre of divine rule and authority for the formation of the book of Isaiah.[11] The words of 40.1-11 take on a new significance once it is understood that, after the catastrophe of 587 BCE, the unanswered question which pervaded the entire *traditio* of Isaiah's prophesying was 'What future can there be for Zion, now that the temple has been destroyed?' Against such a background the connection between the two major parts of the book becomes self-explanatory. A central part of our argument therefore is that, instead of seeking to follow out any sense of connection between 1–39 and 40–66 in terms of two sequential prophetic call experiences, we can find a more explicit linkage through the concern with Jerusalem—Zion as the central theme of the separate parts of the book.

3. *Isaiah—Prophet of Zion*

A major change in the understanding of the relationship between the prophet Isaiah and the centrality of the Jerusalem temple traditions in the Psalter was brought about by S. Mowinckel in his *Psalmenstudien II*.[12] This change was based on the recognition that the Isaiah-narrative tradition of Isaiah 36–37 concerning Jerusalem's miraculous deliverance from the clutches of Sennacherib in 701 BCE has been shaped by the cult mythology of Mount Zion. This is shown by such psalms as 46 and 48 and reflects the belief in the protection afforded to Israel by Yahweh's choosing the sacred mountain as his dwelling-place. Accordingly the influence upon the entire Isaiah book from this Jerusalem psalmic background has been extensive, not only because the prophet himself was affected by it, but because the tradition of his sayings continued to be moulded by it.

The most extensive and far-reaching effect of this influence is to be seen in the way in which the story of what took place in 701 BCE was then given a revised presentation in the light of later events, most especially the disaster of Jerusalem's destruction in 587 BCE.[13] The wider perspectives of this revised presentation have then been incorporated extensively into the whole

---

11. Cf. C.R. Seitz, 'Isaiah 1–66: Making Sense of the Whole', in Seitz, *Reading and Preaching the Book of Isaiah* (Philadelphia: Fortress Press, 1988), pp. 105-26, esp. pp. 115-16.

12. Cf. Seitz, 'The Divine Council', pp. 231-32; Williamson, *The Book Called Isaiah*, pp. 151-54.

13. R.E. Clements, *Isaiah and the Deliverance of Jerusalem: A Study of the Interpretation of Prophecy in the Old Testament* (JSOTSup, 13; Sheffield: JSOT Press, 1980); C.R. Seitz, *Zion's Final Destiny: The Development of the Book of Isaiah* (Minneapolis: Fortress Press, 1991), esp. pp. 119-48.

traditio of the sayings of First Isaiah. The story of the events of the years 705–701 BCE, and the reworking and editing of Isaiah's prophecies which this necessitated, provide the indispensable background for understanding the link between the so-called First and Second Isaiah. It is not only from a literary perspective that chs. 36–39 form a bridge to the fresh continuation of the message of Isaiah; they also provide an essential theological preparation for it. Our argument is that, once the effect of this edited presentation of Isaiah's prophecies is recognized, then the manner in which Isa. 40.1-11 takes up the unresolved question of the Isaiah prophetic *traditio* becomes plain.

Mowinckel's own subsequent suggestions regarding the work of Isaiah's presumed 'disciples' and the cult-prophets of Jerusalem would accord reasonably well with such a perspective[14] Instead of looking for one or two major 'authors' to explain the book, we can better recognize that a series of formative stages are present in it, largely determined by the events which befell Jerusalem between the eighth and fifth centuries BCE. Moreover, it has become evident from the extensive and detailed study of the narrative tradition of Isaiah 36–37 that this is not from a single literary source but has been built up from separate source materials and composed over a period of time by a specific circle of Jerusalem prophet-scribes. That these shared close links with the circles which produced the so-called Deuteronomistic History (Joshua–2 Kings) is also evident. Mowinckel's suggestion that the *traditio* of Isaiah's prophecies was maintained within a group of cult-prophets from Jerusalem would seem to be not far wide of the mark. We can therefore better grasp the nature of the growth of the book of Isaiah by recognizing the work of a plurality of authors from a Jerusalem temple circle than by endeavoring to focus on two individuals—the presumed authors of First and Second Isaiah.

Our contention is that it is this continuing relationship between the different parts of the scroll of Isaiah and the cult-tradition of Jerusalem that establishes its fundamental unity. Succeeding generations of cult-prophets working in the city, even after the temple's destruction in 587 BCE, can more readily be regarded as the authors of the book which bears Isaiah's name than any two individual figures. Moreover, it is the rise and fall, and subsequent re-establishing after 587 BCE, of the cult ideology of Jerusalem that explains the peculiar shifts and apparent incongruities in the book. Its shape has been brought about by the desire to uphold the central claims of Jerusalem as a religious and spiritual centre first in a very positive and triumphalist manner in the wake of the events surrounding Sennacherib's capture of the city in 701 BCE, and then, more than a century later, after the further

14. S. Mowinckel, *Jesaja-disiplene. Profeten fra Jesaja til Jeremia* (Oslo: Aschehoug [Nygaard], 1925).

disasters of 598 and 587 BCE. Its message is clearly 'Let Jerusalem live—even though the temple has been destroyed!'

Once we look away from the concern with individual authorship as a controlling principle and focus instead on the relationship between prophecy and Mount Zion, the site of the most central religious institution of Israel, we can make better sense of the complex shape which the book of Isaiah displays. It gives full weight to the strong evidence that a considerable number of authors and editors have taken a hand in producing the finished scroll. Far from the linkage between chs. 1–39 and 40–55 being a confusing and distorted one, such a connection can be seen to be essential for an understanding of the function which the emergent prophetic book fulfilled. It served to interpret and uphold the controlling authority of Jerusalem and its cultus as the primary religious institution of Judaism. In doing so it had to take account of events which appeared to discredit such a message of hope. Such a goal extended far beyond Jerusalem's original eminence as a national capital where the nation's ruling monarchs were enthroned. It affirmed its over-riding function as the sole legitimate place for sacrificial offerings and as the arbiter of power and truth in the worship of the God of the Jews. Once the first beginnings of the Jewish Dispersion began to emerge, initially exemplified by the fate of those deported to Babylon in 598 BCE, the need for re-establishing Jerusalem's claim to authority became stronger than ever. The existence of several such scattered communities begins to appear very strongly in Isaiah 40–55 and reveals their locations far beyond the relatively small community held in Babylon.

It is the concern to re-assert and re-establish this dominant position of Jerusalem and its religious significance as the holy mountain of God after the debacle of 587 BCE when the temple was destroyed which provides a key to understanding why there are necessary connections between Isaiah 1–39, 40–55 and 56–66. In a rather unexpected fashion it shows that even the seemingly anti-temple sentiment of Isa. 66.1 is important to the theology of the book which strives to uphold that, even though the Jerusalem temple had at one time suffered physical destruction and lain in ruins, the status of Jerusalem as God's chosen centre was never placed in question.

4. *The Remnant from Jerusalem*

In order to substantiate this claim concerning the central importance of Zion as a unifying theme, it is helpful to consider the function of two neglected passages within the book which illustrate the background to Isa. 40.1-11.

The first of these passages in Isa. 37.30-32 occurs as the second of the prophecies attributed to Isaiah at the time when Jerusalem was threatened with siege and capture by Jerusalem. In reality it is undoubtedly the third, and latest, of the three such prophecies to have been composed. Since I have already elsewhere dealt extensively with the narratives concerning the confrontation between Hezekiah and Sennacherib and with these three prophecies attributed to Isaiah in particular.[15] There is little need to do more than to reiterate my conclusions here. The prophecy reads:

> And this shall be the sign for you: This year eat what grows of itself, in the second year what springs from that; then in the third year sow, reap, plant vineyards, and eat their fruit. The surviving remnant of the house of Judah shall again take root downward, and bear fruit upward; for from Jerusalem a remnant shall go out, and from Mount Zion a band of survivors. The zeal of the LORD of hosts will do this (Isa. 37.30-32 NRSV).

By far the most striking aspect of the prophecy is to be found in the acknowledgement in vv. 31-32 that the population of Judah will be reduced to a 'surviving remnant' but that this remnant will again be securely rooted in its land. Most remarkably of all, this surviving remnant is directly linked in v. 32 to the population of Jerusalem and Mount Zion. The historic Zion motif of the divine holy mountain, which clearly exercised a formative role in the composition and theology of the story of how Jerusalem was delivered from the clutches of Sennacherib in 701 BCE, is here linked with a newly devised 'remnant motif', itself clearly drawn from the name of Isaiah's child Shear-jashub of Isa. 7.3. The divine protection for Jerusalem made possible through God's presence on the holy mountain has become the basis for an assurance that a 'band of survivors' will remain, and will flourish again in Jerusalem.

It is necessary to recall a number of widely recognized literary and historical conclusions regarding the setting of this prophecy for its importance to be understood. It is noteworthy that, although the narrative sequence of Isa. 36.1–39.8 shows affinities both with the Deuteronomistic History of Joshua–2 Kings and an early collection of Isaianic prophecies, some measure of independence from both is also evident. Overall these narratives are concerned to show how and why Jerusalem was spared from Sennacherib in 701 BCE. They were clearly not contemporary compositions from Isaiah's time and, as is the case with this particular prophecy, they show a degree of dependence upon a preserved collection of authentic Isaianic sayings. They have been composed no earlier than the time in the late seventh century when Assyrian control over Judah was waning. Taken collectively these narratives show signs of composite authorship and have reached their final form over an extended period of time. Whether or not they formed any part

---

15. R.E. Clements, 'The Prophecies of Isaiah to Hezekiah Concerning Sennacherib: 2 Kings 19.21-34/2 Sam 37.22-35', in R. Liwak and S. Wagner (eds.), *Prophetie and geschichtliche Wirklichkeit im Alten Israel. Festschrift für Siegfried Herrmann zum 65. Geburtstag* (Stuttgart: Kohlhammer, 1991), pp. 65-78 = Clements, *Old Testament Prophecy*, pp. 35-48.

of an original draft of the Deuteronomistic History appears doubtful. For understanding the book of Isaiah their importance is that they show how Isaiah's message was being related to the interpretation of one of the most remarkable events of the prophet's lifetime at some interval after his death. They display a marked theological emphasis upon the power of Yahweh, God of Israel to defend Jerusalem for his own sake and that of the Davidic royal house that sat enthroned there (Isa. 37.35 // 2 Kgs 18.34).[16]

The survival of Jerusalem and its Davidic monarchy in the face of Assyrian oppression appeared as a self-evidencing fact of divine providence which clearly reached a dangerous level of extravagance once that oppressive control began to wane.[17] It is this triumphalist perspective which has not only shaped the content which the narrative reports express, but has brought substantial revision and addition to the collection of Isaiah's prophecies from the eighth century.

The prophetic saying of Isa. 37.31-32 can confidently be attributed to a time after 587 BCE, when its reference to 'a band of survivors' going out from Mount Zion took on a very specific and significant meaning. Virtually all of Judah had been reduced to a ruin by the prolonged Babylonian siege and the deliberate devastation of the land (cf. Deut. 28.38-42; 29.22-23). The identification of the surviving remnant in Judah as the basis for hope of renewal and restoration is remarkable. All the more is this the case, since the regional administration was moved for a period to Mizpah (Jer. 40.6-16; 41.1-10). The saying is little more than a clinging to the belief in the unique role of Mount Zion as a source of divine protection and blessing after events had seriously challenged its older and more comprehensive form.

It is not difficult to relate historically the situation presupposed by the prophecy of Isa. 37.30-32 with that which pertained for a relatively brief period after the events of 587 BCE. Gedaliah's brief control as governor from Mizpah was brought dramatically to an end by his assassination (Jer. 41.18). Eventually all expectation that any immediate return to a situation of stability and social normality, such as the words of Isa. 37.30 reflect, proved to be impossible. We can readily see from the emphatic editorial assertions of Jer. 25.1-11 and 27.1-11 that resignation to a time of chaos and destitution prevailed in Judah (so especially Jer. 25.11). All hope subsequently came to be directed toward the community which had been taken to Babylon in 598 BCE (Jer. 27.22; 29.10), eventually to be augmented by others who arrived there later. No doubt the presence of scions from the Davidic royal

---

16. Cf. R.E. Clements, 'The Politics of Blasphemy: Zion's God and the Threat of Imperialism', in I. Kottsieper et al. (eds.), *'Wer ist wie du, Herr, unter den Göttern?' Studien zur Theologie und Religionsgeschichte Israels für Otto Kaiser zum 70. Geburtstag* (Göttingen: Vandenhoeck & Ruprecht, 1994), pp. 231-46.

17. Cf. C. Hardmeier, *Prophetie im Streit vor dem Untergang Judas* (BZAW, 187; Berlin: W. de Gruyter, 1990).

house in Babylon greatly strengthened such expectations. A return of the scattered remnants of the nation, most especially of that section of the nation which had been removed to Babylon, seemingly by an act of providential wisdom, gave a new focus to the idea of a remnant, no longer directly to be identified with survivors in Jerusalem. In the process the very concept of Israel called for substantial revision and extension. We can discern the same tensions and uncertainties well reflected in the latest stages of revision and addition that have been incorporated into the Deuteronomistic narrative of 2 Kgs 25.27-30. In other passages too the shadow of the events of 587 BCE are to be seen (notably 1 Kgs 8.46-53).

The recognition that the perspective offered by these Isaiah narratives marks a major formative stage in the literary development of the Isaiah tradition represents a considerable advance in understanding its overall theological shape. How the events of Isaiah's time, especially those surrounding Jerusalem's deliverance from destruction by Sennacherib, appeared in the light of the events of the next century became a matter of first importance. After the resurgence of Davidic fortunes under Josiah (639–609 BCE) Hezekiah's survival appeared to have been a miracle! So, after the events of the next half century, the prophecy of Isa. 37.31-32 reflects a sense that the tradition of Zion's unique role for the destiny of Israel remained valid. It was, nevertheless, compelled to undergo significant changes to take account of the realities of later events. We know that, in the political turmoil that followed the murder of Gedaliah, the governor of Judah, even this hope of a renewal arising from within the region did not last for long.

Acceptance that the land would lie desolate for a prolonged period and that the restoration would have to come through a return of those deported to Babylon became the normative expression of Jewish hope. This was the case at least in approved official circles. The transition from a hope based on renewal from within Judah and Jerusalem to one focused instead on a return of the exiles from Babylon can be seen as a fundamental shift of perspective in the tradition of Jeremiah's prophesying and also in that of the final editing of the Deuteronomistic History. It is well to the fore also in the preserved edition of Ezekiel's prophecies. The evidence provided by the narratives of Isaiah 36–39 in their relation to the formation of the book of Isaiah reveals that a similar shift of perspective has deeply influenced this process also.[18]

Once the significance of the narrative tradition of Isaiah 36–39 as a mirror of the reception history of Isaiah's prophesying is taken into account, then

---

18. Cf. P.R. Ackroyd, 'Isaiah 36–39: Structure and Function', in W.C. Delsman *et al.* (eds.), *Von Kanaan bis Kerala: Festschrift für Prof. Mag. Dr Dr J.P.M. van der Ploeg O.P. zur Vollendung des siebzigsten Lebensjahres* (AOAT, 211; Kevelaer: Butzon & Bercker, 1982), pp. 3-21 (repr. in Ackroyd, *Studies in the Religious Tradition of the Old Testament* [London: SCM Press, 1987], pp. 105-20).

the necessity for further explanation and understanding of the divine commitment to Mount Zion and its temple was urgently called for. Not only do the narratives provide an important literary point of linkage between the earliest written collection of Isaiah's prophecies and those which have been added in chs. 40ff., but they also offer the necessary theological basis for the connection. Isaiah's message had been recorded and shaped so as to uphold the traditional mythological understanding of the divine commitment to Mount Zion and its temple, and to the Davidic dynasty which had been inseparably linked to this. The events of 587 BCE in which the Jerusalem temple had been destroyed and the Davidic dynasty removed from its royal throne had set in question all such belief in Mount Zion's role as a place of refuge and a source of light and power to the nations. Could there be any credible feature left of the ancient holy mountain mythology which would continue to command respect when no Davidic king ruled from the city and no temple any longer stood amid its ruins? The unique interest of the short prophecy ascribed to Isaiah in Isa. 37.31-32 lies in its contention that such a belief could be upheld and provide a basis of hope for Judah's future:

> The surviving remnant of the house of Judah shall again take root downward and bear fruit upward: for from Jerusalem a remnant shall go out and from Mount Zion a band of survivors (Isa. 37.31-32).

In a number of respects it is worthwhile to note that this short prophetic saying expresses by its implications many of the same theological characteristics which are to be found in Jer. 3.15-16. This short Deuteronomistic reflection on the future role of Jerusalem, which marks a significant editorial gloss to Jeremiah's prophecies, is concerned to take account of the events of 587 BCE, which are the most likely occasion for the loss of the ark. Its message is clear that, even without such a revered cult-object, Jerusalem, simply as a city, will provide God's earthly throne. In a similar way the Isaianic prophecy that we have considered faces the question: 'What is left for Jerusalem once the temple has been destroyed and the Davidic family taken into exile?' The answer is given in terms of a remnant from which the new nation will arise. Israel's future is seen still to lie with the divine commitment to Mount Zion, in spite of all the setbacks and humiliations that the Holy City had suffered.

It seems highly probable that another brief, and seemingly isolated, passage in Isaiah 1–39 reflects the same situation and emanates from the same general concern:

> What will one answer the messengers of the nation?
> 'The LORD has founded Zion,
>   and the needy among his people
>   will find refuge in her' (Isa. 14.32).

In this case the lack of any reference to a remnant, or any indication that Judah had suffered a severe period of adversity and destruction makes its chronological assignation difficult.

Nevertheless it is the insistence upon Zion being a place of refuge and protection for Yahweh's people on account of its divine foundation that lends it special interest. If it is to be dated after the events of 587 BCE then clearly it is further evidence that even these disasters had not finally put an end to the belief that Jerusalem occupied a special place in the divine government and protection of Israel. It did, however, necessitate a significant shift of emphasis away from the ark-throne theology of a temple sanctuary once the temple had been destroyed. Instead it was necessary to insist that the very location of Mount Zion, as Yahweh's chosen throne-foundation, still fulfilled such a special role. We find many of the same theological shifts in a desire to re-mint the traditional temple theology of divine presence emerging at this time in the Deuteronomic Movement.[19]

However it was not only the desecration of the temple and its altars which presented a problem for the retention of the belief in Jerusalem's special position as a source of divine blessing and enlightenment after the Babylonian destruction. After Gedaliah's murder the rise of new leadership and vitality among the various settlements of scattered Jewish communities shifted Judah's geographical horizons much further afield to new, and in many instances, very distant locations. For these people too the importance of Jerusalem as the site in which all religious power and authority was vested had to be re-asserted. In a real measure the revival of Jerusalem's fortunes as a focus of religious leadership and worship became a paramount concern if the integrity and unity of Jewish worship of the one God Yahweh was to be meaningfully maintained. Jerusalem would have a very different role to play in the world after 587 BCE from that which it had previously fulfilled. Yet this new role was to be built on, and in part validated by, the older tradition of Mount Zion as the cosmic mountain on which Yahweh had settled for his abode.

5. *Good News for the Watchers of Zion*

It is against such a historical and theological background that we can best understand the connection between Isa. 40.1-11 and the prophecies and narratives which have preceded it. Once we recognize that, by the middle of the sixth century BCE, events had raised in a most dramatic fashion the question 'What is to become of Jerusalem and Mount Zion?', then we can

---

19. Cf. T.N.D. Mettinger, *The Dethronement of Sabaoth: Studies in the Shem and Kabod Theologies* (CBOT, 18; Lund: C.W.K. Gleerup, 1982).

see that the new prophetic voice which speaks in Isa. 40.1-11 addresses, not only Jerusalem as a city, but the precise question which the disasters that had befallen the city raised. The theme of Mount Zion's central role as a political centre and symbol of Jewish hope henceforth becomes the dominant one for the remainder of the book of Isaiah, especially in chs. 49–55 and 60–62. In reality, however, it is not simply these chapters, but the final form of the book as a unified whole which exemplifies this.

A further major critical issue calls for careful re-examination in the light of this fact. The first of these concerns the location and setting of the prophetic materials contained in Isaiah 40–55. For too long the theory of 'the unnamed prophet of the exile' has held sway as the majority viewpoint offering the most probable indication of the author's situation. The important references to Babylon, the rise of Cyrus as a threat to Babylon, and the impending downfall of Babylon as the city of oppression have seemed sufficient to support this. Yet a highly respected minority opinion has doubted such a conclusion, taking instead the many explicit forms of address to Jerusalem and Zion as indications that the author cannot have been located far from this city.[20] Moreover, the perspective adopted is that of an observer picturing from Jerusalem's walls the imminent return of lost and distant exiles from the city (Isa. 49.18; 52.1-2, 7-9) like the homecoming of wandering children returning to their parents.

---

20. Cf. especially A.S. Kapelrud, *Et folk på hjemferd. 'Trosteprofeten'—den annen Jesaja—og hans budskap* (Oslo: Universitetsforlaget, 1964); H.M. Barstad, *A Way in the Wilderness* (JSSM, 12; Manchester: University of Manchester, 1989).

Chapter 15

ISAIAH 1.1-31: ISRAEL SUMMONED TO REPENTANCE—
THE INTRODUCTION TO THE ISAIAH BOOK

A widespread agreement is evident among recent commentators on the Isaiah book that Isa. 1.1-31 is designed to serve as an introduction to the book more widely. Plainly this is the case with the opening superscription in 1.1 which conforms to the widely adopted pattern of introducing the prophet by name and providing a historical location for his activity in relation to the kings reigning at the time. However, in regard to 1.2-31 this insight calls for fuller examination and explanation concerning the precise scope of the book which such a long introduction serves. More importantly it demands a fuller understanding of how it functions in relation to the larger work.

1. *The Scope of the Isaiah Book*

It is a major contention of the studies set out here that an especially significant guide to recovering a closer understanding of the documentary units from which the present Isaiah book has been assembled is provided by noting the 'beginnings' and 'endings' which at one time served to provide literary frameworks to separate compositional units. Admittedly such formal categorising of shorter sections cannot be a wholly definitive means for such identification and most commentators have worked on the assumption that a number of additions, transpositions and dislocations are present within these sub-units. These inevitably add to the complexity of the task. In similar vein the intrusion of intertextual allusions and references adds a further dimension since it is not always clear at what stage in the process of composition such allusions were made. Some appear to be primary and to have initiated a new prophetic composition, whereas others appear to be later glosses which draw attention to a connection. Such considerations add to the complexity of the task of retracing the stages through which the present text has passed. Nevertheless in a significant number of cases a clear structural shape and literary coherence is discernible as a guide to the origin of the most important editorially structured units within the larger scroll of Isaiah.

A widely recognized and exemplary instance of such an 'ending' is to be seen in Isa. 12.1-6, where the psalm-like features and introductory 'You will say on that day...' have helped to confirm such a conclusion. The psalm appears to have been intended to serve as the ending of a literary structure of some kind. This, in turn, has encouraged the supposition that Isaiah 1–12 formed an original, *possibly the most original*, literary unit from which the book of Isaiah has been assembled.

This conclusion, however, must be rejected on the grounds that the entire section of Isa. 1.1–4.6 stands apart from the chapters which succeed it.[1] Similar problems reveal themselves in relation to Isa. 65.1–66.24 which also appear to be late additions to the final form of the Isaiah book. They show a number of close links in message and outlook to the opening four chapters. Taken together these six chapters show signs of being among the latest units to have been added to the Isaiah scroll. They provide an all-encompassing message of warning and threat. Effectively, with the exception of the new idea of a 'remnant', they reverse the overall message of hope which the bulk of the book expresses. They share with this an interest in the future of Jerusalem, but now regard the city as faced with imminent threat with its outcome uncertain. These six chapters (Isa. 1–4 and 65–66) anticipate that the future will be a time of judgment for Jerusalem and its leaders who are described as 'princes' in v. 23. Only for a few will the future prove to be a time of blessing and prosperity, since the community is to be purged of wrongdoers, who appear as the majority. Even 'the righteous' of Israel will be tested and refined by the judgment that is to come, leaving only a handful of survivors (cf. Isa. 1.9).

The development elsewhere in the Old Testament of this concept of a remnant in a positive sense tends to alleviate the strikingly negative connotation given to it in Isaiah 1. This in turn tends to mask its importance for understanding the literary implications of the sense in which it is used in chs. 1–4. Although at the beginning the much larger, ideal, community of all Israel as a people is addressed (1.2-4), the actualities of the author's present are focused on the small righteous element within this who have remained faithful (1.18-20). The concept of a 'remnant' therefore occupies a central position in Isaiah 1–4, with Jerusalem representing the spiritual centre of the nation (vv. 8-9), but not even all the citizens of Jerusalem are regarded as faithful (vv. 21-23).

---

1. Cf. M.A. Sweeney, *Isaiah 1–4 and the Post-Exilic Understanding of the Isaianic Tradition* (BZAW, 171; Berlin: W. de Gruyter, 1988), pp. 101-33; cf. also Sweeney, *Isaiah 1–39 with an Introduction to the Prophetic Literature* (FOTL, 16; Grand Rapids: Eerdmans, 1996), pp. 73-87.

The extended section of Isaiah 5–35, with chs. 36–39 added to them, must certainly be regarded as the most basic of the larger documentary units which make up what has become conventionally described as 'First Isaiah'. It contains the oldest material preserved in the book, even though this section too has undoubtedly been much expanded by later additions and reworking, which belong to the post-587 BCE era. The Isaiah book that we possess therefore cannot simply be divided between a pre-exilic and a post-exilic collection of prophecies.

From a literary point of view the whole of chs. 5–39 can readily be seen to fall into carefully planned and relatively self-contained blocks of material which share a common theme. However, this fact strongly suggests that it acquired this present structure from the joining together of collections of prophecies which had already been formed into literary units. As is the case with the entire corpus of the 'Latter Prophets' we are faced with the phenomenon that the needs of preservation and the goals of eliciting fresh interpretations from 'old' prophecies have led to the formation of fresh, carefully edited, literary structures. In this process a considerable degree of 'cross-referencing' has occurred, enabling a larger picture of the future to emerge.

What we are presented with in the present Isaiah book is an assemblage made up from separate compilations, which I have named 'booklets'. These have then been joined together to make up a larger, more comprehensive, work. This cannot have been undertaken any earlier than the Persian period, although some of its component parts appear to have been formed earlier.

In this context the distinctive character and thematic content of chs. 1–4 and 65–66 stands out. They introduce new themes which focus directly and almost exclusively, on problems that had arisen in Jerusalem; in doing so, they presume knowledge of the glorious hope for the city given elsewhere in the book. The city is now no longer portrayed as destined for glory and exaltation, offering truth and peace to the nations, but has become a different Jerusalem, ruled by villains and torn by strife and bloodshed. Those in power in the city are the enemies of the authors of these new warnings and it is the misdeeds of these people which provide the reason for this fresh introduction.

This revised message unashamedly declares that, at this new turning-point in the city's history, all the wonderful visions of the past may remain unrealised; the glorious future that the prophecies of Isaiah 35 and 60–62 had foretold may yet be forfeited and lost. In their future outlook the message of these chapters is so surprisingly different from that which otherwise predominates in the book, that the reader is made startlingly aware that a fresh, unexpected, crisis has arisen. The new message is admonitory, reproving of contemporary wrongs, and sensitive that a deep rift separates those in authority in the city from the authors of the chapter. These identify themselves with a group they call the 'righteous ones' who cling loyally to the demands of *torah*. Moreover, if Isa.1 and 65-66 are of later origin than Isaiah 2–4—a view that bears every sign of being correct—there is a real sense of a progressively deepening crisis. The misdemeanours condemned in Isa.1 are far more serious than those castigated in Isaiah 2–3.

The sense of a rift between those in power in Jerusalem and the authors of chs. 1–4 presents the most marked feature of this striking and memorable introductory unit (so especially 1.21-26, 27-31). The concluding chs. 65.1–66.24 similarly comprise a number of small units which display an irregular and seemingly contradictory character. The supreme assurances that provide the main core of the book with a message of confident hope (e.g. Isa. 35.1-10; 60.1-22) are now interspersed with dire, and even grotesque, warnings. Jerusalem's future is anything but assured. The primary message of the book in its full compass is still focused on the world-encompassing event concerning the forthcoming day of Yahweh; which lies in the future (Isa. 2.12-22). But it will be a day of purging and refining for Israel; those who will suffer Yahweh's judgment include many leaders in Jerusalem! Read against the background of Isaiah 35 and 60–62 with their exuberant optimism about Jerusalem's headship over many nations, this threatening message provides a fresh 'beginning' and 'ending' to the book of Isaiah. It appears sharply out of kilter with the central corpus of it. This includes all the 'First Isaiah' prophecies of chs. 5–39, considered as unit, as well as those of Isaiah 40–55 which shows every sign of having existed at one time as an independent literary composition.

2. The Little Book of Zion: Isaiah 2.1–4.6

If we take the presence of clearly recognizable beginnings and endings as a primary criterion, the prefatory unit of Isa. 2.1–4.6, which follows the introductory chapter, bears the marks of having at one time been assembled to form a complete, self-contained composition. This in no way implies that all the contents are from the same source or period, since there are indications that different units, with different themes, have been brought together in it to make up a single comprehensive structure. Once again the overall impression is that shorter, relatively small, units have been assembled to form a coherent larger 'booklet' characterised by a common theme. It may be described as 'the Little Book of Zion'. In it the wrongdoing and neglect of *torah* by the citizens, especially the women, of the city of Jerusalem are condemned. Some of the misdemeanours listed, however, appear personal, trivial and relatively mundane (so 2.16-17), in contrast to the arrogance and greed that are condemned in 3.13-15. The offences of Jerusalem's leaders in 1.21-23 appear even more serious. Because of this discrepancy in the seriousness of the offences condemned it is useful to consider the longer unit of 2.1–4.6 first before focusing on the opening chapter Isa. 1.1-31.

The 'Little Book of Zion' in 2.1–4.6 is introduced in 2.1 as an address to Judah and Jerusalem and the entire section is framed by the focus in 2.2-4 on the city as the centre from which *torah* is destined to go forth to direct the nations and to usher in an era of world peace (2.3). The concluding unit in Isa. 4.2-6 then returns to the theme of hope for Israel's future, but modifies this from the more assured message of Isaiah 60–62 by declaring that there will occur a final purging of Jerusalem from wickedness. Only after this has taken place can the longed for era of peace begin. The heavy dependence of the whole unit on other parts of the canonical scriptural tradition is particularly marked and points to awareness on the part of its authors that *torah* had by this time become firmly identified with an established body of written texts.

The central focus throughout the whole of 1.1–4.6 is on Jerusalem, its failures and the need for a new judgmental period of cleansing, which must take place before the final elevation of the city to its predestined glory among the nations can be realized. This contrasts strikingly with older parts of the book in 5.1–10.34 which addresses 'all Israel', and even more strikingly with the hope expressed in 60.1–62.12 for the gathering of all Israel's scattered members to Jerusalem as their spiritual 'home'.

The admonitions and warnings of Isa. 2.5–4.1 introduce a significant qualification of this hope. This is then carried still further in the opening ch. 1. The broadly expressed expectations of the coming of 'the Day of Yahweh' set out in 2.12-22 take up the Isaianic theme of the nothingness of all humanity compared to the majesty of God, but they appear to take little account of the contemporary political scene. In Isa. 1.21-31 a similar sharply focused warning declares that no salvation can be expected for Jerusalem until those who claim to be God's servants in the city repent and return to a genuine, *torah*-obedient, piety. In both these prefatory units the promise of Jerusalem's ultimate exaltation is not abandoned, but is reduced to the level of providing no more than a framework for a sharply worded indictment of those who rule the city. The reasons for this indictment form the substance of Isa. 2.1–4.6.

This 'little book of Zion' bears all the marks of being a carefully assembled unit with a coherent structure, either intended from the outset to serve as a preface to the larger book, or possibly at one time existing as an independent prophetic compilation dealing with Jerusalem's fall from grace. It appears highly unlikely that any of the material derives from as early as the eighth century BCE. It introduces the warning that the hope of Jerusalem's blessed future is contingent on obedience to fundamental ethical and religious obligations set out in *torah*. The misdemeanours mentioned that are rife in the city reflect cultic and ethical requirements, familiar from *torah* regulations.[2] The eschatology of the central body of the Isaianic prophetic collection is retained by the use of a literary *inclusio* of a beginning and ending, but is made contingent on the demands of *torah*. From this perspective it is no longer disastrous political decisions, whether of the past or present, which provide the central target of prophetic condemnation, but rather an indifference to *torah*. The issues that establish this accusation take the form of tolerance of foreigners, love of luxury and resort to strange cultic practices. The authorities in Jerusalem stand condemned because they are found wanting in respect of these demands.

M.A. Sweeney is not alone in noting the close links between chs. 1-4 and Isa. 65-66 where similar warnings threaten the inhabitants of Jerusalem. In this way the Isaiah book, as a remarkably long and extensive literary whole, is provided with a broad encompassing framework. It is an assemblage from several literary collections of prophecy which have been brought together in the post-exilic Persian era to present a comprehensive message about Jerusalem and its role among the nations. In their separate origin and development these collections display themes and structures which are still readily recognizable: (1) Isa. 5.1-10.34 has been given a supplement in 11.1-12.6; (2) Isa. 13.1-23.10 has received a supplement in 24.1-27.13 and (3) Isa. 28.1-32.20 has been given a supplement in 33.1-35.10; (4) In similar fashion Isa. 36.1-37.38 has received an additional supplement in 38.1-39.8. A book approximating to the general notion of 'First Isaiah' at one time existed in Isa. 5.1-39.8. The additions of chs. 40.1-55.13 (the 'Second Isaiah') and 56.1-64.12 (the 'Third Isaiah') were joined at later stages to this primary Isaiah collection. Finally the new 'beginning' and 'ending' of 1.1-2.4 and 65.1-66.24 provided a fresh, and sharply revisionist enclosure to the whole extended work.

The surprising feature is that this new framework shifts the message of the book in an unexpected new direction. It was clearly added at a late period and shows a pattern which contrasts with that of the book as a whole. Whereas in the 'Little Book of Zion' the richly optimistic beginning (2.1-4) and ending (4.2-6) enclose a consistently admonitory message, the admonitions of Isaiah 1 and 65–66 achieve the reverse effect. They enclose a message which remains guardedly re-assuring in its contents with sharp words of warning.

---

2. M.A. Sweeney, 'The Book of Isaiah as Prophetic Torah', in Roy F. Melugin and M.A. Sweeney (eds.), *New Visions of Isaiah* (JSOTSup, 214; Sheffield: Sheffield Academic Press, 1996), pp. 50-67; R.E. Clements, 'The Meaning of תורה in Isaiah 1–39', in J.G. McConville and K. Möller (eds.), *Reading the Law: Studies in Honour of Gordon J. Wenham* (LHBOTS, 461; London/New York: T. & T. Clark, 2007), pp. 59-72.

The ultimate hope that Jerusalem would become the head of all nations and the focus of a great world-pilgrimage (Isa. 60.1-20) is shown to be contingent on the demands of *torah*. God's judgment upon nations that oppress the righteous and powerless is intensified to become a deeply alarming portrayal of a 'Day of Wrath' against all human pretensions and ambitions (Isa. 2.12-22), with no exception made for Jerusalem. All human achievements stand condemned and doomed to destruction. Isaiah's message concerning the worthlessness of Egyptian help in protecting Judah (cf. Isa. 31) is elevated into a sharp dismissal of all human pretensions. Only a new heaven and a new earth can fulfil the purposes of God and fulfil the hopes of those who seek to remain the people of God.

In this connection it is significant that the prophecies of Isaiah 5–35 also show evidence of having been subjected to a modest degree of *torah*-redaction. This is most evident in the editorial reworking and re-interpretation of the mystery-laden tablet of 'testimony' of Isa. 8.1 which is interpreted in 8.20 to be a reference to the written *torah*. In this way a quite remarkable, and long-lived, tradition was given birth concerning the opening of the 'sealed book' and the testimony of the 'two witnesses' which would lead to the fulfilment of the promise concerning Jerusalem's glorification. The theme of the 'two witnesses' was destined to occupy a prominent place among the many imaginative and inventive reinterpretations of Isaianic words and metaphors which acquired a new authority in later Jewish and Christian developments. Once the belief in the presence of hidden coded ciphers and mysterious verbal revelations became applied to the written text of Isaiah a whole new genre of prophetic interpretation emerged. No longer were rhetoric and irony the tools of prophetic authority. Instead mystery, verbal imagery and the re-application of popular metaphors to address new situations had become the order of the day. Prophecy was interpreted as though it had been given 'in code'.

3. *Isaiah 1.2-31. The Great Summons to Repentance*

The forthright warning in Isa. 2.1–4.6 concerning Jerusalem's failure to live in accordance with the demands of *torah* relates directly to the even stronger criticism of the city's leadership set out in 1.2-31. The various sections of this unit, like those of the unit which follows, reveal an easily defined structure. Only the concluding vv. 27-31 stand apart suggesting that they were probably introduced at a late stage. They add a further warning concerning the judgmental purging and cleansing of Jerusalem which must take place before the final, still future, redemption of the city can occur.

Isaiah 1.21-23 first sets out an angry admonition:

See what a harlot
  The faithful city has become.
She was once filled with justice.
  Where righteousness dwelt—
  But now murderers!
Your silver has turned to slag;
  Your wine is diluted with water.
Those who rule you are villains
  And accomplices of thieves.
They all love bribes
  And pursue after gifts.
They do not defend the cause of the orphan
  And the widow's case never reaches them.

This fierce invective prepares for the sharp warning that judgment must soon fall upon the city, purging it of wrongdoers and replacing them with worthier persons (vv. 24-31). The message is unmistakeable and makes plain that no salvation can be expected for Jerusalem until those who claim to be God's servants in the city repent and either return to a genuine, *torah*-obedient, piety or are removed.

In both the 'Little Book of Zion' and the opening ch. 1 the hope of Jerusalem's eventual exaltation is not abandoned, but is reduced to the level of providing no more than a framework for a sharply worded indictment of the present leaders of the city. The reasons for this unexpected *volte-face* are elaborated in very different terms from those that have been uppermost elsewhere in the book. No longer does the threat to the city come from great imperial powers and from 'the nations'. Rather it now originates from within Judah, and from within the very citadel of Jerusalem. A remnant is all that remains to take seriously the demands of *torah*—the very embodiment of the knowledge of God which Israel was to share with the nations (Isa. 2.3). The list of the offences perpetrated by the wrongdoers is set out in 2.5–4.1.

The smaller units which make up ch. 1 are not uniform in any respect, either of metre, formal structure or style. Whether they were, at one time, relatively short separate individual compositions can only be conjectured. This variety of form has encouraged the widely canvassed view that some of them may have been taken from elsewhere within the Isaiah tradition.

Certainly the extensive presence in the book of intertextual allusions and citations to other recorded prophecies has encouraged such a view.[3] The references in 1.9 and 10 to the Sodom and Gomorrah narrative show that the author had access to a range of traditional written biblical material which included at least part of the Pentateuchal *torah*. The conjunction of the two verses may point to the influence of a 'catchword' association. Undoubtedly

---

3. Cf. B.D. Sommer, *A Prophet Interprets Scripture: Allusion in Isaiah 40–66* (Stanford: Stanford University Press, 1998), pp. 1-31.

the possibility that some parts of ch. 1 have been drawn from elsewhere in the Isaiah literary tradition has been greatly encouraged by the suggestion that vv. 7-9. These verses portray the land of Judah as devastated leaving only Jerusalem standing apart and intact. This situation has been regarded as fitting that which existed after the *débacle* of 701 BCE. Yet this conclusion must be seriously questioned.[4]

However the conclusion that some, perhaps all, of the contents of this chapter were transposed from elsewhere in the Isaiah collection remains speculative and can have no real bearing on its present purpose as an introductory admonition. Other, very substantial, factors weigh heavily against it. This chapter with its note of urgent appeal was clearly intended to be read by the readers/hearers of the book in a contemporary sense. It demands an immediate response and presents its warnings as a matter or immediate and present necessity. It conveys an underlying sense of betrayal and disillusion which had evidently been occasioned by near-contemporary events. On this score not only is this opening chapter relevant and meaningful to the situation of Israel in a broad historical perspective, but in relation to a situation that was presumed to confront its immediate readers and hearers. This chapter can only make sense when understood in reference to events that had overtaken them, or were about to do so.

When this occurred can only have been sometime, possibly late, in the Persian period of Jerusalem's history.[5] Even the early Hellenistic, era cannot be ruled out. The situation that is presupposed of Jerusalem's isolation in a land torn by conflict is one that pertained for several periods of Judah's turbulent history. It was a situation that pertained not only after 701 BCE but was repeated more than once in subsequent times. No reader could have been expected to undertake a chronological dismemberment of the chapter, applying separate passages to different ages. It appears now as a carefully constructed whole with a well-targeted message:

4. E. Ben Zvi, 'Isaiah 1,4-9 and the Events of 701 BCE in Judah', *JSOT* 5 (1991), pp. 95-111, who proposes a later, post-587 BCE date. Cf. now also Sweeney, *Isaiah 1–39*, and H.G. M. Williamson, *The Book Called Isaiah: Deutero-Isaiah's Role in Composition and Redaction* (Oxford: Clarendon Press, 1994), pp. 148-55; also in *Isaiah 1–5* (ICC; London/New York: T. & T. Clark, 2006), pp. 7-11, 47-73.

5. Both Sweeney and Williamson look for a period early in the Persian period, but it would certainly appear to be the case that the optimism engendered by the restoration of the Jerusalem temple in 520–516 BCE already lay in the past. Some later crisis must be considered as more probable. The entire portrayal of a substantial period of restoration and the ending of 'exile' late in the sixth century BCE appears a highly idealised picture of an obscure period in biblical history. Cf. now G.N. Knoppers, L.L. Grabbe and Deirdre Fulton (eds.), *Exile and Restoration Revisited: Essays in the Babylonian and Persian Periods in Memory of Peter R. Ackroyd* (London: T. & T. Clark, 2009).

If you are willing and obedient,
  You shall eat the good things of the land;
But if you refuse and rebel,
  You shall be devoured by the sword;
  For the mouth of Yahweh has spoken (Isa. 1.19-20).

In its present literary perspective Isaiah 1 appears as a carefully constructed whole, although its independent units can be readily recognized (Isa. 1.2-9, 10-20, 21-26, 27-31). They present a consistent and precisely targeted message, which gives the entire scroll of Isaiah a new significance:

1. vv. 2-9: Israel has become a disobedient people, indifferent to God and disobeying the divine demands. The evidence for this accusation rests on the weakened and impoverished condition of the people (vv. 5-7). Jerusalem stands alone but is itself under threat (vv. 8-9).

2. vv. 10-17: religious zeal is directed towards an elaborate and active cultus, with carefully performed rituals and copious sacrifices (vv. 11-15). However these activities can have no influence upon God in a land ravaged by violence and corruption. God demands a turning from all wrongdoing and only the implementation of justice and compassion for the poor, exemplified in concern for widows and orphans, can avert the present divine anger and heal the wounds of the people (vv. 16-17).

3. vv. 18-20: Such a change in the people's condition can only be achieved by a thoroughgoing change of heart and mind on the part of the entire community (vv. 18-19). Wholehearted repentance is the foremost requirement, but if this continues to be resisted then yet further disaster will come with yet more bloodshed and violence (v. 20).

4. vv. 21-23: Jerusalem and its leaders lie at the heart of the present distress. These leaders are called 'princes' and are branded as corrupt and despicable rebels who flout every requirement of justice and compassion (vv. 21-23).

5. vv. 24-26: Jerusalem is ripe for judgment which will take the form of a fierce conflict in the city. This must lead to the removal of its wicked leaders and the restoration of upright and worthy officials (judges). Only then will Jerusalem recover its honour as 'the city of righteousness and faith' (v. 26).

6. vv. 27-31: A concluding and supplementary rebuke addressed to the city and its leaders condemns the prevalence of forbidden cultic practices. These were linked to ideas of life and fertility so that the condemnation and repudiation of them elaborates on the imagery of life, by insisting that such actions will bring only death and sterility (vv. 30-31).

4. *Isaiah 1–4 and the Structure of the Isaiah Book*

Awareness of the links between chs. 1–4 and 65–66 of the completed Isaiah scroll must be reckoned as an important new insight which research into the structure of the Isaiah book has brought to light in recent years.[6] All six chapters address a fundamentally similar situation. Without this introduction of the new 'beginning' and 'ending' the Isaiah book would have retained a straightforward message regarding Jerusalem and its future which is expressed in 35.1-10 and 60.1-22. Such a positive message is a remarkable visionary outpouring, and it is, in its widest compass, the chief message which Jewish interpreters have drawn from the Isaiah book, as A. Laato has shown.[7]

Beginning with the Song of the Vineyard in 5.1-7 warning Jerusalem of its initial failures, it recounts the upheavals, expectations and disappointments that had coloured the city's turbulent history. Without its new beginning and ending it would, overall, present a vision of the glorious future that awaited the city.

The exuberant portrayal foretelling of the new Jerusalem presented in 35.1-10 conveys an appropriate description of this wonder-laden hope. The Jerusalem of the future will be the 'City of Dreams'—a 'Metropolis of Light and Healing'. In this way a major theme of biblical eschatology, which was later appropriated and developed in the New Testament in the book of Revelation was firmly established.[8] This was then elaborated still further in Christian hymnody and prayer making it a major hermeneutical theme binding the Old Testament to the New.[9] The goal of world history and human aspiration is focused on this promise of the coming of a 'New Jerusalem'—a city blessed with peace and characterized by justice.

A surprising variety of legendary and mythical re-workings concerning Zion's spiritual grandeur were then built up on the expectations that Isaiah's prophecies, and their counterparts in Hebrew psalmody, brought to birth. At the back of this hope lies the belief that a unique divine purpose protected the city in 701 BCE. This has formed the starting-point for the belief that

6. So especially Sweeney, *Isaiah 1–4*, pp. 134-84; also in *Isaiah 1–39*, pp. 70-112, and E.U. Dim, *The Eschatological Implications of Isaiah 65 and 66 as the Conclusion of the Book of Isaiah* (Bern: Peter Lang, 2005).

7. A. Laato, *'About Zion I will not be silent': The Book of Isaiah as an Ideological Unity* (ConBOT, 44; Stockholm: Almqvist & Wiksell, 1998).

8. Cf. D. Mathewson, 'Isaiah in Revelation', in S. Moyise and M.J.J. Menken (eds.), *Isaiah in the New Testament* (London/New York: T. & T. Clark International, 2005), pp. 189-210; J. Fekkes, *Isaiah and Prophetic Traditions in the Book of Revelation: Visionary Antecedents and their Development* (JSNTSup, 93; Sheffield: Sheffield Academic Press, 1993).

9. See further below in Chapter 16.

similar supernatural actions would eventually bring about a new world order. This has become the central message of the Isaiah book and has, through various stages of literary development, determined the structure and formation of chs. 5–64. Yet as far as the present Isaiah book is concerned, this message regarding the city's glorious future has been radically modified. The new 'beginning' and 'ending' that has been given to the book, forms an *inclusio* around its original shape and places this hope in an admonitory framework which no reader can evade. Chapter 1 goes out of its way to drive home this point with great firmness.

Georg Fohrer interpreted the function of the introductory preface in Isa. 1.2-31 as that of providing a summary of the larger message of the book,[10] and others have followed this suggestion. But in what sense can such a claim be upheld? It is quite simply unjustified. In sharp contradiction to such a view the most striking feature lies in the sharp and forthright qualification it brings to the vision of the future that otherwise constitutes the unifying theme of the book. Full acceptance is made of the role to be played in the future by Jerusalem—the core theme of the main part of the book. But now the remarkable feature of the new introduction and admonitory ending to it is the forthright condemnation of the leaders of the city. None of the exultant expressions of hope and triumph that are elsewhere so prominent are present in it. Instead a new warning is placed in the forefront of Yahweh's message that no optimistic vision of the future can have any validity until there has first occurred a thoroughgoing repentance and purging of evil on the part of those who rule the city. Not only is Jerusalem not exempt from this purging, but rather it is the offence presented by the wicked leaders of the city that lies at the heart of the problem. The visionary wonders that are awaited in 35.1-10 and 60.1-62 are absent. Such expectations are shown to be contingent on a more immediate, vital and pressing religious issue.

The exultant and zealously anticipated hopes that form the book's core theme are shown to be unfulfilled and are regarded categorically as impossible of being fulfilled, because the leaders of Jerusalem have betrayed their social and religious responsibilities. In the situation addressed by the book in its final completed form these wicked leaders are continuing to betray those entrusted to their care. Jerusalem is in the hand of godless rebels; pagan rituals are popular in the city; foreigners control much of its administration and wealth. The righteous are spurned and rejected. Who precisely the miscreants are and why such a sharp rift had come to divide the righteous (= the book's editors/authors) from the wicked is not spelt out in any detail.

---

10. Cf. G. Fohrer, 'Jesaja 1 als Zusammenfassung der Verkündigung Jesajas', *ZAW* 74 (1962), pp. 251-68 (repr. in *Studien zur alttestamentlichen Prophetie, 1949–1965* [BZAW, 99, Berlin: W. de Gruyter, 1967], pp. 148-66).

Some measure of fuller clarification of the situation is offered by Isaiah 65–66. What is anticipated is not that Jerusalem will shortly be exalted and set at the head of the nations. On the contrary the immediate future holds only more violence, purging and the necessary removal of these evil men from their positions of power in the city. The just and righteous nature of Israel's God demands no less!

In view of these considerations it is impossible to regard Isa. 1.2-31 as a summarising survey of the message that emerges from the book of Isaiah as a whole. Themes that are prominent in the book from the Song of the Vineyard (Isa. 5.1-7) onwards now recede into the background and are subsumed under the broader concern with the more immediate fate of violence and bloodshed that awaits the city of Jerusalem. At the very most the prominent interest in the book concerning the uniqueness of Yahweh as God, the role of the Davidic dynasty in the redemption of humankind and the glorious future that awaits Jerusalem are pushed into the background and their postponement is left unexplained. There is no reason to suppose that the 'Vision of Isaiah-ben-Amoz' (cf. Isa. 1.1; 2.1) about the wonderful future that Mount Zion was to fulfil among the nations was thought to have been rescinded or annulled. Such a conclusion would belie the very point of constructing the book at all! Nevertheless this hoped-for new Jerusalem of Isaiah's vision cannot appear until a wholesale purging of the present evils which afflict the city has been accomplished.

Undoubtedly an acceptance of the validity and authority of this vision still underlies the warnings and admonitions of 1.2-31. Nevertheless, this new prefatory introduction shows that it had become unrealisable in the minds of the authors/editors who have given the final shape to the book. The problem that hindered its fulfilment was the evil conduct of the men who were currently in power in Jerusalem. Their wickedness is here forthrightly condemned. It was plain for all to see that, because their actions were contrary to the requirements of Yahweh's *torah*, a more immediate problem had arisen and the immediate future had, once again, become uncertain and threatening. Even the possibility of Jerusalem's further destruction could not be ruled out. It is this introduction of the claim that the demands of the God-given *torah* were no longer being upheld which shows why the Isaiah vision was regarded as delayed. Jerusalem's faithlessness and corruption necessarily held back the city's exaltation until repentance, purging and renewal brought about a radical change. The detailed accusations of 2.5–4.1 spell out the particular issues that the book's final editors regard as critical.

Read in this light the sharply admonitory words of Isa. 1.16-17 take on a new urgency:

Wash yourselves clean,
  Remove your evil deeds from my sight,
Cease to do wrong,
  Learn to do what is right.
Seek justice; help the oppressed;
  Support the rights of the orphans;
Plead the widow's case.

Even more far-reaching in their significance is the invitation to repentance and a change of direction in 1.19-20:

If you are willing and obedient,
  You shall eat the produce (lit. 'good') of the land;
But if you refuse and rebel,
  You shall be consumed by the sword,
  For the mouth of Yahweh has spoken.

In front of the grand vision of the book, with its origins far back in the eighth century there has now been introduced a conditional clause: 'If you are willing and obedient...' Jerusalem may not, after all that has been prophesied, enjoy a great and illustrious future. Only the book's readers could make the response necessary to determine one future or the other.

5. David, Mount Zion and the City of Jerusalem

When read in the light of the central themes of the book which follows, the tensions and differences introduced by Isa. 1.2-31 become strongly, and disconcertingly, evident. Not even all Jerusalem is to be saved, but only a remnant of the faithful. Nevertheless, it is not simply a historical downturn in the fortunes of Jerusalem which can have brought about this change. A more fundamental shift in theological outlook, and with this a greatly changed understanding of the nature of prophecy, has been introduced. *Torah*, not apocalyptic eschatology, is the central issue.[11] If the guiding forces that shaped the development of Jewish thought in the third and second centuries BCE are seen as eschatology and *torah*, then it is clearly *torah* that has been accorded an absolute priority.

On any reckoning the book of Isaiah must be reckoned one of the most complicated of all the writings contained in the Hebrew Bible. The presence within it of important narrative sections in Isaiah 7–8 and 36–39 attracts undue attention to them. Besides these 'historical' units other firm references to identifiable historical figures, like Ahaz and Cyrus, tempt the serious reader into constructing a chronological base from which to unravel the complexities of the book's structure. Yet neither of these approaches offers

---

11.   O. Plöger, *Theocracy and Eschatology* (trans. S. Rudman; Oxford: Blackwell, 1968).

more than a partial basis for understanding the final work. Abstract concepts like that of 'unity', and even 'continuity', tend to blur the evident differences; assumptions concerning the 'growth', or 'development' of a single scroll also prove to be inadequate to explain the strong indications that a number of documents, in themselves originating at different periods, have been woven together to form a single extended text. It is the final stages of this, and the renewed tensions that had arisen for the Jewish community in Jerusalem in the late period of Persian domination, that are shown up in Isaiah 1–4 and 65–66.

In such a situation it would certainly be possible to despair of any sense of unity, either of themes, authorial origin, or structural and theological conformity. Whatever unity the extant book possesses cannot be of the order that is familiarly associated with sharply delineated ideologies or carefully planned literary compositions. In such a circumstance the finished scroll would simply have to be regarded as a literary deposit, or compendium of a distinctive urban-nationalistic tradition. Yet more than this appears to have served to shape the literary work which we call 'The Book of Isaiah' as it now exists.

Such unity as lies within it and holds it together is based on continuity—the belief shared by successive generations of Israelites and Jews, or more particularly of some from among their number, that a coherent and consistent purpose of God identified them as a community and shaped their destiny. The book is itself an assemblage of texts which show a measure of inner coherence in their separate identity. In the final analysis the claim to continuity within the whole rests on certain inner spiritual ideals summed up in a concept of *torah*. Neither politics (the divinely privileged dynastic kingship of the Davidic house) nor geography (The distinctiveness of Jerusalem as a political centre), nor even the unexpected outcome of historical events (the survival of Jerusalem from destruction in 701 BCE) can explain this sense of continuity. Each of these factors played a part—sometimes a very substantial part—in the formation of the book of Isaiah. Undoubtedly the rivalry between Jerusalem and Samaria in the aftermath of the disasters of the sixth century BCE played a major role which continued down to New Testament times and beyond.

Nevertheless each of these factors became more complex as Persian authority yielded priority, first to Hellenism and later to Roman rule. Obscure and uncertain, from a historical perspective, as this further slide into disappointment and disillusion remains, it testifies to the many unknown factors which have contributed to the formation of the Isaiah book of prophecy. Nevertheless the inner spirit of hope retained sufficient vitality to re-awaken the choices set out in Isa. 1.16.

In the final analysis it would appear that only this inner sense of a shared experience and a shared range of ideals and values upheld this belief in a continuity that reached across many generations. Without this new introduction and conclusion the unity of the book of Isaiah might well have appeared to rest on the long and turbulent history of the city of Jerusalem from the eighth century BCE down to the late Persian and Hellenistic eras. Yet the sharp warnings and admonitions of Isaiah 1–4 and the altogether unexpected ending to the book in Isa. 66.1-24 show that not even the history of the city of Jerusalem can, of itself, circumscribe the message of the book. The inner spiritual challenge and the repeated re-emergence of hope and renewal build on the ideals of peace and righteousness which are set out in 1.26. Only when they are re-established can the message which the book sets out attain fulfilment:

> Afterward you shall be called the city of righteousness,
>   The faithful city (Isa. 1.26).

Chapter 16

EPILOGUE: THE DELIVERANCE NARRATIVE
AND THE APOCALYPTIC WORLD VIEW

The story of how Jerusalem was spared the horrors of siege and destruction which befell the city of Lachish in 701 BCE by an action of 'the angel of Yahweh' has exercised an immense appeal to generations of readers of the Old Testament. This appeal is all the greater in that much of the Book of Isaiah is otherwise dense and difficult, placing heavy demands on the casual reader to investigate obscure and little-known historical events. Moreover, throughout the history of the Christian Church the belief in angels, divine intervention to bring deliverance in adversity and even to overthrow the expectations of great military powers has been commonplace. Such stories link with the belief that a general providence ultimately orders everything for good in a complex and dangerous world. Secular historians have understandably sought to dispense with the concept of 'providence' and have dismissed such reports of angelic visitations by searching for alternative historical or psychological explanations for unusual experiences and visions. Yet the concepts of 'risk management' and 'mischance' remain as part of human life and the importance of faith and personal assurance are recognized to be essential tools for facing the many unforeseen vicissitudes that occur. Unforeseen factors frustrate many well-planned ventures and the realities of life necessarily include acceptance of risk. Few major volumes of military memoirs dispense altogether with some reference to the concept of 'luck'.

1. *State Propaganda and Voices of Dissent*

A consequence of the remarkable dramatic tension of the Deliverance Narrative of Isa. 36–39 is its highlighting of the concept of trust and its vindication of faith over submission to cruel and oppressive demands. These motifs give to the narrative a lasting appeal. It is an exciting story, in spite of the questions it generates for a long list of historians. The theme of faith as an aspect of courage willing to face both life and death places Hezekiah alongside Samson and the youthful David as biblical heroes with whom a discerning reader can empathise. In some respects Hezekiah's faith bears a recognizably modern character, since he is lifted by the message of a prophet out of despair and acceptance of an inevitable death to new hope and new life. Similarly the arrogance of Sennacherib, expressed through the rhetorical bluster of his deputy the Rabshakeh, arouses in most readers the sense that his untimely end was a case of 'just desserts'. The contemptuous regard shown by the biblical narrator for both figures appears wholly justified. This is all the more apposite in that they are not presented in the biblical story simply as malevolent individuals, but as representatives of a cruel and destructive empire which undermined the foundations of civilized life. It is this cruelty and violence, and the arrogant speeches through which they express their intentions that form the primary target of the author's contempt. This reliance on force and violence suggests to the discerning reader a more fundamental reason for the angelic visitation than simply to save a royal dynasty.

The reader who is able to see the remarkable wall-reliefs displayed in the British Museum that were commissioned to celebrate Sennacherib's destruction of Lachish as a high-point of his 701 BCE campaign in the Eastern Mediterranean may feel that an element of irony pertains to a comparison between these illustrations and the biblical story. Sennacherib's campaign archivists—the media experts of antiquity—unashamedly highlighted the formidable nature of Assyrian power and its ruthlessness. Unquestionably this was the greatest military force in the region at that period of time until Babylon supplanted it by emulating its military and diplomatic strategies. Nevertheless, impressive as the catalogue of Sennacherib's achievements is, and visually moving as the wall illustrations still appear after more than two thousand years, the biblical story has also had a lasting, and strongly contrasting, influence. It retains its appeal as a story of faith conquering violence and mercy overcoming cruelty. It is an ancient version of the theme of a host of stories, novels and films set in religious language. Justice must overcome violence otherwise there can be no civilization.

The story of Jerusalem's escape from disaster in 701 BCE was obviously subsequently elaborated in the city through various accounts, as similar great thematic events have done in popular storytelling. These pose a simple contrast, based on the motif preserved in Isaiah's prophecies between the protection afforded by reliance on human armies and the power of God. My earlier attempt to present some observations about this narrative in the context of a study of the Isaiah book was greeted with much disapproval.[1]

---

1.   R.E. Clements, *Isaiah and the Deliverance of Jerusalem* (JSOTSup, 13; Sheffield: JSOT Press, 1980).

My concern at that time to draw attention to the theological and literary features of the story was regarded as negative and my claim that there is no need to postulate an unreported and unexpected historical setback in order to account for the story of a supernatural visitation was regarded by several scholars as too dismissive of the biblical evidence that something highly unusual must have occurred.

However the many unconvincing attempts to find a historical reverse of some kind to explain the account of a supernatural visitation by an avenging angel are undoubtedly guilty of ignoring many of the central features of the story. They are in danger of trivialising the very features that the narrative emphasises. This is especially brought out in the prophecy ascribed to the prophet Isaiah:

> 'Then the Assyrian shall fall by a sword, not of mortal creatures;
>> And a sword not wielded by human beings, shall devour him.
> He shall flee from the sword,
>> And his youths shall be put to forced labour.
> His defenders (lit. rock) shall flee in terror,
>> And his officers desert the standard in panic',
> Says Yahweh, whose fire is in Zion,
>> And whose furnace is in Jerusalem (Isa. 31.8-9).

It is these theological features, with their focus on faith in God to perform a miracle, that links the story to the prophet Isaiah and which represents its point of greatest appeal. This is the feature which the biblical narrator has been most eager to press home. An action by an Egyptian force to upset Sennacherib's plans would have belied the truth of Isaiah's claim that such help would prove useless (cf. Ps. 33.16-17).

There is no need to repeat again the arguments set out in these studies for a closer look at the complex literary history of the story and its relationship to a wider context of ancient Near-eastern royal ideologies; nor is it necessary to point out the significance of the role of faith in confronting the violent power struggles that are basic aspects of the course of human history. It is not too bold to claim that the Sennacherib Chronicle and its supporting illustrations in the Lachish wall-reliefs represent a typical militaristic world-view based on the use of force. They represent the politics of superior power and are a visual propaganda artefact of remarkable intensity. Once seen, they are not easily forgotten by the serious Bible reader. In contrast the biblical narrator of the Deliverance Narrative has told another version of the same story based on a world-view of faith and trust in a God of justice and mercy.

Historians and critics are perfectly correct in according their approval to the bare historical facts as recorded in the Assyrian chronicle and in accepting that the report of an angelic visitation is a legendary embellishment which is dangerously misleading. There is no reason to doubt that the

Lachish wall-reliefs tell the truth about the horrors of siege warfare and the consequences of defeat. This is precisely what they were meant to do. It is altogether disappointing therefore to find that the alternative biblical version of Jerusalem's escape from such destruction and savagery is regarded as more acceptable if it is trumped by some even more remarkable event brought about by an unreported military reverse or natural occurrence which frustrated Assyrian plans. Sennacherib evidently did return to Nineveh with a wealth of plunder, as his palace illustrations show.

Nonetheless the faith-centred world-view of the biblical story as it is recorded conveys a message about a spiritual dimension to human existence and the importance of spiritual values which force alone fails to reckon with. The supreme test of the story of how Hezekiah and Jerusalem were spared in 701 BCE did not come in its immediate aftermath, but more than a century later by which time the city and temple of Jerusalem had been ravaged by the Babylonians. An even greater test came later still in 70 AD when the temple of Jerusalem was again destroyed. The characteristics of a contest between oppressive force, relying on intimidation and military strength, and faith in a higher order of human life have been repeated too often since. Faith is a weak instrument with which to confront the mighty! As argued above, the authors of the Deliverance Narrative were evidently conscious of the disaster that subsequently overtook Jerusalem in the sixth century BCE since knowledge of this is drawn into the story of what had happened a century earlier. By this time the hostile power behind Jerusalem's misfortune was no longer Assyria but Babylon, which had assumed the role of 'the Evil Empire'. A whole new era of oppression and violence had entered the ancient Middle East.

There is a further dimension to the theological impact that this story has exercised on Christian theology. This concerns the way in which the recording of it in narrative form as a personal story of Hezekiah's loss and recovery of faith shows how biblical prophecy uses the experience of particular persons and events to present the wider unfolding of a message about human history more generally. Through the involvement of Hezekiah the account of what happened in 701 BCE is taken as an exemplary instance of a personal triumph of faith and hope over violence and despair. The account of a national disaster is brought out in highly individual personal terms.

The ability of prophecy to renew hope by telling it in story form is matched in the Isaiah book by the linking together of groups of individual prophecies to form collections and 'booklets'. These were the ancient equivalents of the pamphlets and chap-books with which the oppressed Dissenters of the English Civil Wars upheld their faith in a power of God that was greater than human force. Collections of written prophecies were part of the relatively novel process of using literary—book—form as a means of perpetuating and revitalizing the message of prophecy. Such booklets believed passionately that there is a spiritual dimension to human history which reckons not simply with one event, or one victory, but looks to a great final triumph. In this way written prophecy, and stories of prophets, became a literature of hope.

In the Isaiah book prophecies from different periods were linked together to make up a pastiche of images and themes about Jerusalem as 'the City of God'. If any single title beyond that of the original prophet properly describes the vision of the prophet Isaiah (cf. Isa. 1.1) it is as a book about the origin, history and purpose of the city of Jerusalem. No aspect of the study of the biblical prophets has received greater attention in the twentieth century than its transformation from the spoken words of poet-orators to a literature of a series of apocalyptic visions. It became the canvas for painting a picture embracing all world-history. At times the late biblical examples of this type of literature relapse into a disturbing, seemingly nonsensical, world of mythology, filled with symbols, ciphers, and code-names of persons too dangerous to identify openly. Nevertheless prophecy revealed the cosmic irrational dimension of evil and perceived it as the ultimate threat to the survival of the human race.

2. Prophecy in the New Testament

The quest to understand the methods, intentions and techniques used by scribes in the formation of this prophetic literature of the Old Testament provide an important bridge towards understanding some of the most striking Jewish writings of the Hellenistic and Roman Ages.[2] In turn these provide an essential background to the use by Christians of prophetic citations in the New Testament. In this development a further factor enters into the story. The writings of the prophets were translated into Greek which was not simply a mammoth literary achievement but presupposes a remarkable cultural and intellectual transposition. The prophets required to be understood in a new political setting and their manner of working required to be understood in the light of fresh ideas.

The Gospel of St. Matthew is a striking example where the citation of prophetic texts is used to inject meaning and significance into a narrative. However all four Gospels use allusion to Old Testament texts extensively, regarding them as prophetic in character even in cases where this appears

---

2. Cf. Craig A. Evans (ed.), *From Prophecy to Testament: The Function of the Old Testament in the New* (Peabody, MA: Hendrickson, 2000); Evans (ed.), *The Interpretation of Scripture in Early Judaism and Christianity: Studies in Language and Tradition* (Studies in Scripture and Early Judaism and Christianity, 7; Journal for the Study of the Pseudepigrapha Supplement, 33; Sheffield: Sheffield Academic Press, 2000).

not originally to have been the case.[3] The claim that long established prophecies foretelling the coming of a Messiah identifies who Jesus of Nazareth is stands in the forefront of the message. Not only in the use of ancient royal titles, but also through specific incidents and experiences the life of Jesus of Nazareth is interpreted as fulfilling Old Testament prophecies. The coming of a new kingly figure, rooted in the traditions regarding King David, the rise of the 'Church' as a community of the faithful who constitute a 'new Israel', as well as the coming of a new Teacher and Lawgiver supplanting the role of Moses, are all themes by which New Testament authors relate their message to that of the Hebrew prophets.

Alongside the claims to prophetic fulfilment the New Testament writers introduce ideas of closure and completeness which inject into the message of Christianity a degree of final authority. At the same time they link the present to the past, and to the work of the historic heroes of Judaism; in this way they serve as a means of authorising changes and innovations in much the same way that earlier prophets had done. By doing so they promoted the Christian separation from Jews and gave the Christian Church an independent identity as 'the people of God'.

Some of the techniques and strategies that are used in this assertion of a separate Christian identity can already be found in the later stages of the interpretation of Old Testament prophecy at Qumran. The concept of a faithful 'remnant' and belief that the 'true' people of God would be identified by persecution and suffering form part of such a pattern. The concept of an ecclesia—a chosen community of the faithful—drew authority from several specific prophecies in the book of Isaiah.

Consistency of method and aim are present throughout all these New Testament writings, even though they derive from different periods. They repeatedly adopt and project forward hopes and expectations which originated with earlier writings. These hopes are then re-focused into a new hope for the future in which the role of the Christian Church as the new Israel occupies a central place. The idea of a continuity of belief and purpose develops themes which already appear earlier in the editorial framework of written prophecy. The result is that history is seen as a single purposive movement, or 'destiny', foreseen as a plan of God. The belief becomes dominant that a final consummating event of world history, that had long been foretold by prophets, would shortly occur which would herald the dawning of a 'new heaven and a new earth'.

---

3. Cf. especially, S. Moyise and M.J.J. Menken (eds.), *Isaiah in the New Testament* (London/New York: T. & T. Clark International, 2005); J.F.A. Sawyer, *The Fifth Gospel: Isaiah in the History of Christianity* (Cambridge: Cambridge University Press, 1996); B.S. Childs, *The Struggle to Understand Isaiah as Christian Scripture* (Grand Rapids: Eerdmans, 2004).

What in literary terms is a 'collection', or 'canon' of written prophecy translates in theological terms into a claim that a historical series of events conform to a divine 'plan'. This is held to encompass the entire span of human history (1 Pet. 1.10-12). One sequence of events is related to other earlier events even though the latest in the series shows considerable freshness and novelty. Prophecies given long in advance are fulfilled in unexpected ways by events which are held to make plain their true meaning. Arguments by appeals to written texts that these had been foretold earlier provide a mode of authentication proving that they conformed to a divine purpose.

The study of Hebrew prophecy, both in respect of its ancient Near Eastern roots and its unique Jewish literary development, reveals the high level of significance that was attached to it in antiquity and which has survived into modern times. The very labelling of the Hebrew Scriptures as constituting an *Old* Testament owes much to the imposition of this hermeneutic of 'Promise and Fulfilment' on the two distinct collections of writings. As a result the retention of a canon of Jewish (Hebrew) writings to constitute a Christian Old Testament was a significant feature of early Christian life, even though these Hebrew Scriptures required to be re-interpreted in their new Roman setting. In this context the 'Argument from Prophecy' filled a prominent place. It was not simply an argument depending on popular forms of religious inspiration and foretelling, but a broader argument about the nature of history and the belief that historical events could be understood and interpreted as revealing a divine plan for the world.

In the modern era a great many illuminating, and often disarmingly engaging, attempts to interpret the prophets in terms of their own 'Life and Times' have been constructed. The aim of these reconstructions has been to recapture the message and religious intensity of the prophets as preachers to an obtuse and indifferent audience. Yet these have demanded a major work of re-editing the present books, dismembering and re-ordering them, usually abandoning the present literary order and reconstructing a fresh chronological one. The paucity of information for doing this, however, has necessitated that during the latter half of the twentieth century such efforts have had to be almost entirely abandoned. In their place has come recognition of the literary complexity of prophecy as a body of writings. Prophecy, once it was written down and recorded, became the subject of elaboration at the hands of many biblical editors. The transition from spoken word to written text had far-reaching consequences so that written prophecy developed into an intricate vision of the future history of the world.

No book is more intimately bound up with this shift of interpretation than that of Isaiah and a certain irony attaches to the point that, by separating it into two or three books and ascribing it to different prophets, this feature was, for a time, obscured.

Within the book that eventually emerged the story of how Jerusalem was saved in 701 BCE performs a pivotal role in providing an exemplary anticipation of other future events. These events will be a 'final showdown' of all human history when the faithful people of God will be confronted by unnamed hostile nations. The religious and political popularity of such a message in the twentieth and twenty-first centuries has earned for such a world-view both opprobrium and alarm. The oppression of the faithful 'people of God' by 'the evil empire' has served as a many-sided parable of the violence that prevails in the modern world. Expectation that this confrontation will finally be brought to an end provides a perspective of hope to the many seemingly intractable problems that human history creates. How and when all this will happen has provided researchers, seers, and enquiring human beings with a teasing glimpse of a different world order. Regrettably it appears no nearer realisation now than in did in the eighth, sixth, or first centuries BCE. It fully justifies the description of Isaiah's book as constituting a 'vision' (Isa. 1.1).

There is nevertheless a profoundly religious dimension to such a title in that the central motif of the story how Jerusalem was saved from Sennacherib and his mighty forces is one of faith over unbridled violence and intimidation. When the ruined city of Lachish testified to the barbaric consequences of defeat, Hezekiah faced a sentence of death. But, when challenged by Isaiah, the Bible's version of this near-disastrous episode tells that he recovered hope and, by doing so, he gained a new life (Isa. 38.1-8, 21-22). In one sense this story of a personal encounter with the reality of death provides a parable of the city of Jerusalem which did, after 587 BCE, enjoy a rebirth from the disaster that had engulfed it under Nebuchadrezzar.

3. Zion—Symbol of Trust

The belief that a miracle of divine intervention saved Jerusalem in 701 BCE was later enlarged upon and expanded in the Psalter to express a wider belief that Jerusalem-Zion was a unique place of refuge—a city of supernatural majesty that offered peace to its citizens and to the world. Such a belief gave rise to the unique 'Zion Tradition'. This belief, or cluster of traditions, belongs to the post-587 BCE era when a majority of Jews were domiciled beyond the comfortable range of access to the literal Jerusalem and Mount Zion.[45] It represents an unusual, and highly distinctive, literary and theo-

---

4. Cf. F.F. Bruce, *This Is That* (Exeter: Paternoster Press, 1968, 1976)

5. The theme is extensively explored in a number of books. Cf. especially C. Körting, *Zion in den Psalmen* (FAT, 48; Tübingen: Mohr Siebeck, 2006); J. Dekker, *Zion's Rock Solid Foundations: An Exegetical Study of the Zion Text in Isaiah 28.16* (Leiden/Boston: E.J. Brill, 2007). Dekker's study is particularly informative in showing the extensive

logical development which has built firmly on a positive re-assuring interpretation of the events of 701 BCE. This message is particularly expressed in
the 'Psalms of Trust' in Psalms 120–134 (cf. also Pss 46, 48, 65; etc.). The
imagery of refuge, protection and security are elevated to become central
aspects of the concept of divine providence, closely allied to traditional
language of a divine presence. A remarkable aspect is the extension of such
language in a manner that is semi-mystical in that the actual physical location of the holy Mount Zion is never clearly maintained and is sometimes
wholly absent. 'Zion' becomes simply a metaphor of divine protection and
assurance. This practice has carried over into Christian worship through the
adoption of the Hebrew psalms into worship and hymnody. The affirmation
of Isa. 14.32 is taken as a broad assurance in which the name 'Zion' is used
as a title embracing all those who put their trust in God:

> What will one answer the messengers of the nation?
> 'Yahweh has founded Zion,
>   and the weak among his people
>   will find refuge in her' (Isa. 14.32).

This tradition in the language of Christian worship is an unusual mixture
of spiritual, geographical and military terminology which conveys a mys-
tical, symbolic understanding of the divine presence. It leaned heavily on the
fact that, in a post-Reformation era, the established practice of using the Old
Testament Psalms in Christian worship became, in the eighteenth and nineteenth centuries, the basis for a new expression of Christian hymnody. The
military language of refuge and defence—of 'standing firm', 'finding shelter', 'standing on a rock' along with metaphors of God as 'Shield' and
'Defender', become stock images expressing faith and trust. The 'Songs of
Zion' become poems of faith which provide a personal focal point for a
Christian world-view which puts trust in God as a central resource for cop-
ing with the trials of life. Most familiar in this regard are the Christian
Protestant interpretations of Psalms 46 and 48 which apply the idea of Zion
partly to the Christian Church generally, partly to Protestantism, but most of
all to a conviction that justice and peace must overcome violence and chaos.

Assertions regarding an unseen divine 'presence' and 'going up to Zion'
are transformed into a quasi-geographical map of the spiritual life. The use
of this traditional language in Christian worship served a dual purpose: it
upheld and re-interpreted the belief in a divine presence which originated in

development of the theme of Zion as a metaphor of divine protection and security in later
biblical contexts. Noteworthy also is the fact that John Betjeman could entitle a series of
popular radio talks given in the mid-1970s dealing with the history of Christian hymnody
as 'Sweet Songs of Zion' (J. Betjeman, *Sweet Songs of Zion* [ed. S. Games; London:
Hodder & Stoughton, 2007]).

an obsolete temple theology. At the same time it retained a sense of mystery and 'otherness' which avoided notions of an actual physical, divine reality. In this way the language of an obsolete mode of worship, combined with the story of a prophetic reaction to a painful military defeat, became stock images of a new religious vocabulary. This affirmed strong belief in an ultimate divine providence, without shunning the harsh realities of violence and destruction. It is a linguistic symbolism of a very distinctive kind. Instead of the vocabulary of cult and ritual, with the strange technical terminology which this implied, it replaced this with the readily explicable language of security, protection and defence drawn from everyday threats to life. Cult concepts became re-interpreted as spiritual aspirations and the jargon of military prowess became interpreted as progress in the attainment of spiritual maturity.

Popular nineteenth-century reconstructions of the life and prophecies of Isaiah ultimately expressed only a very partial interpretation of the wider message of the book. In many respects the renewed concern to return to a strictly 'historical' exposition of the message of the prophet became a deceptively alluring path which led nowhere. It forfeited the spiritual dimension with which Jewish and Christian history had invested the message of prophecy and it failed to reach a convincing account of the historical achievements of prophets in their own time. As critical eyes scrutinised the details of the biblical texts they were increasingly compelled to set aside larger and larger portions of it. So far as Isaiah is concerned, not only did Isaiah 40–66 have to be assigned to another anonymous prophet, but much of Isaiah 1–39 soon followed. The passages that can be ascribed to an eighth-century prophet living in Jerusalem became increasingly difficult to relate to the use made of the book's best-known passages in Christian worship. Seen in its entirety it is as an apocalyptic vision about world history awaiting the coming of 'a new heaven and a new earth'. It anticipates another world order altogether. The story of how Jerusalem was saved in 701 BCE stands on this undefined border between faith and historical reality. In places the book goes on to foretell further divine visitations comparable to, but even greater than, that ascribed to 701 BCE (so especially Isa. 17.12-14). The fundamental problem posed by human violence is seen as resolved by further supernatural intervention.

Not only is this tension between reality and the expectations of faith unresolved in the biblical book, but it is similarly unresolved in the impact that it has had in Christian history. Hezekiah's prayer of submission to God in his time of trial reflects something of this tension (Isa. 38.10-20; cf. also Isa. 17.10-11). For this ancient king the transition from despair to faith is not presented as a straightforward experience in which the moment of darkness passed and the time of light and assurance was securely established.

Furthermore Hezekiah's reprieve from death did not bring permanent security for the Davidic dynasty, as he himself was to learn when Babylonian emissaries brought a new contender for power into his kingdom. His acquiescent acceptance of the judgement given by Isaiah that the future of his royal house would later face new threats (cf. Isa. 39.8) lapses into a degree of fatalism. In the story of Jerusalem's (and Hezekiah's) Deliverance faith and despair live close together as uncomfortable companions; Hezekiah's initial lack of trust generates the longing for its return; at the same time his submission to despair re-awakens the inevitable necessity of trust (Isa. 38.17).

In Christian theology the influence of prophecy has been ambiguous. Scholars have, at times, tried hard to present it as a purposeful understanding of history that promotes belief in human progress, that uncovers deep social and ethical insights and that generates new creative effort. Yet, in this context, is has, all too often, encouraged forms of Christian nationalism and imperialism which are dangerous secular ideals. At other times, and perhaps more consistently, biblical prophecy has been interpreted as overturning all such expectations of human progress.[6] The horrors of human violence are seen as incurable and the majority of humanity is regarded as doomed to extinction in a great final catastrophe, with no more than a remnant escaping the ultimate destruction. In the former case reconstructions of the rise and fall of prophecy have been dovetailed into a presentation of an optimistic purposeful and progressive view of human history. In the latter case a more disconnected and pessimistic viewpoint prevails. The biblical canon of prophecy cannot be said to offer an unqualified endorsement of either one, since both views appear.

The message of Isaiah is neither an unqualified affirmation of an optimistic belief in inevitable human progress nor an assurance that, in the end 'all manner of things shall be well'. The two disturbing final chapters of the book preclude any such conclusion. Throughout its course it laments the horrors of warfare and cries out against the oppression of the innocent by the powerful. Both its beginning and ending recall the fragility of hope for humankind and offer no assured outcome for the immediate future; not even Jerusalem is exempted from this since its leaders are singled out as among the foremost of the guilty (cf. Isa. 1.21-23). This dualistic character appears and re-appears throughout its sixty-six chapters. As a 'Book of Hope' it is also a confrontation with despair.

---

6. Cf. Paul Boyer, *When Time Shall Be No More: Prophecy Belief in Modern American Culture* (Cambridge, MA: Harvard University Press, 1992).

SELECT BIBLIOGRAPHY

General Introduction to Prophecy

Blenkinsopp, J., *A History of Prophecy in Israel: Revised and Enlarged* (Louisville, KY: Westminster/John Knox Press, 1996).

Clements, R.E., *Old Testament Prophecy: From Oracles to Canon* (Louisville, KY: Westminster/John Knox Press, 1996).

Davies, P.R. (ed.), *The Prophets: A Sheffield Reader* (The Biblical Seminar, 42; Sheffield: Sheffield Academic Press, 1996).

Gitay, Y. (ed.), *Prophecy and Prophets* (SBLSS; Atlanta: Society of Biblical Literature, 1997).

Gordon, R.P. (ed.), *The Place is Too Small for Us: The Israelite Prophets in Recent Scholarship* (Sources for Biblical and Theological Study, 5; Winona Lake, IN: Eisenbrauns, 1995).

Hauser, A.J., *Recent Research on the Major Prophets* (Recent Research in Biblical Studies, 1; Sheffield: Sheffield Phoenix Press, 2008).

Koch, K., *The Prophets*. I. *The Assyrian Period* (trans. Margaret Kohl; London: SCM Press, 1983).

— *The Prophets*. II. *The Babylonian and Persian Periods* (trans. Margaret Kohl; London: SCM Press, 1983).

McConville, G., *Exploring the Old Testament*. IV. *Prophets* (London: SPCK, 2002).

Mowinckel, S., *The Spirit and the Word: Prophecy and Tradition in Ancient Israel* (ed. K.C. Hanson; Minneapolis: Fortress Press, 2002).

Orton, David E. (ed.), *Prophecy in the Hebrew Bible: Selected Studies from Vetus Testamentum* (Leiden/Boston/Köln: E.J. Brill, 2000).

Petersen, David, *The Prophetic Literature: An Introduction* (Louisville, KY: Westminster/John Knox Press, 2002).

Redditt, Paul L., *Introduction to the Prophets* (Grand Rapids: Eerdmans, 2008).

Seitz, C.R., *Prophecy and Hermeneutics: Towards a New Introduction to the Prophets* (Grand Rapids: Baker Academic, 2007).

Prophecy and the Rise of Literacy

Millard, A., *Reading and Writing in the Time of Jesus* (The Biblical Seminar, 6; Sheffield: Sheffield Academic Press, 2000).

Ben Zvi, E., and M.H. Floyd (eds.), *Writings and Speech in Israelite and Ancient Near Eastern Prophecy* (SBLSS, 10; Atlanta: Society of Biblical Literature, 2000).

Toorn, K. van der, *Scribal Culture and the Making of the Hebrew Bible* (Cambridge, MA: Harvard University Press, 2007).

Isaiah and the Threat to Jerusalem in 701 BCE

Ackroyd, P.R., *Studies in the Religious Tradition of the Old Testament* (London: SCM Press, 1987).

Aubin, H.T., *The Rescue of Jerusalem: The Alliance between Hebrews and Africans in 701 BC* (New York: Soho Press, 2002).

Beuken, W.A.M., *Isaiah*. II. *Isaiah 28–39* (Historical Commentary on the Old Testament; Leuven: Peeters, 2000).

Childs, B.S., *Isaiah and the Assyrian Crisis* (Studies in Biblical Theology, 2/3; London: SCM Press, 1967).

Deijl, A. van der, *Protest or Propaganda: War in the Old Testament Book of Kings and in Contemporaneous Ancient Near Eastern Texts* (Studia semitica neerlandica; Leiden/Boston: E.J. Brill, 2008).

Evans, P.S., *The Invasion of Sennacherib in the Book of Kings: A Source-Critical and Rhetorical Study of 2 Kings 18–19* (VTSup, 125; Leiden/Boston: E.J. Brill, 2009).

Grabbe, L.L. (ed.), *'Like a Bird in a Cage': The Invasion of Sennacherib in 701 BCE* (JSOTSup, 363; Sheffield: Sheffield Academic Press, 2003). NB extensive bibliography, pp. 324-46.

Seitz, C.R., *Zion's Final Destiny: The Development of the Book of Isaiah* (Minneapolis: Fortress Press, 1991).

Smelik, K.A.D., *Converting the Past: Studies in Ancient Israelite and Moabite Historiography* (OTS, 28; Leiden/Boston: E.J. Brill, 1992).

Forming the Book of Isaiah

Blenkinsopp, J., *Opening the Sealed Book: Interpretations of the Book of Isaiah in Late Antiquity* (Grand Rapids: Eerdmans, 2006).

Broyles, C.C., and C.A. Evans (eds.), *Writing and Reading the Scroll of Isaiah: Studies of an Interpretive Tradition* (2 vols.; Leiden/Boston: E.J. Brill, 1997). NB extensive bibliography, II, pp. 717-71.

Melugin, R.F., and M.A. Sweeney (eds.), *New Visions of Isaiah* (JSOTSup, 214; Sheffield: Sheffield Academic Press, 1996).

Sommer, B.D., *A Prophet Interprets Scripture: Allusion in Isaiah 40–66* (Stanford: Stanford University Press, 1998).

Sweeney, M.A., *Isaiah 1–39, with an Introduction to Prophetic Literature* (FOTL, 16; Grand Rapids: Eerdmans, 1996).

Williamson, H.G.M., *The Book Called Isaiah* (Oxford: Oxford University Press, 1994).

— *Variations on a Theme: King, Messiah and Servant in the Book of Isaiah* (Carlisle: Paternoster Press, 1997).

The Book of Isaiah

Commentaries

Childs, B.S., *Isaiah: A Commentary* (Louisville, KY; Westminster/John Knox Press, 2001).

Oswalt, J.N., *The Book of Isaiah*. I. *Isaiah 1–39*. II. *Isaiah 40–66* (NICOT; Grand Rapids: Eerdmans, 1986, 1997).

Seitz, C.R., *Isaiah 1–39* (Interpretation; Louisville, KY: John Knox Press, 1993).
Wildberger, H., *Isaiah 1–39* (3 vols.; Minneapolis: Fortress Press, 1991–2002). A General Introduction to Isaiah 1–39 with bibliography in III, pp. 494-49.

Isaiah and the Zion Tradition

Dekker, J., *Zion's Rock-Solid Foundations: An Exegetical Study of the Zion Text in Isaiah 28.16* (OTS, 54; Leiden/Boston: E.J. Brill, 2007).
Ollenburger, Ben C., *Zion: The City of the Great King—A Theological Symbol of the Jerusalem Cult* (JSOTSup, 41; Sheffield: JSOT Press, 1987).

Isaiah in Christian Interpretation

Childs, B.S., *The Struggle to Understand Isaiah as Christian Scripture* (Grand Rapids: Eerdmans, 2004).
Moyise, S., and M.J.J. Menken, *Isaiah in the New Testament* (London/New York: Continuum, 2005).
Rowland, C., and J. Barton, *Apocalyptic in History and Tradition* (Journal for the Study of the Pseudepigrapha Supplement Series, 43; London/New York: Continuum/ Sheffield Academic Press, 2002).
Sawyer, J.F.A., *The Fifth Gospel: Isaiah in the History of Christianity* (Cambridge: Cambridge University Press, 1996).

INDEX OF AUTHORS